Street Economies
in the Urban Global South

KU-295-667

Publication of this book and the SAR seminar from which it resulted were
made possible with the generous support of The Paloheimo Foundation and
The Brown Foundation, Inc., of Houston, Texas.

**School for Advanced Research
Advanced Seminar Series**

James F. Brooks
General Editor

Street Economies
in the Urban Global South

Contributors

Florence E. Babb
Center for Women's Studies and Gender Research, University of Florida

Ray Bromley
Department of Geography and Planning, University at Albany, State University of New York

Gracia C. Clark
Department of Anthropology, Indiana University

Karen Tranberg Hansen
Department of Anthropology, Northwestern University

Maria Hedman
Department of Human Geography, Stockholm University

Ilda Lindell
Department of Human Geography, Stockholm University

Walter E. Little
Department of Anthropology, University of Albany, State University of New York

B. Lynne Milgram
Faculty of Liberal Arts and Sciences (Anthropology), OCAD University

Wilma S. Nchito
Geography Department, University of Zambia

Suzanne Scheld
Department of Anthropology, California State University Northridge

Linda J. Seligmann
Department of Sociology and Anthropology, George Mason University

Lydia Siu
Department of Anthropology, Chinese University of Hong Kong

Sarah Turner
Department of Geography, McGill University

Kyle-Nathan Verboomen
Department of Human Geography, Stockholm University

Photo: Karen Tranberg Hansen, North West Province, South Africa, 2007.

Street Economies
in the Urban Global South

*Edited by Karen Tranberg Hansen, Walter E. Little,
and B. Lynne Milgram*

School for Advanced Research Press
Santa Fe

School for Advanced Research Press
Post Office Box 2188
Santa Fe, New Mexico 87504-2188
www.sarpress.org

Managing Editor: Lisa Pacheco
Editorial Assistant: Ellen Goldberg
Designer and Production Manager: Cynthia Dyer
Manuscript Editor: Cecile Kaufman
Proofreader: Kate Whelan
Indexer: Margaret Moore Booker
Printer: Cushing Malloy, Inc.

Library of Congress Cataloging-in-Publication Data

Street economies in the urban global south / edited by Karen Tranberg Hansen, Walter E. Little,
and B. Lynne Milgram. — First edition.
    pages cm. — (Advanced seminar series)
  Includes bibliographical references and index.
  ISBN 978-1-938645-14-3 (alk. paper) — ISBN 978-1-938645-15-0 (e-book)
1. Public spaces—Developing countries. 2. Street vendors—Government policy—Developing
countries. 3. Cities and towns—Growth. 4. Developing countries—Politics and government.
I. Hansen, Karen Tranberg.
  HT153.S857 2013
  307.76—dc23
                          2013007491

MIX
Paper from
responsible sources
FSC® C044104
www.fsc.org

Cover illustration: Detail of photo by Karen Tranberg Hansen, North West Province,
South Africa, 2007.

*The School for Advanced Research (SAR) promotes the furthering of scholarship on—and public
understanding of—human culture, behavior, and evolution. SAR Press publishes cutting-edge scholarly
and general-interest books that encourage critical thinking and present new perspectives on topics of interest
to all humans. Contributions by authors reflect their own opinions and viewpoints and do not necessarily
express the opinions of SAR Press.*

Contents

Figures

Acknowledgments

Producing *Street Economies in the Urban Global South* has been a rewarding experience from start to finish. From the beginning, we believed that the topic was timely and promising for consideration from both anthropological and geographical perspectives. Our explorations of street economy issues took root in two invited sessions at the American Anthropological Association meetings in 2007 and 2010. From our initial 2007 panel focus on street vending activities, we broadened our inquiry in 2010 to investigate street economies more generally. Most of the volume authors were involved in these AAA sessions as either discussants or paper presenters, assisting us through their subsequent discussions to lay the groundwork for our School for Advanced Research (SAR) advanced seminar residency in March 2011.

We are indebted to SAR for extending the funding support that made it possible for a group of ten scholars—young to senior cultural anthropologists and human geographers—to convene on the SAR campus and engage in extensive discussions about the nature and scope of this book. Indeed, we feel that this scholarly mix fostered unique insights into our street economy inquiries. Our veteran scholars do not simply return to their past accounts, but in all cases, they include significant new field research to trace the shifting dynamics of the street in their different locales. The up-and-coming scholars similarly provide nuanced and rich analyses of street economies, perceptively teasing out new directions in their specific accounts, and Ray Bromley and Florence Babb insightfully contextualize the volume chapters in introductory and concluding sections. We were fortunate to work with such a distinguished and international group of researchers who, importantly, delivered their papers in a timely fashion throughout the multiple stages of writing and revision and whose provocative suggestions kept collective discussions animated and productive throughout our collaborative process. It certainly made the job of editing this volume a smooth one.

We also wish to thank the two external reviewers of the volume, who provided thorough and incisive comments and contributed to our achieving a better piece of scholarship. We extend our special thanks to Lynn Thompson Baca, director, and to Lisa Pacheco, managing editor, of SAR Press and to their production team. They supportively shepherded us through the challenges of preparing an edited volume.

ACKNOWLEDGMENTS

As coeditors, we value this opportunity of working together on this volume. Each of us brought particular strengths to different parts of the presentation and production process, and, indeed, each of us acquired new skills along the way. With this book, we hope to build on the energy and insights we established during our residency at SAR and encourage further research that charts the street economy developments arising in response to ongoing economic and political volatility. We believe that this collaborative and collegial process has helped us produce a strong and useful book.

Street Economies
in the Urban Global South

1

Introduction

Street Economies in the Urban Global South

**Karen Tranberg Hansen, Walter E. Little,
and B. Lynne Milgram**

When a young fruit and vegetable vendor, Mohamed Bouazizi, set himself on fire in Sidi Bouzid, a small city in central Tunisia, on December 17, 2010, he ignited demonstrations that helped topple the country's autocratic ruler (Fahim 2011). The volatility of the economy of the street helps explain his desperate act: he might have conducted business without a permit, city officials confiscated his goods, they even slapped him, and, meanwhile, his debt grew, making him unable to bribe officials to overlook his vending. In fact, changing combinations of circumstances like these give street economies their ambiguous nature and complicate the explanatory power of worn-out analytical dichotomies like public–private, illegal–legal, and informal–formal.

Focusing on economic, political, social, and cultural dynamics of street economies across the urban Global South,[1] this volume showcases the embeddedness of street economies with cultural practices and norms shaping vendors' life worlds and their spatial and organizational shifts in conflict with, or accommodation to, regulatory efforts at different levels of society. The street economies we showcase are fueled by socioeconomic and political changes influenced by market-driven shifts in postsocialist Vietnam, a struggling democracy in the Philippines, former command economies in Africa, and previous authoritarian regimes in Latin America.

3

This volume differs from recent works (Bhowmik 2010; Brown 2006c; Cross and Morales 2007), some of which center on policy and advocacy, because it focuses on the Global South and the recent global conjuncture of profound politicoeconomic changes and their sociospatial consequences. At the turn of the twentieth century and beginning of the twenty-first century, the street economies we describe here were experiencing far-ranging transformations that make the very recent past a unique moment for analysis. For although contestations over public space have a long history, we argue, the contemporary dynamics that drive them have changed, namely, the recent conjuncture of neoliberal economic policies with unprecedented urban growth in the Global South. At the local level, diverse sociospatial processes are unfolding in the wake of urban economic restructuring on a global scale guided by international development institutions and concurrent development projects coordinated by nongovernmental organizations (NGOs). This economic and political environment shapes how vendors sell and organize, and it helps give rise to new conceptions of civil society.

THE URBAN GLOBAL SOUTH AND STREET ECONOMIES

The unprecedented urban growth in the Global South at present and predicted in the future takes place against a demographic and economic backdrop that challenges livelihoods in several ways. The rapidly growing cities in the Global South are divided along lines that in many places are accentuating and extending long-existing polarizations in new ways (UN-Habitat 2011). When combined with socioeconomic and political inequality, divisions along lines of age and gender have sociospatial exclusionary effects. Such processes are affecting young people particularly adversely because almost everywhere in the Global South, they compose a very large segment of these growing urban populations. What is more, these processes are unfolding at the same time as urban space is becoming reconfigured in at least two interconnected ways. One of them involves private or foreign investments that are changing conventional land values. The second is exemplified by new urban master plans that may include multiple-lane ring roads, face-lifted city centers for tourism consumption, shopping malls with upscale entertainment centers, high-rise hotels, and gated communities for the very rich. These new topographies of inclusion and exclusion define large proportions of urban residents such as the workers in the street as out of place in new spectral urban politics (De Boeck 2011). But while street vendors may appear not to be part of the new urban master plans, they have not been evicted. In fact, turning space into a resource, street vendors are probably the most conspicuous urban economic actors throughout the Global South.

Street economies are livelihoods that are practiced on the street and in urban public space—for example, on sidewalks, in office corridors, in aisles of public markets, around train and bus stations, and in vacant spaces where vendors sell fruits and vegetables, prepared foodstuffs, drinks, handicrafts, toiletries, items of hardware, pirated music CDs, new and secondhand clothes, shoes, books, and many other goods and services. These vendors set up temporary stalls in urban public spaces and move around with their goods, changing locations, strategies, and commodities, depending on the level of surveillance. The street economy serves the vast majority of urban populations in the rapidly growing cities of the Global South by providing basic commodities and services at affordable prices in convenient locations to residents with limited means.

Because street economy livelihoods frequently are the bane of city administrations and occasionally are the target of development initiatives by NGOs, the street economy is not bounded by the street but forms an integral part of urban life in general and is shaped by the rules and regulations that govern it. Relations between vendors and regulatory agencies are not always and everywhere hostile. Some cities have pro-vendor policies, and vendors and politicians may depend on each other for protection and votes. In other settings, vendors become their own government. Vendors may organize themselves into associations based on the goods they sell or on their selling locations, and some vendor associations form broader umbrella federations. In both instances, such collective organization enables vendors to better advocate for their access to city streets for business and their rights to socioeconomic and political participation as urban citizens. Yet, several problems beset vendors' efforts to develop institutional linkages. Some organizational strategies trap them in clientilistic relations with power holders; others are short-lived or fragment into opportunistic survival networks.

Urban authorities intent on ridding streets of vendors, markets, and shoppers who contribute to congestion and disorder have occasionally formed alliances with NGOs in programs to incorporate informal vendors into the formal economy. In cities throughout the Global South, municipal administrations, NGOs, and vendors have become embroiled in confrontations varying from the forceful removal of vendors by the police, riots, and public demonstrations by vendors to mutual suspicion among city officials, NGOs, and vendors. Such embroilments have contributed to the rise of vendor-based New Social Movements, some of them with transnational participation (Butcher and Velayutham 2009; Lindell 2010c). In the current global economic recession, especially since 2008, these political and economic phenomena will only be exacerbated, raising key questions for scholarship and policy formation and implementation.

Above all, streets are multifunctional spaces whose changing resource environments—buildings, commodities, street-savvy economic and social practices, and rules and regulations—both enable and restrict the livelihoods of female and male street vendors of different ages and backgrounds. Depending on the dominant sociocultural norms, the street as a place for vending is distinctly gendered, as in Lusaka, Zambia, where male mobile vendors far outnumber women. Focusing on the street, literally or not, connects our preoccupation with economic practices to the social and cultural dimensions of urban life in a more general sense. In this view, street economies link micro and macro processes and their variable interaction, as well as their politics. Joshua Barker identifies the broader problematic in research on street life: "the street is a terrain for creativity and a starting place for democratic or oppositional politics, or it is a terrain pre-structured by political, legal and economic forces that reinforce existing social hierarchies and patterns of exclusion" (2009:156). The contributions to this volume demonstrate vividly how changing, context-dependent forces affect this problematic. They also illustrate that rules and regulations frequently exist on the books but rarely are successfully implemented. Instead, when regulatory authorities continually fail to manage street activities, vendors may set up their own management and governance strategies. In short, street vending conveys many creative potentials yet is almost everywhere volatile, subject to the vicissitudes of everyday life and government politics.

RECENT POLITICOECONOMIC GLOBAL CONJUNCTURES

In most of the cities in the Global South that we discuss in this volume, the 1980s and 1990s were characterized by neoliberal structural adjustment reforms advocated by the World Bank and the International Monetary Fund (IMF) and aimed at fiscal restraint while encouraging foreign investment and private enterprise under the aegis of market forces. The increased poverty rates such programs generated in many places have been addressed in the most recent development approach of the World Bank and the IMF in the so-called Poverty Reduction Strategy Papers (PRSP), now pursued in several countries in the South. Some of the adverse effects of fiscal restraint, for example, in education and health, are being relieved, and poverty reduction is expected to result from economic growth of selected sectors with investment potential. Although these programs contain few explicit concerns with urban employment and vulnerable parts of the labor force like women and youth, they hail entrepreneurship and self-employment as avenues toward poverty reduction.

The PRSP approach is tied up with reforming corruption through new accountancy and budget-keeping practices and a process of political and economic decentralization. Ideally, in such programs, municipalities should operate independently from central governments in decentralized governance structures composed of various local-level participatory stakeholders. Yet, the involvement of supra- and international-level agencies with governance practices impinges on the role of the state and other regulatory agencies, blurring lines of authority and unhinging power flows. Because of the limited resources available for local-level development in many countries in the South, decentralization programs rarely operate smoothly but rather draw on existing power constellations, in which vendors rarely get the opportunity to speak in their own voice.

Much current economic development discourse is replete with notions of self-employment and entrepreneurship as solutions to widespread poverty. Yet, the observations we present in this volume provide far less base for optimism than the view expressed in a recent work on street entrepreneurs with worldwide coverage. Characterizing the present as a "postmodern" economic/political system, John Cross and Alfonso Morales suggest that "street commerce is often seen as a source of growth and flexibility" (2007:2). By contrast, we are struck by the many constraints that circumscribe the actors in the street economy across the Global South, hampering their ability to break through their economic marginalization in social and legal terms (Lindell 2010c). Indeed, in this volume, we note not less, but increasing, antagonism between vendors and regulatory agencies. Some repressive regimes have been extraordinarily heavy-handed and physically violent against vending in public space (Kamete 2008). We have the impression that street vendors themselves would rather not sell in the streets, if they had a choice, but instead would prefer to do something else, a conventional job. In fact, we found in many places that local-level discourse does not support the widespread development ideal that everybody is or can be an entrepreneur. As this volume demonstrates, small-scale economic actors are well aware of obstacles toward expansion, and, more striking, today's youth generation rarely wishes to follow in the footsteps of its vendor parents.

More and more urban residents in the Global South make a living on the street because they are faced with weak or ineffective state and local governments, no social safety net, and few opportunities for secure employment. Not only is the street economy the first resort for people with few marketable skills, but it is also often the last resort for formerly employed persons who have lost private or public sector jobs due to economic retrenchment. Their economic ventures connect with the overall economy in complicated ways, not always licitly, and crisscross public and private space. This is why it may make constructive explanatory sense to approach informality as an urban organizing logic rather than as a specific sector of the economy (Roy 2005:148). The pervasiveness of street vending in a time of economic liberalization and globalization testifies to the interpenetration of formal and informal economic practices. The activities that states consider legitimate ("legal") and the pursuits that vendors view as acceptable ("licit") raise questions about taken-for-granted understandings of legality (Van Schendel and Abraham 2005:4–5). What is more, street vendors' organizational efforts across formal-informal and legal-illegal divides provide evidence of alignments between groups of workers who are not conventionally linked and whose interests may conflict or become reconciled.

STREET VENDING AND ANTHROPOLOGY

Markets and vendors are a foundational domain of anthropology's economic inquiry (Bohannan and Dalton 1962; Geertz 1963; Plattner 1985). The role of market trade in the sociopolitical integration of complex society and the rise of urban civilization has been extensively studied, yet the persistence and growth of street economies, particularly street vending, have received far less attention (Smart 1989) until recently. This volume takes up critical issues in the contemporary relationship between vendors in the street economy and agents of the state in the context of ongoing global economic transformations. Drawing on personal expertise in sociocultural anthropology, human geography, and development, the contributors explore several theoretical issues, including (1) how culture, power, and difference are mutually shaped and reconfigured in the public sphere; (2) how changing from a politicoeconomic approach to an analysis of cultural politics within the context of governance yields insights into activism and emerging conceptualizations of public space and citizenship; (3) how commodified cultural identities go beyond simple touristic consumption practices; and (4) how street vendors participate in social movements that are part of larger, transnational political and economic forces. Through ethnographically informed case studies, contributors cast fresh light on the complex array of livelihood decisions, resistance strategies, and mobilization practices street vendors pursue.

Local authorities, national governments, and international agencies often place limitations on urban informal livelihoods in efforts to modernize and globalize (Elyachar 2005). Vendors, because of their frequently illegal status in urban public space, are extraordinarily vulnerable in their attempts to earn a living, protect their goods from confiscation, and avoid fines, prosecution, and imprisonment. They have developed a variety of strategies to evade, circumvent, or negotiate restrictions on their trade. As we noted earlier, some have organized into trade-specific groups and networks and established transnational umbrella associations. StreetNet International, for example, a South Africa–based NGO established in 2002, supports organizations of street vendors, informal market vendors, and hawkers, with branches in Africa, Asia, and Latin America. Inspired by a class-based model, StreetNet seeks to create alliances between labor and social movements rather than to focus on micro-enterprises and the NGO development sector. Such alliances provide new approaches to appropriating public space and pursuing political action that cut across established divisions.

By examining how street economies are embedded in local systems of regulation, cultural practices, and norms that shape the life worlds of street vendors, the rich comparative and cross-cultural perspectives provided in this volume raise several important questions: How do street vendors defend and improve their livelihoods? How do wider global urban economic transformations affect them, and how, in the context of these transformations, do their actions shape urban space? What are the relations among street vendors, NGOs, and state and municipal institutions, and how do these relations influence urban politics?

Our discussions of broad debates about informality, urban development policy (Ramsamy 2006), and the effects of globalization on economic life in the Global South cast important light on the interrelationship between culture and economy in some of the world's fastest-growing cities. Above all, individual contributors identify processes by which differentially positioned vendors act on the sites and ways in which globalization plays out, not simply by responding to such processes but by actively engaging them and, in effect, redefining civil society.

ORGANIZATION OF THE BOOK

In order to explain the diverse life and cultural worlds of street vendors, the contributors explore several aspects of the street economy within local-to-transnational contexts. These aspects include considering the composition of central actors in gender, generational, class, and ethnic terms and identifying their protagonists, including clients, patrons, police, urban and state authorities, and international regulatory agencies such as the World Bank and the European Union, whose policy agendas affect the conduct of informal economic activity. Some of the contributors focus on the nature and scope of organizational activism from the perspective of vendors and NGOs. In terms of methodology, the authors describe the circumstances within which they conducted their field research, and they firmly ground their analyses of street economy practices by documenting the connections between local everyday life events and transnational processes.

At grassroots and international levels, and between them, are emergent economies and politics that invite scholarly inquiry into the significance of street vending (Brown, Lyons, and Dankoco 2010). The contraction of the global economy that has contributed to the expansion of informal economic activities in the Global South, as the urban poor seek out livelihoods and reconceptualize ways to organize (Edelman 2001; Tostesen, Tvedten, and Vaa 2001), is making nuanced analyses of street vending even more important to policy makers and social scientists studying economic and political phenomena.

Ray Bromley's (chapter 2) overview anchors the volume chapters by exploring the social, economic, and political functions of streets as public spaces and the changing ideas about the role street vending has played in the economy and labor market. Building on his long-term research of urban planning and street trade, Bromley outlines that over the past half-century, descriptions of street vending by scholars and policy makers have moved from depicting this activity as folkloric, temporary, and essentially outmoded—a superfluous occupation soon to disappear—to resituating it as mainstream, growing in worldwide significance, and supplying much needed jobs, goods, and services. Because street vending does not easily fit into traditional models of communist, modernist, or capitalist development, Bromley argues, its persistence and proliferation have contributed to a major rethink of development alternatives, turning attention to questions of social justice and environmental sustainability. He maintains that any viable future for our rapidly growing cities depends on finding a balance among citizens' rights to services and participation in governance, livelihood, mobility, safety, security, and a pleasing environment realized in multipurpose public spaces.

Gracia Clark (chapter 3), drawing on her more than thirty years of research with Kumasi market women in Ghana, provides a historical analysis of Kumasi street vending practices with a focus on food provisioning. Clark investigates how street traders have negotiated or resisted the Ghana government's ongoing local-to-national interventions to ban this work and the driving forces that fashion the constant reshaping and perseverance of trading practices. Focusing on the city of Kumasi, she identifies the disjuncture between the government's marginalization of street economy work and the lived reality that vendors' provisioning activities are already integrated into the local economy, fulfilling urbanites' demands and needs. Clark's fine-grained historical analysis traces the integral role vending plays in the relationships of marriage and parenthood for the predominant Asante ethnic group and the historical timelines of hostile government interventions and vendor resistance. She explores alternative explanatory frameworks to make sense of apparent contradictions in policy making, implementation, and impact. Clark concludes that the continuing denial of legitimacy to street trading precludes its potential to enable vendors' upward economic mobility and belies its integration into the fabric of daily life for Kumasi residents and for Ghanaians more generally.

Karen Tranberg Hansen and Wilma Nchito's (chapter 4) research in Lusaka, Zambia's capital, focuses on the long-term interconnections between street vendors and formal market traders. Regarding mobility as street vendors' main advantage, the authors argue that vendors' occupation of locations with high pedestrian traffic, including some market locations, and their reluctance to move beyond the city's Central Business District are tactics of resistance. Specifically, the authors investigate the channels through which vendors operationalized in-between spaces for business within the New Soweto Market, Lusaka's newest ultramodern market, when the market's formal opening was delayed. Displaced street vendors turned the inside of the new market into the street, occupying open space in front of formal shops. One result of vendors' actions was to renew tensions between marketers, that is, the people with stands and shops and the vendors, who need to be highly mobile. Yet, during the impasse, even some shop owners did not occupy their shops but worked from the open space in front, or both. The authors suggest that in the process of such an "interiorizing" of the street, the social attributes that make street vending a lively enterprise also play out in this changed setting. Resonating with the inquiries of other chapters on the changing dynamics of space relations, Hansen and Nchito's Lusaka case study highlights the context-specific changes in spatial regulation that have accompanied restructuring of Zambia's economy in the wake of economic liberalization since the transition from a socialist command to a market economy in 1991.

In a related street-vendor movement from street to formal market, Lynne Milgram's chapter 5, situated in Baguio City in the northern

Philippines, charts how competition among vendors for street locations has prompted some sellers to occupy alternative spaces (aisles) inside Baguio City's public market—the regional hub for fresh produce. Milgram argues that the early success of vendors' relocated businesses within the market demonstrates that consumers want their trade and that it is already incorporated into the city's economy. She maintains that female ambulant vendors' claims to rights to their Baguio City market spaces not legally sanctioned for commercial use encourage us to reconsider categories of space use and legal/illegal practice. Indeed, Milgram reports that the Baguio City Market management collects daily rental fees from these vendors, allowing them to occupy their illegal locations, and some permanent market traders expand their businesses by selling products in the same in-between sites. Like street vendors in Turner's Hanoi study and those in South Africa explored by Lindell and her collaborators, Baguio City street sellers activate business spaces that are subject to conflicting claims by making personalized agreements across market sectors, forging uneasy alliances with city officials, and organizing associations to advocate their collective rights. Milgram concludes that female vendor actions that straddle notions of what is legal and illegal point to alternative and transformative uses of space, facilitating the viable livelihoods they demand and deserve.

In a case study about street vendor political subjectivities in Antigua, Guatemala, Walter Little (chapter 6) draws on twenty years of experience to describe transformations in the ways vendors view themselves as economic and political actors. Unlike the vendors discussed by Milgram and by Hansen and Nchito, mobile Maya vendors who sell handicrafts to tourists do not see formal marketplaces as sites to develop and maintain sales. They are keenly aware of what their primary clientele is interested in purchasing, from whom, and where. This puts them, ideally, on the Spanish colonial–style streets, but also right where the municipal government does not want them. Little argues that in their self-recognition that they are part of the tourism spectacle for tourists, vendors are gaining small ways to resist municipal regulations and police seizures of their merchandise. As in Seligmann's discussion of street vending in Cusco, Peru, the relationship between vendors and the municipality in Antigua is contentious. In effect, Maya vendors are not recognized as an important part of Antigua's tourism economy, much less as part of the touristic landscape the tourists expect to see. Much like the vendors described by Turner in Hanoi and by Lindell and her collaborators in South Africa, Maya vendors find themselves struggling against street vending bans, forced expulsions, and heavy fines. With limited success through formal collective organizing, they have nevertheless come to better recognize how integral they are to the national and international representations of Antigua, which has emboldened them against local law enforcement and municipal officers.

Drawing on twenty years of field research in Cusco, Peru, Linda Seligmann (chapter 7) argues that municipal authorities' current promotion of tourism as a significant source of revenue has resulted in dramatic shifts in the use of urban space that do not necessarily coincide with resident, tourist, or vendor expectations and needs. To realize the potential of tourism for the city's economy, city officials have removed vendors from the city center, formalized and individuated them according to the type of commodity they sell (crafts, fresh produce, souvenirs), and moved vendors, both ambulatory and those who work from makeshift stalls, to permanent market spaces in high-rise buildings with improved hygienic and electricity services but located far away from the city center. Seligmann demonstrates that such development initiatives have widened the fissures between more and less established craft and food vendors, in particular, through licensing mechanisms differentiated by locus. Like other contributors, she analyzes the ways in which vendors actively take advantage of and/ or resist these policies that have affected their access to and use of space, and she charts the ongoing challenges vendors face with the government's neoliberal agendas. Seligmann concludes by identifying the paradox that has emerged with the Cusco government's urban development initiative. Although most vendors have not benefited economically in any substantial way from formalization and relocation, increasing the number of stalls in the new buildings and regrouping enterprises by type may, in fact, prove lucrative to some sellers.

Sarah Turner's (chapter 8) exploration of street economy trades in Hanoi, Vietnam, introduces a different dynamic by exploring tensions that arise when a socialist regime incorporates neoliberal economic practices. Turner focuses on the ramifications of the city government's 2008 ban on street vending activities in key downtown city streets and in public spaces around hospitals, schools, and bus and train stations. The vast majority of street vendors targeted in this ban were rural migrants who used the city's streets as a setting for their only alternative livelihood. Also pursuing a living via street vending are long-time Hanoi residents who feel fully entitled to their small slice of public space. Turner demonstrates that by carefully negotiating spatial routines, drawing on social capital, and negotiating power relations with state officials, street vendors in both groups continue to trade on the streets of Hanoi, circumventing the ban and defending their "counterspaces." Distinguishing between fixed-stall and itinerant sellers, she dispels any idea of a homogenous street-vending population. Her study highlights the importance of recognizing such heterogeneity among vendors when she concludes that Hanoi residents operating fixed stalls have maneuvered themselves into working relationships with officials that to some degree are tenable and resilient whereas itinerant street vendors remain in a far more precarious position. Turner's Hanoi case study, like the other chapters, highlights political context and heterogeneity in order to identify the variable dynamics of street economy practices.

Suzanne Scheld and Lydia Siu's (chapter 9) investigation of street economy practices in Dakar, the capital of Senegal, focuses on racism and racialized discourse among vendors and marketers. Exploring how racism is initiated and perpetuated by immigrant Chinese storeowners and native Senegalese street vendors, they analyze the extent to which vendors are advantaged and/or disadvantaged by such race-based communication. Scheld and Siu note that for the past ten years, Chinese traders have been immigrating to Dakar and several other African countries to open small shops that offer clothing, home decorations, and other inexpensive Chinese goods. Although the increasing number of Chinese traders in Dakar has created competition for Senegalese importers, it has also opened opportunities for Senegalese street vendors who sell Chinese goods on the sidewalks in front of Chinese shops. Their co-habitation and interdependent relationship, the authors argue, have generated a discourse debating the "problem" of Chinese trading in Dakar—a discussion that carries distinct racial undertones. Whereas Senegalese vendors use economic arguments to question whether the government should permit Chinese trading in Dakar while African traders struggle to survive, the Chinese merchants talk of Senegalese street vendors in clearly race-based terms. Scheld and Liu demonstrate how racialized discourse "in the street" provides evidence of the globalized nature of the city's localized street economy.

Like the work of Scheld and Liu, Ilda Lindell, Maria Hedman, and Kyle-Nathan Verboomen's (chapter 10) case study of World Cup 2010 in South Africa showcases the global dynamic of locally based street economy practices. The authors argue that according to municipal authorities in the host cities of Port Elizabeth and Durban, mounting a mega-event such as World Cup 2010 would generate economic benefits for everyone. The reality proved to be very different for people working in the street economy, as evictions, relocations, and restrictions caused many vendors to lose their livelihoods or restricted them from benefiting economically from the event. The authors argue that although street vendors were promised a voice in how their services could be incorporated into those offered to city visitors during this event, in fact, vendors' informal activities were treated as a nuisance to be eradicated and as an unhealthy deviation from internationally accepted standards of modern, tidy, urban centers. In some cases, new bylaws were introduced that criminalized street vending. Charting the different experiences and resistance strategies of street vendors in Port Elizabeth and Durban, the authors document how vendors formed associations and aligned themselves with international civil society organizations to advocate for their collective demands. Vendors in Durban were more successful in their collective actions than those in Port Elizabeth because the former gained broad-based support from the city's substantive civil society organizations. The authors conclude that vendors achieved some of their goals by local-to-transnational collective organizing but the results varied because of the different place-based politics of the two cities.

Florence Babb's (chapter 11) concluding commentary invites a reading across and beyond the collected ethnographic essays, addressing such themes as how street economy workers navigate economic and political marginalities and how to understand processes of formal and informal work. She considers contributors' attention to social differentiation, gendered and racialized identities in street economies, and the often fraught relationships between street vendors and states. She underscores the quickening pace of change in street economies that has come with rapid urbanization and globalization. Notwithstanding the changing currents in the urban Global South and in the scholarship on street economies, Babb suggests that it is important to trace intellectual genealogies and to recognize precursors to current work. She points to significant conceptual work in an earlier generation's scholarship and describes how it influenced her own thinking in the 1970s and 1980s on marketers and street vendors in Andean Peru. Even so, Babb concludes that more recent postcolonial and poststructural critiques have added a much needed dimension to the discussion, notable here in the work of volume contributors. Most fundamental, Babb argues, we are better positioned today to raise the vexing question of who has the right to make a living on the streets when informal economies reach the breaking point.

Given the uncertainty and immediacy of rapidly changing global economic circumstances and the uncertain ramifications for street economy vendors, who are working on the edge, the detailed ethnographic accounts of *Street Economies in the Urban Global South* will inform the current process of urban transformation in several ways. The contributions provide vivid accounts of the diverse experiences of street vendors in urban, globalized, social contexts by focusing on often marginalized street workers who describe their projects and plans. Bringing together ethnographic evidence that traces the numerous processes and factors instrumental in exacerbating the marginality and disempowerment of street economy work, the chapters simultaneously highlight individual and collective resistance by street vendors to overcome such processes. We expect that this book will make the precarious local life worlds of the street economy challenge the far too common exclusion of activities on the edge—street economy practices—from analyses of political and global market forces.

Note

1. We use the term *the Global South* in preference to *the Third World* because of the normative developmentalist associations of the latter.

2

Rethinking the Public Realm

On Vending, Popular Protest, and Street Politics

Ray Bromley

In 2008–2009, the world economy hovered on the verge of economic collapse because of the reckless behavior of many banks and brokerages, the negligence of several key governments, and the combined forces of economic financialization and globalization. Though a global meltdown was averted, the future for many countries is far from rosy. Japan and the Euro-zone fell into crisis in 2011, growth slowed in most major national economies in 2012, and in many parts of the world, there are intractable problems associated with combinations of fiscal deficits, trade deficits, high unemployment, high rates of loan default and mortgage foreclosure, and pervasive negative equity resulting from the collapse of over inflated real estate markets.

The recent phase of world economic instability has triggered widespread social unrest. Food prices are rising worldwide as climate change, population growth, freshwater shortages, rising fertilizer costs, and the diversion of food grains to meat and ethanol production put pressure on global agricultural capacity. Rapidly growing access to cellphones and the Internet have created new communication channels that cannot easily be controlled by government censorship. Popular awareness and mobilization has been facilitated, and political actions and protests are spreading across regions and countries. The Arab Spring of 2011 is the most dramatic change, of course, with the overthrow of governments in Tunisia, Egypt, and Libya and serious rioting and repression in Syria, Bahrain, and Yemen (Agathangelou and Soguk 2011). Meanwhile, protests are on the rise in Russia, China, and India with growing public recognition of official corruption and the widening gulf between a tiny but massively wealthy elite and the striving middle and working classes. The recent 2011 "Occupy" movement emanating from the United States has redrawn the class map in response to the fast-growing gap between CEOs and their struggling workers. Instead of the old Marxian paradigm, which viewed the middle class as a "petty bourgeoisie" allied to the elites and working to serve their interests (Marx and Engels 1998[1848]:20–21), now the middle class is re-imaged as part of the 99 percent, allied with the workers and the impoverished against financial speculators, greedy CEOs, and self-serving plutocrats.

As new forces for democratization have emerged arguing for redistribution and a new social order, wealthy elites and major corporations have fought back. In autocratic political systems, they have supported the most repressive forces, but in most of the world, they have simply used the power of money—controlling the mass media and the flow of information to the public, buying large amounts of media time to support their preferred political parties and candidates, and paying the best lobbyists handsomely to promote their objectives. Through a mix of lobbying, ideological advocacy, and outright bribery, they have persuaded politicians and judges to cut taxes for the ultrarich and corporations, facilitate tax avoidance by offshoring jobs and assets, and allow corporations to usurp the rights of citizens.

In the midst of such rapid financialization, globalization, and growing socioeconomic inequality in both rich and poor countries, more people have taken to the streets in protest, and amateur digital images and videos have shown the world what is going on, spreading public outrage around the globe. Facebook, Twitter, cellphones, and Al-Jazeera have fanned the flames of unrest and converted incidents like the self-immolation death of Mohamed Bouazizi in Sidi Bouzid, Tunisia, in December 2010 or the vicious beating of "blue bra girl" in Tahrir Square in Cairo in December 2011 into catalysts for change. It is not the first time in history that major public protests have overthrown governments or been brutally suppressed. The French Revolution of 1789–1799, the fall of Venezuela's Marcos Pérez Jiménez in 1958 and of Iran's Shah Mohammad Reza Pahlavi in 1979, and the frustrated uprisings of Paris and Mexico City in 1968 and of Tianamen Square in Beijing in 1989 are all powerful examples of mass protests in public spaces. What we may be seeing now, however, is a wider international diffusion of protest, fueled by popular resentment of government repression, political corruption, corporate manipulation of democracy and the financial system, rising unemployment, and growing economic inequality. In some countries, the poor are more impoverished, but in most of the world, resentment focuses on rising popular expectations and the specter of elite enrichment.

As twenty-first-century elites imitate ancient monarchs, separating themselves from the masses behind high walls, gates, security guards, and electronic sensors or in skyscrapers, limousines, and executive jets, the street acquires enhanced significance as the quintessentially public place in an increasingly urbanized and privatized world. But this enhanced significance is under tremendous pressure from the dominant global transportation technology, namely, motor vehicles: cars, motorcycles, trucks, and buses. Drivers and passengers are frustrated by congestion, traffic jams worldwide are becoming more frequent and serious, and governments respond by clearing the streets to facilitate the flow of traffic. The private car is the archetypal global consumer commodity, a mark of identity and status, a source of security and comfort, and a protected space that travels through the public realm. Even politically conscious, middle-class professionals who sympathize with blue-collar workers and resent the greed of the elite one percent become frustrated in traffic jams, detest congestion, and try to avoid parking charges.

The rise of motor vehicles is associated with "sprawl" and "ribbon development"—the outward expansion of urban areas at lower densities and the growth of commercial strips along the roads connecting towns and cities. Throughout the world, the main features of twentieth-century US cities are being replicated in the twenty-first century—suburbanization, the emergence of drive-in commercial strips, malls, and office and tech parks, the construction of divided superhighways closed to pedestrians and bicycles, and the dedication of anything up to half the total space to roads, driveways, and parking. Density is sacrificed in exchange for traffic flow, suburban utopias, and free parking at every drive-in business, and the public realm becomes increasingly hostile to pedestrians and vendors. Powerful commercial interests help to sell the suburban dream, associating it with healthful family living, avoidance of urban crime, the protection of a gated environment, and the joys of home and car ownership.

The battle over the significance of public space is particularly intense in the Global South, where most households still do not own cars and where large numbers of workers seek to make a living in small businesses including street and market trading and in small off-street shops, services, and repair enterprises. Acute contrasts emerge within large metropolitan regions. In Metro Delhi, for example, there is a tremendous contrast between the densely populated neighborhoods packed with street-level commerce in Old Delhi and Karol Bagh; the wide and often empty streets of planned governmental New Delhi, with its scattered ministries and official bungalow residences; and the emerging high-tech suburbs of Gurgaon and Noida, built for corporations, apartments, and motor vehicles, where incipient street life is an irritant to motorists. The same tension is found in most metropolitan zones in the Global South separating traditional and relatively high-density areas with abundant pedestrian activity from the emerging low-density sprawl zones, where motor vehicles dominate the streets and business is concentrated on private properties. Street vending, mass transit, and pedestrian movements all depend on maintaining urban densities and restraining sprawl, but all too often, city planning focuses on reducing density and facilitating new urban development on Greenfield sites. Such policies foster the image of a city free from congestion, pollution, and visual disorder, but they increase vehicle dependency, fuel consumption, and air pollution and reduce the potential for cost-effective mass transit systems.

MAINSTREAMING STREET VENDING[1]

Street vending is one of the world's oldest and most widespread occupations, yet only recently has it begun to receive substantial scholarly attention. For many years, it was viewed as a quaint and insignificant occupation, destined to disappear as more modern forms of retailing out-stripped it with scale economies; greater choice, security, and consumer convenience; better hygiene and customer service; and climate-controlled retail environments. Officials and intellectuals have typically viewed street vending as outmoded, insanitary, and a potential public nuisance.

Early academic writings on street vending were largely anthropological—a "hawkers and higglers" literature, either focused on rural marketing or presenting vendors as unsophisticated rural migrants maintaining their old traditions. The literature celebrated the vendors' exotic dress, picturesque carts and stalls, traditional products, and concentration at festivals and other public celebrations (Dewey 1962; Katzin 1959; Vansina 1962). Viewed as transitory and apolitical, street vendors were much less studied than traveling traders or market vendors.

In the 1950s, however, rapid urbanization took place in much of the Global South, and street vending grew as the old marketplaces and downtown areas proved inadequate to house the rapidly expanding commerce of burgeoning cities growing by 5, 10, and even 15 percent a year. A new paradigm emerged, namely, W. Arthur Lewis's dual economy model (Lewis 1954). Street vending came to be viewed as part of a traditional sector, together with peasant farming, handicraft production, domestic service, marketplace trade, and neighborhood stores. These occupations played crucial roles in the economy, providing livelihoods for a large proportion of the population in the Global South. They were seen as a reserve army of labor, occupied until the modern/formal sector could expand sufficiently to absorb everyone into better jobs with contracts, minimum wages, sickness and disability benefits, pensions, and the protection of labor legislation.

Though some policy experts envisioned a rapid transition to development and modernity for the whole Global South (Rostow 1960), most observers were more cautious, realizing that many countries would remain "underdeveloped" for decades and that the global system might not be able to sustain the accelerated economic development of all nations. Applying old Keynesian perspectives on employment and the role of government derived from analyses of the Great Depression in the Global North, many development economists assumed that there would be widespread unemployment associated with the poverty of the Global South. In the burgeoning cities of the South, however, they saw large numbers of people doing jobs that did not appear in official employment statistics—vendors working on and off streets, artisans, porters and transporters, servants, recycling and repair workers, queue standers, and many more—so they developed a concept of "underemployment" or "disguised unemployment" somewhat similar to the Marxian "lumpenproletariat." The underemployed or disguised unemployed were portrayed as effectively unemployed, performing useless functions as parasites on the real and productive economy. The concepts of underemployment and disguised unemployment were particularly associated with urbanization, reflecting a pro-rural bias that assumed that rural occupations, though often low in productivity, were somehow more wholesome and useful than those of the poor in rapidly growing cities (Lipton 1977:216–227).

A major turnaround in the literature occurred during and after the Conference on Urban Unemployment in Africa, held at the Institute of Development Studies at the University of Sussex in England in September 1971. The key paper presented was by the anthropologist Keith Hart (published 1973), based on ethnographic fieldwork among Northern Ghanaian migrants in a slum neighborhood of Accra. Hart described a resilient "informal sector" of self-employment and small enterprises, unregulated, some legitimate, like urban agriculture, tailoring, and petty hawking, and some illegitimate, like pawnbroking, prostitution, and petty theft. He had a major impact on the conference organizers, Richard Jolly, Hans Singer, and other economists who were preparing for a mission to Kenya under the auspices of the International Labour Office (ILO) as part of its World Employment Program (WEP), an ambitious effort to rethink economic development strategies for the Global South. Hart demonstrated the absurdity of believing that most of the urban poor were unemployed or that they suffered from underemployment or disguised unemployment doing useless and dysfunctional jobs. Instead, he showed that most people work long hours and that most create goods and services that improve the quality of life of the workers and their households. Primarily through a case study of Atinga's Bar, a small and highly precarious business created by a former soldier who had been medically discharged, Hart demonstrated how even the most undercapitalized enterprises can provide social support and community services. The bar began unlicensed, but later Atinga purchased a liquor sales license and for twenty months, his bar acted "as a buffer, for those…'out of work,' against destitution and dependence on others" (Hart 1973:81). Whereas Hart was merely seeking to describe life as lived by the urban poor, the future members of the ILO Kenya Mission were seeking an organizing concept for a new set of policy recommendations, and they co-opted Hart's "informal sector" idea (Hart 2010). In adopting the concept, however, they changed its character by avoiding significant discussion of questionable and disreputable occupations like barkeeping, pawnbroking, or prostitution, minimizing discussion of retailing, emphasizing the positive values of hard work, self-reliance, recycling, technical ingenuity, and entrepreneurship, and reducing dependence upon foreign imports, capital investments, and loans.

The highly influential International Labour Office (ILO) Kenya Report (1972) that Jolly and Singer coordinated introduced the informal sector concept into the published policy literature, effectively renaming Lewis's traditional sector as the "informal sector" coexisting with an expanding modern sector of corporate and governmental employment in mines, plantations, factories, banks, clinics, hospitals, schools, universities, supermarkets, department stores, and other firms and institutions of the growing economy. Crucial to the ILO reasoning was the idea that it would take a very long time to expand the formal sector and that the informal sector could be harnessed in the meantime to build employment, human resources, production, and consumption. The informal sector was reframed as an active agent in a long-term development process rather than as a reserve army of labor engaged in traditional and subsistence activities or as urban unemployment or disguised unemployment. Though the ILO focused more on peasant farmers, artisans, and recycling workers than on street vendors, the 1970s policy discussions triggered a fundamental reevaluation of street vending. Several authors pointed out that most street vendors were not folkloric, that their merchandise was not traditional, that the latest manufactured goods were sold on the street, and that many street vendors had links with larger, off-street businesses (Bromley 1978a, 1978b; Dasgupta 1992). Some emphasized the entrepreneurial dimension of street vending, portraying the occupation as a training ground and fount of innovation (van den Bogaert 1977). Nevertheless, many authors and policy experts continued to assume that, sooner or later, more modern modes of economic activity would supercede street vending and that the occupation was unimportant and destined to disappear.

Why, even in the 1970s and 1980s, was street vending so pervasively ignored and disdained? The answer to this question is not that street vending was invisible or economically insignificant or a censored or taboo topic. It was all too visible, but it could not be reconciled with the standard paradigms of Marxism, modernity, and capitalism that prevailed in this period. Those who chose to study street vending were often dismissed as anarchists, neo-Marxists, or simply lovers of the quaint, exotic, and disorderly.

In orthodox Marxist-Leninist analysis, street vending was petty trading, varying from marginal and lumpenproletarian to micro-entrepreneurial and petty bourgeois. Street vendors were "urban kulaks"—inconvenient nonpeasant, nonproletarian, nonrevolutionary remnants. Their views and occupations were considered irrelevant to the inevitable revolution. After the revolution, it was assumed that they would be replaced by rational, planned distribution systems (Anchishkin 1980:108–126) and that they would have to be reeducated to perform new roles in the new economy. Street vendors were viewed as archetypal "parasitic middlemen" in economies where all real value derived from the extraction and processing of raw materials and from industries manufacturing commodities. Services were mere adjuncts to the fundamental commodity-producing activities that underpinned the economy.

To advocates of modernity, both socialist and capitalist, street vending was a disorderly and superfluous activity that cluttered the urban environment, interrupted efficient traffic flows, and competed unfairly with new, large, hygienic commercial establishments. Street vending was the antithesis of everything modern—the supermarket, the department store, and the shopping mall. Most modernists believed that these gleaming commercial establishments enabled shoppers to obtain all they needed under a single roof with maximum speed, economy, comfort, and hygiene. In sharp contrast, they thought that street vending had no future and vendors could survive only by dodging taxes, hoodwinking customers, selling illicit goods, and pandering to antiquated traditions. The world was seen to be increasingly dominated by giant corporations, and pushcarts, stalls, shops, workshops, handicrafts, and peasant farms all seemed uncompetitive.

Corporate success under capitalism is usually attributed to modern management, scale economies, horizontal and vertical integration, sophisticated research and development (R&D), and aggressive marketing campaigns through the mass media. Seeing major corporations grow, take over rivals, and expand transnationally, many twentieth-century observers assumed that small businesses would disappear or be concentrated in narrow, specific niches of the economy such as high-tech business services and fashion-trend start-ups. Such ideas seem crude and absurd now, but they were prevalent just a quarter-century ago, in a Cold War era shaped by the titanic struggle between the capitalist West and the Soviet Bloc. Just as few envisioned the fall of communism until the Soviet Bloc collapsed, few imagined before this collapse that street vending would continue to proliferate for several more decades.

By mistakenly seeing street vending as disappearing, irrelevant, or parasitic, most twentieth-century scholars and policy makers thus ignored its economic, social, and political significance. Street vending is a potentially fruitful research area, providing insights into many aspects of society, economy, and politics in the Global South. It has obvious importance in studying household economies, child labor, the gender division of labor, occupational health, worker organization, the resolution of workplace conflicts, and worker organization into cooperatives, associations, and trade unions. It is also a laboratory for studying entrepreneurship, the determinants of microbusiness success, and the dynamics of microcredit (de Soto 1989; Harper 1998; Peberdy 2000). Furthermore, the regulation of street vending has never received the serious attention it deserves. Studying street vending provides a perfect laboratory for understanding "street-level bureaucracy"—how government and policing work at the lowest level (Lipsky 1980). In most countries and localities, street vendors have had to deal with petty officials who sometimes behave high-handedly, seek bribes, and administer outdated and impractical rules. Very often, local officials selectively target only a small proportion of those who break official rules and regulations, and their selection processes provide powerful insights into social dynamics, discrimination, and concepts of who is "deserving" and "undeserving."

I came to street vendor studies after doing spatial and socioeconomic analyses of marketplace trade. Like many other researchers, I participated in the 1970s informal sector debates, using case studies of individual occupations in specific places as ways to illustrate much broader arguments. I studied street vendors because of their capacity to illustrate features of the overall economic system (Bromley 1985; Bromley and Gerry 1979). Most researchers, however, preferred to focus on other small-scale participants in the system—peasant farmers, artisans, and small industries—activities that seemed more productive, following the prevailing commodity obsessions of the era. They directed their attention to what they perceived as "engines of growth" rather than what they saw as "petty services" that would eventually disappear. Ironically, however, many of the so-called productive occupations have shrunk over the past three decades, and street vending has grown in significance amidst a massive global shift toward service occupations (Soubbotina 2004:50–54).

The transitions of the past quarter-century have included the fall of communism, the decline of developmentalism, the rise of China, India, and Brazil, accelerating globalization, massive international financial flows, the rising power of transnational corporations, growing awareness of resource depletion and climate change, and the diminishing power of most nation-states to make independent policies. Manufacturing industries have declined in many parts of the world, and new technologies have emphasized electronics, software, and the elegance of miniaturization. The service sector is now the principal employer in the Global North and most of the Global South. In the midst of all this global change, street vendors have continued to innovate and grow in numbers. They should no longer be forgotten, condemned, ignored, or bundled into some much larger sector. The occupation is economically, socially, and politically important, and it meets substantial and enduring consumer demands. The population of vendors, customers, and their dependents is too large to ignore.

BRINGING THE PUBLIC REALM BACK INTO THE DISCUSSION

The street is both a contested space and a space for contested visions where different uses and activities, both real and envisioned, compete for significance. In the mid-twentieth century, architects', engineers', and planners' images of cities of the future typically showed wide, straight streets in daylight and good weather, with low traffic densities, beautiful trees, a few strolling pedestrians, and an aura of calm and prosperity (Garnier 1917; Le Corbusier 1933; Lewis 1949). The city was to be sanitized and problem free, with consumers going to their nearest supermarkets and malls and enjoying a middle-class life. When such environments were created, however, whether in Chandigarh, Brasilia, Milton Keynes, or Columbia, Maryland, the public response was apathy. The new utopias proved to be boring, boredom did not attract tourists, and bored consumers reduced their consumption. The response from real estate developers, planning consultants, and retailers has been to reintroduce history, seasonality, and variety, emphasizing enjoyable shopping, dining, and strolling and how unique each outing can be. The archetypal project, replicated from Boston and Baltimore to Hong Kong and Cape Town, is James Rouse's "festival marketplace," a shopping mall enriched with historic theme making, seasonal decorations, food courts, pushcart vendors, and street performers (Hall 1988:347–351). The aim is to make places exciting, and from Las Vegas to "Old" Shanghai, developers often choose historic architectural styles, retail designs, and costumed vendors to create a fantasy history. Even more striking is to replicate buildings, monuments, costumes, and stalls from all over the world, in the Vegas tradition, so that traveling is no longer necessary to experience places. Many cities in the Global South have ethnic stores, restaurants, and stalls offering their wares in alien environments—sometimes products of migrant diasporas, sometimes suppliers to migrant communities, and sometimes merely franchised replicas like Taco Bell and McDonald's.

Globalization has been accompanied by a blurring of place, space, and time and also by a blurring of the distinction between public and private space. Public authorities have long regulated the use of private property and public spaces, but the issues and forms of regulation have become increasingly complex. Real estate developers may be required to provide affordable housing and publicly available plazas on their sites, yet they retain powers to limit public protests and assembly on their property. Meanwhile, public authorities routinely require prior applications and permits for parades and protest demonstrations in public places, and citizens are often forbidden to engage in anything the authorities define as begging, loitering, and lewd behavior. The battle over freedom of assembly and the occupation of public space is ongoing, and increasingly complex forms of "semi-public" and "semi-private" spaces have emerged (Bell et al. 2012; Blomley 2011). For centuries, some off-street businesses have extended themselves out onto the sidewalk or sent employees and family members onto the streets to sell merchandise or distribute publicity. Much more recently, however, mall developers have begun to hire and rent space to small-scale vendors who sell from pushcarts and kiosks in the mall hallways, adding visual and seasonal variety and enabling the malls to exceed 100 percent occupancy.

Perhaps the most ironic dimension of rediscovering the significance of the public realm in the Global North is the new interest of urbanists in re-creating traditional elements of urbanism that are still prevalent in the Global South—livable neighborhoods, congenial public spaces, recycling, and walking and bicycling for healthful exercise, social interaction, and energy efficiency. The "New Urbanists" have created twenty-first-century visions of ideal communities, inspiring some planners and real estate developers and influencing projects around the world (Calthorpe 2011; Duany and Plater-Zyberk 1991). They link closely to "neo-traditionalists" like Leon Krier (1992) and Prince Charles (1989), rejecting modernity and consciously re-creating elements of history in both architecture and urban design. Though they have mainly impacted middle-class communities in the Global North, their influence is also to be seen in some visionary schemes in the Global South, notably, Shanghai's New Towns and Pune's Lavasa. In addition, they build upon the older traditions and influences of the early twentieth-century Garden Cities Movement, which inspired model neighborhoods in many parts of the world (Hall 1988:86–135). In the Global South, there is even an incipient worldwide "streets for all" movement, mainly promoted by bicycle and pedestrian advocates arguing for widespread "traffic calming" and a public realm that is equitably shared by motor vehicles, bicycles, pedestrians, and vendors (de Langen 2005; Khayesi, Monheil, and Nebe 2010).

Ideally, and following a new urbanist model, street vending complements pedestrian activity by making the streets more interesting, convivial, and full of amenities and by putting "eyes on the street," vigilant citizens to witness and report crime and thus deter delinquent behavior (Jacobs 1961). On May 1, 2010, in a spectacular example of eyes on the street, three street vendors, two of them disabled Vietnam veterans and the other a Senegalese Muslim immigrant, alerted police to a suspicious vehicle in New York City's Times Square,[2] preventing what could have been a horrific terrorist bomb attack in one of the world's busiest and best-known public spaces (Fernandez 2010). Despite this high-profile case and many less well-known incidents, however, most media portrayals associate pedestrian congestion with crime, and better-off citizens are shown traveling by car and thus avoiding the supposed hazards of street life.

From the viewpoint of street vendors in the Global South, new perspectives on the public realm offer genuine hope, whether as spaces of democracy, expressions of postmodernity and commercial pluralism, or crucial elements in a socially and environmentally sustainable new urbanism. Sadly, however, the overwhelming majority of elites, technocrats, and officials still cling to the values of modernism, seeing streets as traffic corridors, disorder as disfunctionality, commercial pluralism as the survival of outmoded institutions, and pedestrians and cyclists as deprived individuals who will buy motorcycles and cars after a few more years of economic growth. Street vending remains in a precarious and fluctuating situation. It creates jobs, provides basic goods and services, and helps sustain millions of households, but it irritates officials, competes with off-street businesses, and sometimes contributes to urban problems like congestion and pollution. It takes up valuable and contested space that could be used for vehicle movement, vehicle parking, or real estate development.

For many years and in most parts of the Global South, street vending will continue on the margins—often tolerated, rarely supported, often regulated and pushed from place to place, and frequently persecuted (Bromley 2000). Yet, despite negative elite, official, and media portrayals, street vending is a crucial element in the broader public realm. Its future is closely related to the worldwide struggles currently gathering momentum in the public realm—struggles for democracy, community, social justice, and environmental sustainability.

Notes

1. This section of the chapter is an expansion and updating of the foreword to *Street Entrepreneurs* (Bromley 2007).

2. Wikipedia provides a comprehensive overview of this incident at http://en.wikipedia.org/wiki/2010_Times_Square_car_bombing_attempt, accessed July 17, 2012.

3

Twentieth-Century Government Attacks on Food Vendors in Kumasi, Ghana

Gracia C. Clark

Street vendors find themselves at the center of political controversy in many parts of the world and perhaps nowhere more than in Ghana, West Africa. Government crackdowns on street vendors in Kumasi, Ghana, have been repeated so often that their occurrence requires less explanation than their absence. Hostility from officials is taken for granted as much as the vendors' legendary resilience, rooted in their tireless flexibility in trading practices. The disjuncture between this apparent marginalization and yet the central place of vendors in the consumer economy raises these questions: How can the city government so contemptuously disregard street vendors' rights and needs when vendors provide cheap goods that keep the citizens quiescent? If such a large proportion of Ghana's urban population either works as traders or buys from them, why is targeting traders so popular that many Ghana governments have seen this action as an easy way to gain public respect? Why did this tactic succeed so well, on the whole, for heads of state like former President J. J. Rawlings?

This chapter explores the factors that maintain the contradictions behind those initial questions, by closely analyzing the historical dynamics of the relationship between street vendors and their governments in Kumasi, Ghana's second largest city. The first section explains in some detail the integral role vending plays in the relationships of marriage and parenthood for the predominant Asante ethnic group and some major minority groups.

The second section sketches the timelines of hostile interventions through a slightly extended twentieth century, showing how and why hostilities continued. The third section explores alternative explanatory frameworks for making sense of these apparent contradictions.

I draw on material collected as a by-product of more than thirty years of fieldwork in Kumasi from 1978 to the present. My focus changed over those years from the organization of Kumasi's legendary Central Market, to food security, to development policies, and, most recently, to life histories of Asante women and discussions of contemporary Muslim life (Clark 2010). The central place of street vendors in the economic life of Ghana meant that their consistent marginalization affected these topics, so I learned how vending fit into the lives of the people who taught me about all of them. I interviewed traders and their families, spent time in their markets and homes, and searched the National Archives in Accra and Kumasi and those at the Asantehene's archives on his Kumasi palace grounds. I also draw on my experience in Ghana as a consumer while living for a total of about seven years, including four stays of a year or more. Many traders I came to know well worked in marginal market locations and unregistered or streetside clusters or had moved up and down through the well-populated and fluid continuum from head-tray peddler to Central Market stallholder.

In order to engage these questions, the first step is to assess the integration of street vending into the local economy in both its indigenous and its global aspects. The crowds of strong, well-connected, well-accepted women traders found across coastal West Africa suggest that they would find many local defenders, yet very few stepped forward in times of crisis in Ghana (see Clark 1988b). On closer examination, strong linkages are evident between street vending and the formal sector (both public and private) and also in familial exchanges of work and material support. Its flexibility or variable fluidity, like synthetic engine oil, constantly adjusts to fill the gaps that would otherwise bring the engine to a halt. Vending has woven itself so tightly into the fabric of social relations at home and at work that actually removing it would trigger major realignments in marriage, parenthood, and neighborhood power relations.

Clearly, street vending is important for keeping the wheels of the status quo turning, but this close fit does not preclude friction or pressure. Street vendors are highly effective as a magnet for, and reminder of, social anxieties in many dimensions. Urban streets overflowing with vendors advertise the inability of the formal sector (public and private) to provide jobs for all who need to work, as Bromley (chapter 2, this volume) notes. The size of the informal customer base shows that a substantial proportion even of those with formal sector jobs cannot afford to buy food and services from formal sources.

Skilled workers like teachers, clerks, and nurses who go into trading demonstrate that their salaries have failed to keep up with inflation, despite their valued schooling. Formal employment shrank in Ghana, as it has in many Sub-Saharan countries, under the combined weight of structural adjustment programs and global recession. Workers laid off from the public and the corporate sectors end up trading alongside youths still waiting for that first job. As Hansen reports from Zambia, the youth are particularly hard hit. In the next generation, many of those who finish higher education may eventually join the ranks of vendors, threatening the social reproduction of impoverished middle-class professionals (Hansen 2008b).

As regimes change (and they have changed dramatically in Ghana), their rationale for repressing street vending shifts accordingly. Over the past hundred and twenty years, Kumasi and its surrounding Ashanti Region have experienced many changes of government that have radically shifted major aspects of public commercial policy. In practice, relations between street vending and successive state regimes show the same ambiguity of opposition and clientelism so apparent in kinship relations.

Both international and local trading have been economically important in this region of West Africa for many centuries. Asante emerged as an inland empire with its capital at Kumasi in order to control trade routes between the coastal European forts and older trans-Sahara networks in the dry grasslands to the north, called the savanna. Asante history, family roles, and values assume wide participation in commercial activity. The British made the Asante Empire their colony in 1896 and relinquished control in 1954. An only slightly extended twentieth century thus includes the entire colonial period and an equal time of independence with a wide range of regimes in power.

When British colonial conquerors opened roads and built railroads for military access, they cemented the foundation for Kumasi's commercial dominance in the then Ashanti Region. Its rainforest location already provided gold and kola for export and had suitable land for planting the new crop, cocoa. Kumasi became a key collection and transfer point for exports, imports, and local staples between the coast and the dry grassland zones. Its population has grown to nearly one million at last count, including immigrants from many ethnic groups and neighboring countries.

The African socialism of Ghana's first president, Kwame Nkrumah, yielded in turn to free market capitalism, import substitution, protectionism, cronyism, populism, and globalization over the next fifty years. Traders in official and unofficial markets also faced government raids on an annual or occasional basis, intensified in 1979 and again in 1984, under the military regimes led by J. J. Rawlings. Yet, the same extra degree of vulnerability for street vendors noted by Milgram (chapter 5, this volume) and Babb (chapter 11, this volume) remained remarkably consistent. Physical raids on Ghana markets largely ceased after 1985, under neoliberal pressures, except in the case of relocations of entire markets. By contrast, roadside vendors and ambulatory vendors without permanent sites (called "hawkers" in British parlance) met with very little respect for their livelihoods and private property at any time.

Each successive regime has apparently felt that very similar action would promote its goals and its image. Whether such an action has been presented as price control, sanitation, crime fighting, civic beautification, or just clearing land for a new polyclinic that never materializes, when one looks up from the newspaper account, each episode of demolishing stalls, confiscating goods, and physical attacks on vendors looks very similar and has much the same effect. Likewise, the exclusion of traders from eligibility for various government subsidies, consultations, or protections and from externally funded projects such as microcredit has been consistent across ideologies from left to right and between corrupt and more honest ruling groups, even though the material relations each ruling coalition had with street vendors were quite different.

Since 1990, Ghana has been held up as a shining example that whole-hearted neoliberal reforms will bring economic growth. This makes the Ghanaian experience particularly revealing of the contradictions between neoliberal ideology and its implementation. Conditions attached to World Bank and IMF structural adjustment loans since 1985 mandated deregulation of business and privatization of state enterprises, triggering massive layoffs. World Bank policy principles valorize self-employment and entrepreneurship and rely heavily on the small business sector to provide employment and growth. Yet, attacks on street traders are still accepted as legitimate and commonplace in Accra, Kumasi, and other major cities. The makeshift stalls of street vendors are still broken up, their goods confiscated or destroyed with impunity, and their persons beaten or arrested.

Despite such individual catastrophes, street vending as a whole has been surviving and proliferating. The fluidity and adaptability of vendors, though not unlimited, as Babb (chapter 11, this volume) notes, allow them to continue providing important commercial services and employment options. This becomes a threat to government because control of the economy takes a higher priority than the efficient supply of consumer goods. Low-

FIGURE 3.1

Women frying yams, with children helping and customers looking on. Photo: Gracia Clark,
Kumasi, Ghana, August 28, 2010

entry capital requirements make vending an accessible employment of
first resort for the upwardly mobile and of last resort for the downwardly
mobile, both being politically charged categories in most circumstances.
The visibly rapid expansion of street vending suggests that more desperate
people find themselves near the bottom now, whether looking up or falling
and about to crash. Street and open market locations continue to recapture
contemporary consumer markets in urban Ghana today despite the concomitant expansion of elite consumption, mainly in Accra.

"PART OF OUR WAY OF LIFE"

Street vending, especially of cooked food, has been thoroughly integrated into the social organization of daily life and work for Asante and
for many of the minority ethnic groups in the Kumasi population (figure
3.1). Cultural values and practices that Asante share with many other West
African ethnic groups still rely today upon prepared food sellers to grease
the wheels of commerce, employment, and family life. Both women and
men depend on cooked food sellers to facilitate domestic management on
multiple levels. Vendors provide the equivalent to a convenience store or
delivery service, bringing to the home or workplace the staple items a cook

normally needs to buy every day. Certain foods, such as oranges, bread, or fried doughnuts, almost always reach the consumer from a street vendor, even in residential areas.

The daily routine for many Kumasi families includes breakfast and lunch bought ready-to-eat from the familiar hands of local vendors. Parents and children may leave for school and work at different times, complicating shared meals. British influence popularized the consumption of tea and white bread for breakfast. Bread can be bought the night before and kept out and requires no heating. Bread consumption peaked during the early 1930s and 1950s, but the scarcity and high price of bread during the 1970s and 1980s renewed consumption of local snack foods. Buying snack foods in the immediate neighborhood creates a built-in quality check because any major disease outbreaks among local customers would promptly become public knowledge.

Many of these local foods are rarely prepared for home use, like the Ga and Fanti steamed corn dumplings called *donkono*. Their multistage preparatory process spans several days, first soaking corn and fermenting the prepared corn dough overnight before wrapping portions in corn husks for steaming. In Accra, these dumplings are the historic staple featured in annual rituals, but they are more usually bought daily from vendors there as well. Home production of donkono in Accra takes place only on major holidays, when the labor of visiting relatives is available, as when Mexican-Americans gather to make tamales. Even when a Kumasi woman knows this process herself, it is not worth the trouble for the small quantities that a family would normally consume.

Ghana's informal restaurants, or chop bars, have a shady connotation due to the close association of cooking with marital sexuality (Clark 1989). This local "fast food" outlet creates tension over the power balance between husband and wife, which can be largely avoided by buying meals from vendors in the open air. Farm gate buyers are traders who purchase directly from farmers and stay in a familiar supply area for a week or more. They may also contract with food vendors for regular meals while they arrange for the purchase and pickup of goods. One middle-aged trader jokingly referred to a younger village woman as her village wife because the latter routinely cooked meals for her when she was in town on her buying trips.

Cooked-food vendors save both time and money for Kumasi families and individual workers because many cost factors here work in favor of the vendors. The majority of Kumasi residents cook on charcoal-burning "coal pots" prepared by burning a generous amount of charcoal down to coals. Lighting the coal pot for preparing traditional Asante breakfast dishes,

such as boiled plantain with green leaf stew, burns up more expensive charcoal, as well as more labor time, than buying cornmeal porridge or rice
and beans from a neighbor selling outside her house. Without refrigera-
tion, food left over from meals cannot safely be saved, so it is distributed
among the neighbor children, who help with dishwashing. Formal-sector
fast food, by contrast, costs more than eating at home. Burgers, pizza, and
fried chicken are luxury treats for the upper middle classes in Kumasi, not
a working-class shortcut, as in the United States. Construction sites and
other temporary worksites soon attract vendors who daily supply breakfast
and lunch to the workers, and for larger jobsites, a vendor takes advantage
of the assured demand by setting up a temporary chop bar in the vicinity.

Without completely internalizing European concepts and values about
time, Kumasi residents are well aware that taking time away from their work
or business loses them money. Virtually all Kumasi women, whether from
north or south, Christian or Muslim, do expect to work to earn money for
their children. Any self-respecting Asante adult, male or female, should
have an independent income and support matrilineal relatives, as well as
their own children. Local gender ideals legitimate women's work as an
essential aspect of motherhood (Clark 1999). Mother and father both
should contribute to the subsistence and educational expenses for their
children as much as possible.

Kumasi women are not necessarily available for preparing meals on
demand, even those whose standards of modesty encourage them to work
at home. Kumasi residents include patrilineal Muslim ethnic groups among
which most wives work to earn income that remains under the wife's control. One Muslim husband, who traded in the Central Market and lived
quite nearby, looked surprised when I asked whether he ate lunch at home.
He dismissed the idea with the comment, "My wife would be busy with her
work [as a seamstress]." Although he was pleased that she worked inside the
home, which was more respectable for Muslim women, he clearly found it
unreasonable to expect her to stop work and cook for him during the day.
Meeting with customers and supervising apprentices turns the house into a
workplace during the day. Going home for lunch and stopping to prepare
it are not viable options when every penny counts.

Access to street food vendors also underpins many common strategies
for childcare. Schoolchildren need to be sent off daily with a handful of
coins as lunch money. Children just under school age can be left at home
with their lunch money; they learn to buy food from familiar vendors near
the house long before they can cook for themselves. This low-risk option
enables children aged six or seven to care for their even younger brothers

and sisters, especially when an elderly neighbor is available in the compound to give instructions in emergencies. Toddlers are almost always seen clutching a piece of roasted yam or a handful of rice, whether at home or on their mothers' backs. They actually need these frequent snacks, given their small stomachs, to get enough food in the course of a day. Few Kumasi mothers would stop to cook this often for a child, even if they were at home. Buying food in small amounts helps prevent the malnutrition that can make a difficult weaning year even more hazardous.

Children are also the major labor force in street hawking. As part-time workers, they sell before and after school or at lunch and recess to their classmates and teachers. Those whose families cannot keep them in school sell full-time for family members or neighbors from a young age, starting with a safe round of neighboring houses. Women whose family responsibilities or Muslim values put pressure on them to remain at home can still maintain significant business activities by employing children as hawkers and messengers (Hill 1969; Schildkrout 1978). Bread bakers report taking on apprentices or "girls" who help with the baking before taking the fresh bread out on head trays. Mothers with market stalls often bring a child to serve more customers during the busiest hours and send the child out with a head tray when business is slow. The level of retail food service Kumasi residents expect would hardly be possible without the participation of children earning sub-adult incomes (figure 3.2).

Street vending also serves an important training function for children. It builds skills and confidence that prepare them for more substantial trading later. Many of the elderly traders I interviewed told fondly of their first trading experience vending snack foods. One had had an aunt who sold groundnuts and gave her a bowlful on credit to roast and sell to her classmates at school recess. Another had borrowed some flour from her mother, a baker, and made pancakes to sell to her friends. I noticed that several older traders deliberately trained their grandchildren by setting them up as vendors on their own account. One older woman even bought some cheap peppers for her granddaughter to learn on, rather than risk her own, more expensive yam stock. She tested the six-year-old girl on dividing the peppers into heaps and making change and scolded her when she fell asleep over her tiny corner table. Another middle-aged trader tested her group of young hawkers in a series of complicated mental math problems, involving a customer buying several heaps and asking for a reduction, before sending them out with head trays of her smoked fish.

In very poor families, of course, children need to feed themselves with their daily earnings. One seven-year-old girl from a marginal family looked

FIGURE 3.2

A tree gives free overhead for several vendors beside a major street. Photo: Gracia Clark, Kumasi, Ghana, September 8, 2011.

startled after her first day selling when her mother announced proudly that the girl would now be buying her own lunch from her own earnings. Still, the credit or contacts even a poor Kumasi family can provide set their children one step ahead. The stereotypical destitute child works for even less as a *kaya-kaya* (head carrier),[1] perhaps even with a rented basin. Older traders often mentioned accumulating their initial trading capital by carefully saving such childhood vending earnings. They bemoaned that it was more difficult for the new generation to do so now because of increased competition.

Preadolescent girls were very proud of their commercial success, bragging that they made more money than some adults. One teenage egg seller boasted excitedly to her friends, "I'm hot! I'm hot!" A pre-teen who sold secondhand children's clothes for her aunt after school and on weekends explained with a laugh that she was often able to sell them at more than the set price and keep the difference. Her aunt was delighted when she reported selling them all at the full price and would often give her something from the stock to wear. Besides learning skills, these young traders start building the reputation and contacts that will be important assets for their future ventures. In this light, Robertson (1984:147) noted that in trading families in Accra, girls who finished school had to catch up with peers who had already spent years trading.

Over time, a hawker's status as a good customer of the supplier should increase the amount of goods credited to her, eventually enough to maintain a fixed location and finally, perhaps, a market stall to supply other hawkers in her turn. Cooked food sellers hope to begin as hawkers and develop a customer base and network of contacts, gradually spending longer periods at some regular stop or resting place along their daily route and ultimately managing to establish a lucrative chop bar or roadside restaurant. Those hawking goods for mothers or older relatives may eventually divide or take over their market stalls. Conversely, one Central Market cloth trader who had all her stock confiscated in 1979 started over by hawking secondhand clothes. A yam wholesaler bankrupted by illness in 1990 turned to making and hawking doughnuts to make a new start, finally turning over the hawking and later the production itself to her children and grandchildren. Different kinds of two-way connections between hawkers and stallholders or shopkeepers are described throughout this volume.

Though hawking is perfectly respectable and even laudable for children, showing their reliability and initiative, it should lead to something better as an adult. The constant walking is exhausting and undignified for an older woman. One retired stallholder mentioned leaving hawking long ago for a different line of trade because she "got older." Market and roadside traders turned to hiring young people "with strong legs to run away" as hawkers to sell their goods in 1979 and 1982, when price control enforcement made their fixed premises too vulnerable to confiscation (figure 3.3). An increasing proportion of hawkers now say that they are doing it because they have no option. Even if their mothers are traders, the supplier credit that started the mothers off on their own has now dried up. It is also difficult now to find selling space in the Central Market at any price. All the stall frontages and walkways have long since been filled in and subdivided.

In one life narrative, an elderly Muslim woman who married young in an Ashanti Region small town managed to support all her children with cooked food sales alone after her husband moved to Nigeria. Her young daughters hawked her cooked food outside school hours, and they remembered that it tasted good enough to sell fast. Before long, she had a busy chop bar with several employees and subsequently was able to build a house. Illiterate herself, she paid for law school for her husband in Nigeria

FIGURE 3.3

Vendors on a downtown street corner. Photo: Gracia Clark, Kumasi, Ghana, March 9, 2012.

and put all her daughters through college. Such examples of upward mobility are rare, but for the otherwise desperately disenfranchised, these carry a powerful message of hope that is as compelling as a lotto ticket since the chances for success seem more responsive to individual effort. For the vast majority, however, immediate survival is reward enough because it is by no means assured.

THE HAWKER WARS

Like local African chiefs before them, the British authorities took many steps to create and protect a dominant, profitable role for merchants of their own nation. Street vending emerged as a contentious issue very early in Kumasi's colonial period. The first local government body in Kumasi was the Kumasi Public Health Board (KPHB), established before 1920 by the Chief Medical Officer in response to several plague outbreaks (NAK6 1914). After an initial focus on building large street drains, the KPHB took up arms against street hawkers. The regulations it enforced applied equally to all vendors operating outside registered city markets, but it showed special hostility to vendors of ready-to-eat foods. By 1926, the KPHB minutes show the Provincial Ministry of Health Officer taking a hard line on street hawkers. He referred to food hawkers as injurious to public health, arguing for a limit on their numbers and for setting high license fees (KPHB 1926d). He advocated applying a punishing monthly fee of 15 to 20 shillings; the British-led Chamber of Commerce representative counseled a more reasonable 2 shillings and 6 pence (2s 6d or a half-crown coin).

Local African leaders managed to negotiate limited concessions on some abuses of power by claiming cultural privilege and stressing their cooperation with the authorities. The KPHB had appointed only members who represented segments of the resident British population. The organization had no African members until 1932, when the Asantehene and two educated men were allowed to attend, but these new members were not allowed to vote or to discuss KPHB issues (KPHB 1932b). In 1930, the Asantehene made a special appearance at the KPHB locale to caution against proposed punitive licensing that might make hawking impossible. He then asked that an area in Manhyia, near his new palace, be set aside for legal hawking, explaining, "It is part of our local culture" (KPHB 1930a). Nonetheless, the Health Officer insisted on licenses for all bakeries, laundries, and public eating houses (KPHB 1930c).

Colonial records most frequently accuse vendors of evading market fees, raising price levels, creating an eyesore, and spreading disease—all themes that can still be heard today. The Public Health Officer seemed particularly concerned about the hawkers who sold in the main city market, those selling food to the traders, and other craft workers operating here. He asserted that it would even be better if traders cooked for themselves in the market, despite the constant threat of fires. Licensed hawkers had to stay healthy, avoid selling near dustbins or latrines, and protect their wares from dirt and filth (KPHB 1926b). To be held legally accountable for their actions, they had to be of legal age, disqualifying the large proportion of children doing this work.

A few more supportive measures were mentioned, but these were not actually pro-hawker as such. Like Seligmann's (chapter 7, this volume) modern markets for Cusco vendors, they rather promoted formalization through fixed premises and modern facilities. As an early example, the Kumasi Central Market was rebuilt starting in 1925 in a new spacious site designed to replace the overcrowded old site pinched between downtown stores. Street vendors were expected to rent stalls in recognized markets when available, bolstering the market revenues, which already provided a substantial part of the city's income (KPHB 1926a). A more sympathetic

Chief Medical Officer reportedly designed hygienic, glass-walled display boxes, made by local carpenters and light enough for vendors to carry on their heads (KPHB 1930c). By 1930, the Chief Commissioner of Ashanti recommended that small towns and rural villages throughout Ashanti construct public market buildings and use the revenues to fund local sanitary facilities (NAK14 1930). In 1932, stalls were built for bread sellers and food sellers in Kejetia, the truck and bus station adjacent to the Central Market (KPHB 1932a).

Older traders remembered the Sanitary Inspector as a "bogey man" of their youth, to be feared or outwitted. In rural areas, the Sanitary Inspectors fined married women for their dirty kitchens or confiscated roaming pigs. Those in Kumasi reported to the Chief Engineer, who had built the market and also kept the market plans. These "sanitary boys" waged an undeclared "Sanitary War" against hawkers. Inspectors had considerable discretion in enforcing the rules, leading to petitions for relief by those victimized by their tactics. In 1926, a firewood seller complained that he had been waylaid and beaten by the sanitary inspectors (KPHB 1926b). Also, in August 1926, a baker was arrested because she thought that her baker's license covered sending her "boys" out to sell the bread (KPHB 1926c). Five women bakers petitioned inspectors in 1931, protesting that their "hawking boys" had been harassed by the "sanitary boys," who had seized the hawkers' pans and tables and eaten their bread (KPHB 1931).

These raids and the regulations behind them, despite their notoriety and evident lack of success in reducing the number of hawkers, retained firm official backing until the end of British rule. In 1934, the Health Officer in Kumasi proposed a regular twice-weekly roundup of hawkers, which, in practice, caught frustratingly few (KPHB 1934). Kumasi's six "hawker controllers" stayed very busy even after World War II and petitioned in 1951 for more assistants and "less conspicuous uniforms" to enable them to capture more hawkers, whom they would hand over to the police (NAK8 1951).

The 1947 Commission of Enquiry into trade malpractices during World War II documented numerous measures taken to preserve the dominance of the major expatriate firms and protect British hegemony (Trade Malpractices 1965). British employers in Ghana had two economic concerns with the growth of street vending. By providing at least a barely viable work alternative to the mines, the military, the civil service, and labor on cocoa farms, a thriving street economy reduced the supply of desperate men (surplus labor) and reinforced a wage floor. It pushed further upward on wages by evading colonial attempts to keep wages low by keeping prices low for farm produce. During both world wars, military recruitment led to shortages of urban and farm labor, but food purchases for the barracks and prisons increased. Price controls were tried for local produce in regional capitals like Kumasi and mining towns like nearby Obuasi, but these measures only drove food sales to backstreets and transient locations (NAK6 1914).

Despite meticulous research by Rowena Lawson, the commission report proposed a solution to shortages and rising prices that repeated a familiar colonial formula: gradually reduce the number of licenses granted to traders outside shops. Nationalist leaders in the postwar period (including Kwame Nkrumah, the future president) blamed the same conditions of scarcity and high prices on British rule. They refuted the demonization of street and market trading and relied on financial and organizing support from market traders. The eminent Dr. J. B. Danquah gave an impassioned speech in their defense, calling them "our mothers" in response to the 1947 trade irregularities report (NAA6 1947).

When independence came in 1957 and Nkrumah became leader of the new country, Ghana, the nationalists quickly reoriented commercial policy to remove provisions protecting British firms. The Nkrumah government switched the focus of price control enforcement from local food production to imported goods. However, because Nkrumah was accountable for the rising cost of living and for paying adequate wages to office staff and to other salaried workers, he likewise needed a convenient scapegoat. Near at hand was colonial rhetoric that deflected responsibility for the higher prices of both imports and local foods onto traders' deliberate hoarding and other conspiratorial practices. As price controls began with the import list of "essential commodities," initiatives like the State Farms and the Ghana Food Trading Corporation also sought to limit or eliminate traders' range of control.

Government spokesmen continued to blame traders for national economic problems that deepened through the 1980s (Robertson 1983). Although socialist, populist, patronist, and free market regimes had different relations to the informal street trader and expressed these in the language of their regulations and their enforcement, their street tactics of rounding up traders to beat them and confiscate their goods echo eerily across the decades. Each successive regime announced its seriousness by raiding informal markets and streetside kiosks, and these attacks continued to be violent and arbitrary—demolishing sheds and confiscating goods, even those of hawkers who had received permission from other parts of the government. Busia's free-market policies and Acheampong's "Operation Feed

Yourself" had quite different aims and structural relations to street vending, but their episodic raids looked and felt the same.

Flight Lieutenant Jerry Rawlings headed several regimes that confronted traders in and out of the official markets. Rawlings' first brief stay in office in 1979, between the military Akuffo and the elected Limann, aimed at eliminating the most corrupt individuals, but in his second term, which lasted ten years (1983–1994), he attempted to institute more comprehensive reforms of the distribution system through producer and consumer cooperatives and brigades. Grappling with rampant inflation and dizzying price levels for daily foodstuffs, he targeted food-crop vendors with draconian price controls that had disastrous results (Clark 1988b). Quality and serving size of ingredients for prepared foods like bread and donkono made a mockery of the official price lists because vendors simply reduced the portion size. When soldiers started confiscating foodstuffs in 1983, Kumasi and other towns endured acute food shortages because farmers stopped selling their crops (Clark 1988b). A few months after initiating both of these directives, the government tacitly suspended its enforcement in order to restore the flow of food, even though price controls were cancelled legally only as a condition of World Bank loan assistance in 1985.

Repeated government efforts at controlling trade continue to target hawkers and roadside food vendors through ongoing street clearance campaigns, civic beautification initiatives, and decongestion exercises. Trade deregulation has afforded some protection to traders in designated marketplaces, and commercial policy has stabilized for the past twenty years, reflecting a long-term commitment to free-market principles. Since elections began in 1994, several peaceful handovers of power have taken place between political parties after close elections earned Ghana its reputation as a stable democracy. Still, each new head of state has apparently felt compelled to prove his mettle by promptly removing street vendors in Accra and in regional capitals like Kumasi. Street vendors remain highly vulnerable and highly effective scapegoats for conflicts and grievances over urban land use, unemployment, household budgeting, child labor, and economic development.

Democratic governments do not escape the pressures that drive more authoritarian regimes to act against the street economy. Indeed, in some ways, their greater accountability for the state of the economy presses them to exert more control. Under indirect rule, the colonial British sought mainly to generate revenue and reduce costs; hence, their interventions quickly retreated to ensuring tax collection and low-cost foodstuffs for government purchase. The fluidity of street vending facilitated escape from these demands, so it was repressed in favor of registered marketplaces. Independent governments faced similar revenue and cost pressures, but in addition, they promised to deliver a rising standard of living. In Ghana, this promise led them to reorient colonial price controls to focus on the imports that symbolized progress. Military rulers likewise modified the colonial theme of discipline to assert central control of economic processes. For African-led regimes, the organized traders in marketplaces presented a stronger structural threat to their extended agenda than did street vendors. Market groups gradually emerged as the central target of both vitriolic discourse and repressive action, though street vendors' second place offered them little protection. Despite their structural vulnerability, vendors remained the most visible category of trade because their presence contradicted the narrative of government-led progress. Meanwhile, the self-exploitation and competition in these so-called refuge employment sectors offered few real opportunities for sellers.

THE STREET ECONOMY KEEPS COMING BACK

The narrative genre of governments that is grounded in how they lead the nation ahead by successfully managing the economy encapsulates the evolutionary, statist assumptions shared by leftist and rightist regimes even as they overthrew each other in postwar Ghana. Although visions of economic utopia and the strategies for arriving there might radically diverge among supporters of socialist, free-market, and personalist forms of government, they all expect their government to create the necessary conditions to move away from the present disorderly, stagnant conditions toward a more orderly stage that includes higher efficiency, advanced technology, more wealth, and a higher standard of living. The persisting street economy continually defeats all these aspirations for such order, both materially and symbolically, and hence attracts hostility from those who endorse such visions.

Modernization analysts in the 1950s, like socialists in the 1930s, assumed that street vending and other informal trade would wither away naturally over the decades that followed, starved out by the superior efficiency of modern economic institutions. Factories and stores would grow and multiply, taking over their market share until the Global South came to resemble the North, or else state farms and cooperatives would expand to mimic the Eastern Bloc. Each side in the Cold War assumed this process to be historically inevitable, as well as desirable, making its reversal even more shocking. Not only did the metaphorical train to development utopia suffer serious delays, but also its track was turned upside down. Instead, flexible and contingent work relations and subcontracting have multiplied in the industrial nations, making the industrial economies look and feel more like the Third World, street vendors included (Bromley 2000). Street vendors in their numbers contradict the legitimacy of the national journey narrative, whether they prosper or suffer, because they have no place in any of these narratives.

The street economy also diverts significant material resources from the national project, however this is formulated. It is not capital intensive, but its open access and labor intensity deprive the corporate economy of the dispossessed, undervalued labor through which corporations accumulate capital. Street vending not only deprives the state apparatus of tax revenue but also hampers the corporate and state sectors' preferential access to prime real estate, transport infrastructure, and ordinary consumers. These material rivalries lay a material basis for the declared public antagonism between the street economy and both of the formally documented spheres—private and public. The street, a quintessentially public space, presents a direct challenge to the state's hegemony over what is public. Various symbolic connections can intensify this structural opposition by ideological and psychological reinforcement, giving the symbolic its actual material effects.

In a parallel way, hostility to street vendors draws energy from other arenas of social conflict by association with their resources. Health and safety concerns about food vending have a reality beyond the imagination of colonial officers. Poor working conditions in the market or on deteriorated side streets do multiply ill health and injuries among stallholders, hawkers, carriers, customers, and the general population. Equally strong connections link street food and the ubiquitous chop bar with significant gender anxieties over sexual fidelity and child support, placing cooked-food vendors at the center of some of the bitterest contestations. Cloth also carries strong moral connotations from its association with marriage, child-birth, and funerals, and it has also long been a focus of political argument about trade practices.

Continuing repression of this intensity might easily weaken the street economy, so why does it persist so tenaciously? The fluidity that seems to show structural weakness produces an elastic strength, enabling street traders to adapt rapidly to changing patterns of opportunity and also to dangers of extinction. Street vending always stands in intimate interaction with formal sector institutions such as government marketing boards, corporations, and cooperatives and with more organized parts of the spectrum of commercial activity, such as registered marketplaces. It is constituted in relation to them, so its membership and sales strategies constantly reshape to fill the ever-shifting gap between them.

The same fluidity that underpins their fabled resilience also reproduces the hostility and neglect they endure. Traders compensate quickly for hostile rules and actions and therefore reappear promptly even after repeated raids. This rapid bounce back leads development analysts to underestimate the losses of capital and time caused by arbitrary enforcement of licensing and other regulations, notably, price controls. They likewise overestimate the capacity of the "informal sector" to absorb new entrants ejected from the formal private and public sectors under neoliberal austerity programs. Meanwhile, the self-exploitation and competition in these supposed refuge employment sectors offer little real refuge.

Constant adaptation means that the street economy quickly reflects shifts in the relationships between other economic and ethnic sectors that it mediates. It not only fills the cracks in the system but also makes them more visible, which is not always welcome. Such cracks are, in fact, not anomalies, but an integral part of the economic structure. They shift in order to maintain the core inequality whose stability fuels this system. These constant changes help the street economy survive, often with new individuals populating it, but they also ensure a connection between its current shape and emergent problematic issues. The street economy thus remains a relevant symbol of discontent and a relevant scapegoat for social tensions. For example, swelling numbers of vendors signal the failure of a government to manage a suitable formal economy that meets the consumption and employment needs of the country. Displays of smuggled goods testify to porous borders and lax enforcement of foreign exchange and import regulations.

Because of vendors' relative lack of political leverage, the enforcement of licensing and business regulations, mainly, price controls, has a disproportionate impact on them. Crackdowns on street vendors are a cheap thrill that costs a regime little, politically or financially, while demonstrating that it cares about economic hardship and national progress. Neoliberal loan conditionalities rule out exercising most other regulatory options, but they still allow street clearances. Street vending frequently turns into a flashpoint for political or social tensions that have their roots in other economic sectors. Traders act as proxies for confrontations with more dangerous protagonists, such as corruption, ethnic and racial inequalities, illegal immigration, and gender relations within the household or family.

Prices and capital arrangements in the street economy reflect sensitive balances of economic power across the world system, within the

Kumasi market's institutions, and between rural and urban communities. Impoverished migrants from remote dusty villages inside Ghana's borders trade alongside refugees from its war-torn neighbors, considering themselves fortunate to be street vendors instead of carrying loads or begging. The battles for vending space on sidewalks, in parks, and in vacant lots cast a spotlight on corruption and inequality in access to prime, central, urban land and competition with formal businesses for scarce consumers and supplies. Neoliberal aspirations only raise the price of land and storefronts, from higher rents offered by foreign investors and from large-scale government appropriation of land for modernist displays of public investment. Construction has begun in Kumasi on a gated community downtown on land near its Central Market. Though nowhere near the scale of South African suburbs or World Cup facilities described by Lindell and her colleagues (chapter 10, this volume), it displaces a thriving market where city authorities had already relocated traders displaced by a highway bypass. Chronic disputes over who has legitimate access to public space and for what purposes test the boundaries of recognized citizenship, both literally and figuratively.

Analysts commonly classify street vendors as extremely marginal to the national or urban economy, metaphorically operating at the farthest edges of the global corporate system. Such socioeconomic locations should logically be quiet and neglected, remote from the attention of government and the private sector. Instead, street vendors typically find themselves at the center of public attention, the first rather than the last to attract government intervention in any sort of crisis. This historical pattern suggests that their location is closer to the center of the globalized economy but structurally subordinated so as to conceal the inequality at the core of that globalized economy's sustainability. The fluid economic position of vendors matches their fluid ideological position generating repeated shifts in friends and enemies. These fluid political alliances place vendors in an ambiguous political category, not a neutral or forgotten social location but rather a highly charged and volatile intersection that sparks frequent explosions (Clark 1999).

The continuing denial of legitimacy to street trading belies its integration into the fabric of daily life for Kumasi residents and for Ghanaians more generally. The public might be expected to take this economic sphere for granted and the government to shrink from ruining its subsidy of social reproduction costs. Food, consumer goods, and services sold on the streets keep the urban population fed, allow real wages to dwindle without immediate catastrophe, and enable mothers to combine work and childcare. The

47

option of trading or hawking goods also serves as a safety valve for the job-less, young or old, keeping them frantically busy selling instead of idle and desperate enough to rebel.

The antagonism between street vendors and national or local authori-ties is so common globally that it is taken for granted, as Bromley's overview (chapter 2, this volume) states very clearly. Many linkages in the supply chain and its personnel mitigate this oppositional dynamic, but it remains a pervasive reality in many contexts. Street and market vendors appear as emblems of political opposition and volatility, in localized forms, across Latin America, Asia, and other parts of Africa, justifying drastic repression in one country after another (Clark 1988a). Depending on local circum-stances, street vendors may be caught up in these hostilities or dodge them; they may be special targets or be likely to avoid arrest because they are underage and ready to run. In Ghana, I witnessed repeated clearances of street vendors in Accra and Kumasi from 1978 to 2011, and I heard or read reports of many other incidents. These persistent enforcement measures, now routinely called "decongestion exercises," have driven vendors away from specific locations at key urban intersections but have not dislodged them from their critical place in the distribution system.

These patterns of attack and resistance show that the street economy inhabits an unusual social location, at once highly vulnerable and strate-gically central to the constellation of more powerful social forces. Street vendors reflect the contradictory pressures of those forces so directly that they threaten to display the actively obscured but fierce subordination that lies at the core of global economies. Ideally, they would perform their func-tions invisibly and unseen, but in reality, the formal sectors of the economy do not function as noiselessly as elites perhaps expect (Sassen 1996a, 2001). The occasional scream and grind emerge from powerful but imperfectly aligned social forces that call on the vending sector to keep them moving against one another. To be useful in this way, street vendors need to be con-tinually present in the center but also reliably fluid, that is, securely subor-dinated, to respond effectively to its ever changing demands. Since no such control is completely successful, street traders do resist, at least passively, and it is their centrality that makes the sparks fly when they do.

Note

1. The kaya-kaya (pidgin English for "carrier") stands ready for hire with a large basin or basket to carry purchases to and from the lorry park or within the market for a small fee.

4

Where Have All the Vendors Gone?

Redrawing Boundaries in Lusaka's Street Economy

Karen Tranberg Hansen and Wilma S. Nchito

At a news briefing in June 2009 in Lusaka, Zambia, the minister of Local Government and Housing (LGH) confidently asserted that street vending would become history by June 10, the date set to remove vendors from the capital's central business district (CBD) in preparation for the opening of the recently completed New Soweto Market (Zambia Daily Mail 2009b). But even though street vendors and itinerant traders were conspicuous by their absence in the CBD during the summer months of 2010, the minister was wrong. For rather than reaching the end of street vending, Lusaka's street economy is undergoing one of many processes of boundary redrawing.

Focusing on the impasse over the formal commissioning of the latest ultramodern market in Lusaka, the New Soweto Market, this chapter explores some effects of changes in the regime of spatial regulation that have accompanied the restructuring of Zambia's economy in the wake of economic liberalization since the transition from a socialist command to a market economy in 1991. We argue that the delay in the formal opening of the New Soweto Market reveals a new configuration of a long-contested relationship between street vendors, marketeers, agents of the state, political parties, and external agents. Because power, according to Foucault (1991), rarely is entirely totalizing, conflicts between regulatory agencies at different levels of society and political bodies leave scope for the complex dynamics in Lusaka's street economy. We suggest that the current spatial politics has contributed to placing the street within the market and, in the process, fueled fresh tensions between vendors, marketeers, and regulatory agents. According to the marketeers, the street vendors who mill around outside the market take away their customers yet do not pay market fees. The street vendors for their part argue that they cannot return to the streets because vending in public space is illegal.

Our research question, where have all the street vendors gone?, arises from long-time engagement with Lusaka's streets and markets and is based specifically on research we conducted in Lusaka around the Soweto Market complex between mid-August and mid-October 2010 (Hansen 2004, 2008a, 2010; Nchito 2002, 2011; Nchito and Hansen 2010). Our work contributes to a growing body of scholarship on public space and informality in urban street economies in both the North and the South (Brown 2006c; Cross and Morales 2007; Lindell 2010c). Although governing authorities both past and present have worked against street vendors to recover public space by means of repressive action, in some cases, they have also worked with vendors to facilitate vendors' livelihoods (Dobson, Skinner, and Nicholson 2009; Donovan 2008; Hunt 2009; Skinner 2008). Still, the conditions of street vendors are rarely legally protected, and they seldom participate in urban governance (Brown, Lyons, and Dankoco 2010:679).

The chapter begins with a sketch of recent economic restructuring and spatial regulation in Zambia. Then we briefly describe Lusaka's changing street vending scene, focusing on markets. This is followed by a discussion of management and politics in markets. Next we present some of our research observations, along with case studies as illustration.[1] In the conclusion, we showcase not the end to street vending but what may likely turn out to be a brief historical moment in the recurring, always contested, boundary-making relationship between actors and agents in Lusaka's street economy.

ECONOMIC RESTRUCTURING AND SPATIAL REGULATION IN ZAMBIA

Zambia's copper-based economy has performed well in recent years, thanks to rising world market prices and the increase of nontraditional exports. Although it continues to be characterized in United Nations terms as one of the world's least developed countries, Zambia's GDP has grown steadily since the early 2000s (EUI 2010:15).[2] Privatization of the mining industry has attracted investors from Australia, Canada, India, China. The infrastructure is undergoing upgrading of roads, schools, and hospitals largely financed by external donors in support of International Monetary Fund (IMF) and World Bank development approaches. Urban administrative decentralization is one of these approaches that has specific bearing on our discussion in this chapter.

These are welcome changes against the backdrop of the 1980s and 1990s' IMF/World Bank–initiated structural adjustment programs (SAPs), which saw growing inequality, rising unemployment, deteriorating health, declining access to education, and a crumbling infrastructure. In 2002, the SAPs were succeeded by a World Bank–initiated Poverty Reduction Strategy Papers (PRSP), the compliance with which in 2005 qualified Zambia for debt relief under the Highly Indebted Poor Countries (HIPC) Initiative. Aiming to reduce the adverse effects of SAPs, this pro-poor policy pursues poverty reduction through democracy, open markets, and a competitive business environment. The Fifth National Development Plan 2006–2010 (FNDP) succeeded PRSP, targeting agriculture growth as the key to poverty reduction. FNDP promotes an environment supportive of private sector growth, infrastructure, health, and education. The urban sector policies include plans for housing, safe water, sanitation, and waste management (Republic of Zambia 2006:20–41) yet do not reference markets and their management.

Two decades of SAPs and recent neoliberal reforms have had political, economic, sociocultural, and spatial ramifications that affect the livelihoods of different population groups in unlike ways, sharpening inequalities and extending them in new ways. In Lusaka, with an estimated population of nearly two million, the reforms are altering the nature and availability of urban space, including land and infrastructure and access to markets. Changes in land values have adversely affected the availability of housing and its location, as well as the place and nature of commercial activity. The vast majority of Lusaka's population lives in informal housing on the outskirts of the city. Here, inadequate provision of electricity, water, and transport reduces the possibility for residents to pursue small-scale manufacturing activities.

Many poor urban residents have turned the designated markets and streets in Lusaka's city center into a major stage in their struggle for economic access. But vendor access to public space has become increasingly limited by foreign investment in the retail sector. Urban retail space has been reconfigured as investors, especially South African and Chinese firms, participate in selective upgrading resulting in new patterns of spatial segregation. A visible result is several shopping malls financed by British and South African capital and by local business interests. Additional malls and upgrading of existing markets are underway. The New Soweto Market, financed by the European Union and built between 2005 and 2009, adds to these efforts as "the Manda Hill of markets," referencing the name of Lusaka's first modern shopping mall.

Political interference in markets has complicated the Ministry of Local Government and Housing's (MLGH) efforts to implement donor-required decentralization of the urban administration (Resnick 2011). The scope for politics in markets grew after the enactment of the Local Government Act of 1991, when city councils became elected rather than appointed by the governing party (Mutale 2004:41–42). Today in Zambia's urban areas, almost all mayors and councilors are members of opposition parties, whereas the LGH minister is a political appointee and central government controls finances (Chikulu 2009). As a result, the city councils have neither total control over the street economy nor sufficient resources to enforce the Markets Act. The LGH Ministry is supposed to oversee market operations through the city councils, but the governing party, the Movement for Multi-party Democracy (MMD), keeps offices and staff in many markets, where opposition parties such as the Patriotic Front (PF) also interfere intermittently. This situation enables a variety of actors to affect the operation of urban markets and promotes continual friction.

MARKETS AND STREET VENDING IN LUSAKA

On the pages that follow, we briefly overview the market scene close to Lusaka's CBD.[3] Our concern is to highlight the contested relationship between marketeers (traders who occupy authorized stands or stalls), unauthorized vendors, and regulatory agencies in a context where new regimes of urban governance are being implemented.

In the late 1990s, Lusaka had several designated city and township markets (Hansen 2004:68) (figure 4.1).[4] Vending is illegal in spaces not designated as markets, such as streets and other areas not authorized for vending. Street vending developed during the colonial period, especially in the African townships, and spread rapidly into the downtown area when the economy slowly declined in the mid-1970s. Then as now, the Lusaka City Council occasionally removed vendors from the streets, confiscating their goods and fining them. Vendors who are unable to pay serve prison sentences.

Lusaka's largest market is called Soweto, named after the large African township outside Johannesburg. Beginning informally, Soweto Market developed in the late 1970s as a center for the produce trade at the edge of the light industrial area. It soon featured the capital's largest auto-part section and trades in small-scale manufacture, repair, and services. Toward the end of 1994, several traders were relocated because of the construction

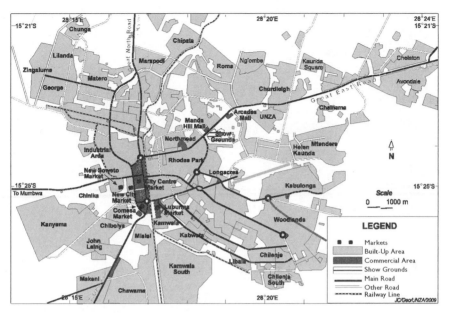

FIGURE 4.1

Map of Lusaka and new markets. Redrawn from Greater Lusaka Surveyor General, Lusaka,
2009.

of a new market. In return, the City Council promised them stands in the
new market. Several months of trouble preceded the move. Some vendors
set up beyond the market area underneath tall pylons carrying high-power
electric cables. Others went outside Kamwala, Lusaka's oldest market, trading next to the railway tracks.

Above all, traders spilled into the streets. The 1997 opening of the new
market at Soweto, called City Market, did little to halt the process. Many
stand-holders who had fought for space in the new market gave up their
stands, complaining of high fees and lack of customers. A few days after the
market's formal opening, the City Council burned the makeshift stands
outside the market. Yet, stand-holders continued to leave the new market
for the streets in ongoing conflicts between marketeers and vendors, police,
the City Council, management, and political cadres.[5]

By Christmas 1998 in Lusaka, vendors seemed to rule the streets, having turned main streets, alleyways, and shop corridors in the city center
and many other places into one huge outdoor shopping mall (figure 4.2).
The crowding in this least capitalized and most labor-intensive part of
the economy caused traffic problems and public health dangers and gave
pickpockets a field day. In the pre-dawn hours of April 28, 1999, council

FIGURE 4.2

Street vendors in Lubumbashi Road. Photo: Karen Tranberg Hansen, Lusaka, Zambia, 2009.

workers, police, and paramilitary razed the makeshift stands in Lusaka's city center, extending the demolition the following night and weeks across the city, into the townships, and, in June, into the Copperbelt and other towns. For a few months, Lusaka's main streets remained almost free from vendors, yet they soon returned in a variety of disguises, among them, car boot sales, sales from containers, and mobile business conducted during rush hours.

Before and after the 1999 massive clearing of street vendors, the City Council encouraged vendors to move to designated markets in the townships, apply for stands in the new City Market, or move to Chibolya, a site that was west of the light industrial area and in 1997 had been slated for a market. It took several years to be completed and consists merely of a perimeter wall behind which marketeers build stands. In 2004, it served as a center for the fish trade. Vendors complained that Chibolya was too far from the city center. Meanwhile, at City Market, it took the construction of a bus station for marketeers to set up stands within the market and for customers to frequent it. With subdivided stalls, today it accommodates some four thousand marketeers, and vendors in the thousands display their goods outside the market, including on a site reserved for a parking lot.

Kamwala, Lusaka's oldest market, was built during the colonial era's racial segregation to serve Africans. At independence in 1964, it constituted the capital's liveliest shopping area for people with limited income. By the mid-1990s, the space outside Kamwala had filled up, absorbing vendors displaced by the development of the City Market. When a Chinese-funded redevelopment project began at Kamwala in 2001, it displaced hundreds of marketeers and vendors. Redeveloping parts of the old market appeared to be a solution to the oppressive crowding inside the market. But rental fees catering to higher-end traders, including many Chinese operators, pushed out less well capitalized traders, forcing vendors and small-scale marketeers who had operated there for years to look for alternative locations.

Higher-end traders were also the target for the redevelopment of Lusaka's Town Centre Market, constructed in 1966 in the heart of the CBD. In the 1990s, it functioned as a convenience market for city center workers. This market redevelopment is a joint enterprise between the City Council and local businesses (with Lebanese background). The project experienced problems resembling those at Soweto and Kamwala, including delays caused by the unwillingness of traders to relocate, excessive shop rentals, and allegations of foreigners' "taking over" the market. After several warnings in 2008 and again in 2009, council police demolished stalls in the City Centre Market and nearby streets, promising vendors a site on the edge of the Soweto Market complex (Zambia Daily Mail 2008, 2009a).

The COMESA flea market on Lumumba Road not far from the Soweto Market complex is a rare exception to the pattern of authorities cracking down on vendors. In this case, mobile cross-border traders successfully dealt with regulatory authorities. In 1998, the Zambia Cross-Border Traders Association purchased land near the COMESA headquarters (Common Market for East and Central Africa, a customs union) (Nchito and Hansen 2010).[6] Successfully contesting efforts to regulate informal activities, the cross-border traders rather than the LGH minister proudly asserted ownership. Commonly referred to as the COMESA market, it is used solely by cross-border traders. Popular because of its reasonable prices, the COMESA market offers a wide variety of items from dry goods, to clothing, bedding, and beverages.

Throughout these years, the Soweto Market complex expanded. Bordered to the west by a secondary school, Namununga, the area under the high-power pylons continued to be a thorn in the eye of the City Council. After a cholera outbreak in February 2004, the area under the pylons that in the past had absorbed many vendors was razed. The vendors filled up the sides along nearby Los Angeles Road. Others returned to the streets,

FIGURE 4.3
New Soweto Market. Photo: Wilma Nchito, Lusaka, Zambia, 2011.

where conflicts over space keep arising. Although several new markets have been built in Lusaka, they have not solved the contentious street-vending problem. In effect, vendors move on and off the streets depending on the resolve of the City Council and the political climate.

THE NEW SOWETO MARKET

Ten years after the largest-ever clean-up exercise of street vendors in Zambia in 1999, the New Soweto Market (figure 4.3), with stalls for more than two thousand vendors, was completed (in March or April). In July 2009, it was ready to be formally commissioned. Its construction, financed by the European Union as part of a Market Rehabilitation Project across Zambia,[7] had begun in 2005 on the western edge of the Soweto Market complex next to the power pylons. This "Manda Hill of markets" is an ultra-modern market consisting of several buildings with shops; open sheds with stands for the sale of fresh vegetables, fruit, and dried goods (fish, grain, dried vegetables); maize and oil grinding mills; and storage space. There are electricity, water, and fee-paying toilets with showers and bathtubs. The market features banks, a post office, a police post, a taxi rank, and many other facilities.

Hoping to undertake a site visit in July 2009, we were not allowed to enter the new market. By September 2009, when entry was possible, only

FIGURE 4.4
Demolishing market stalls at the old Soweto Market, Lusaka, Zambia. Photo: The Post, 2001.
Published with permission of the National Archives of Zambia.

a few shops appeared to be occupied. This brand new market was nearly deserted. Meanwhile, on Lumumba Road bordering City Market and new developments to the north, street vendors crowded several street blocks. Rumors of a major removal abounded, including the one with the June 10, 2009, deadline we mentioned. But the previous year, an opposition party, the Patriotic Front (PF) controlling the Lusaka City Council, had obtained a court injunction, restraining the LGH minister from removing the vendors (Zambia Daily Mail 2009b). Not until September 13, 2009, did police forcefully move vendors from the streets, demolishing their stalls in an action said to cost the LGH Ministry K2 billion (Times of Zambia 2009) (figure 4.4).[8]

One year later, in October 2010, the New Soweto Market had still not been formally commissioned. Yet, it was crowded by vendors working in open space, not from designated stalls but in front of shops, and several shops appeared vacant (figure 4.5). Along the perimeter wall were *salaula* (secondhand clothing) stands. For more than one year, rumors of a formal opening circulated. City Council personnel and market management explained the delay by lack of transparency in the allocation of stalls and shops and political interference. Indeed, an initial allocation was nullified

FIGURE 4.5

Street vendors occupying space in front of formal shops in the New Soweto Market. Photo: Wilma Nchito, Lusaka, Zambia, 2011.

and another undertaken. But several persons who initially were allocated space lodged court cases, delaying the formal opening of the market (Nchito 2011:100–101).

MARKET MANAGEMENT AND POLITICAL INTEREST GROUPS

Most markets in Zambia are state property. The Markets Act empowers the LGH minister to delegate management to local authorities (district, municipal, and city councils). In the past, markets were managed by city councils or cooperative societies. Stand-holders paid levies to the council, rent to the cooperative society, and daily fees. Many also paid fees to funeral societies, football associations, and security guards.

Because markets are strategic places for party recruitment, their management has been a target for political maneuver. During the one-party state (1972–1991), the ruling party, the United National Independence Party (UNIP), usurped power under the Markets Act, often through the

cooperative societies, controlling or taking control of the stand allocation in many markets through its youth wing (Beveridge and Oberschall
1979:84–86). UNIP membership became a prerequisite for access to a
stand, with stand-holders paying fees or levies to the party.

The new City Market, opened in August 1997, was the first market
to experience decentralization of governance through the management
regime of a private firm. The idea of establishing management boards had
been introduced in the late 1990s as part of the EU market rehabilitation
project in Lusaka and on the Copperbelt and implemented in some markets in 2005 (Nchito 2002). Including a variety of stakeholders, such boards
were expected to depoliticize the running of markets and lessen the conflicts between councils, different groups of marketeers, the LGH Ministry,
and political parties.

But the decentralized strategy of governance through stakeholder participation reinforced the role of interest groups instead of democratizing
market management. Board membership was based on party allegiance
and special interests, with cadres, political factions, and associations collecting or soliciting levies. The private management of the City Market,
for example, lasted only a couple of years, after which the City Council
resumed its management. In 2006, the LGH minister dissolved the management boards and through the city councils took charge of the markets
again. A new Markets and Bus Stations Act of 2007 came into effect in
2008, vesting power in the LGH minister to appoint local authorities or
boards to manage markets (Republic of Zambia 2007). Not exactly in the
spirit of decentralization, the minister appointed several board members.
Top-heavy, the new act banned associations from operating within markets
managed by local authority or a board, clearly in an effort to prevent interest groups from setting up bases in markets. In 2010, most regulatory discussions of new markets made reference to management boards, invoking
a participation model aimed at broader representation and less political
maneuvering than when boards were introduced in the late 1990s.

During the impasse caused by the delay in the formal opening of the
New Soweto Market, the MMD allocated space to vendors outside the
shops and stalls in the open sheds. "There is nothing we can do about it,"
explained a woman council police officer, "until the market has been formally opened. Then we have the power." The City Market employs an anti-
vending team of market and council workers who remove vendors from the
premises. A member of the management team observed the futility of such
exercises. "At times, it gets very political," he said. This is the case close to
the election campaign period, when there are challenges from all corners

and the team cannot "push vendors too much around." Referring to the upcoming 2011 presidential and parliamentary elections, he no doubt recalled the riots instigated by MMD and PF cadres in several urban markets after the 2009 presidential election. Markets have become a political tool because the City Council's efforts to run markets are subordinated to management directives of the LGH Ministry, which the MMD controls.

What of the street vendors? The new approaches to market management relate to vendors through control rather than assistance. In the view of regulators, street vendors constitute an economic and political nuisance. The new markets constructed since the late 1990s and exhortations to vendors to rent stalls in designated markets have been ineffective. Market upgrading and redevelopment have largely excluded vendors through high rental fees. Taken together, these developments are threatening the earning potential and livelihoods of the thousands of vendors whom investment-driven market liberalization has displaced.

LUSAKA'S STREET ECONOMY

Ten percent of the Zambian labor force is employed in the formal sector, and 68 percent work in the informal sector (CSO 2003, cited in Republic of Zambia 2006:227). While overall poverty (defined as living on less than one US dollar a day) declined from 70 percent in 1991 to 64 percent in 2006, it increased in urban areas from 49 percent to 53 percent (CSO 2006:1). Lusaka's streets and markets are among the most important sources and sites of nonformal employment for the city's large poor population. But where had all the vendors gone?, we asked when approaching the Soweto Market complex to study the situation between mid-August and mid-October 2010. Only the previous year, vendors had crowded several street blocks of Lumumba Road bordering the market complex. Looking more closely, we located some vendors on one side of Lumumba Road, around busy access roads with pedestrian and vehicle traffic. And vendors still crowded Los Angeles Road along the southern border of the market complex, as well as on the corner of Los Angeles Road and Lumumba Road along the front of the Simoson Building, a privately owned complex built in the 1980s. On the northern end, along Mumbwa Road, there were also several vendors.

As we interviewed vendors, we noticed new market developments toward the north in an area set aside for a car park. Over the preceding two years, new stalls had been erected there. We learned that the area had been reserved for vendors displaced by the redevelopment of the City Centre Market in 2008 and 2009. In addition to some displaced vendors, the area accommodated vendors from other locations, especially people who had traded outside the City Market and been chased away by council police or the anti-vending team. Most striking, we learned that the area was run by the MMD, whose cadres called it the Lumumba Roadside Market and charged levies. The vendors called it Munyaule Market, *munyuale* meaning, in the Nyanja language, "to scratch someone's back."

Vendors, not marketeers, had also settled within the New Soweto Market in walkways in front of the shops and the open market sheds, many of them displaced when the trading area under the power pylons was cleared. Expressing wariness, they all knew that they would be removed once the new market was formally commissioned. A few said that they would like a stall and could afford it but that all stalls had been allocated. Many spoke of returning to the streets.

Most of the fifty vendors we interviewed around the Soweto Market complex were drawn from Lusaka's large population of really poor people. They traded all kinds of goods, from salaula, Chinese clothing and shoes, DVDs, and small hardware items, to toiletries, vegetables and fruit, dried fish, snacks, and cigarettes. Only two were manufacturers, one man selling metal containers for food preparation and one woman selling door mats she crocheted using unraveled wool from salaula sweaters. There were a few itinerant vendors, selling men's trousers they had ironed from garments purchased from salaula vendors. Itinerant vendors who sell their goods in the traffic lights at street intersections are called Eagle Eagle for the speed and quickness with which they move between passing cars to catch customers. They iron the trousers within City Market in a tailor's stall, paying a fee. Vendors displayed their goods on the ground, in used makeshift stands, or on rented wheelbarrows.

The vendors we interviewed included a nearly equal number of women (twenty-three) and men (twenty-seven). Most were in the age range of twenty-one to thirty-two years, the few vendors below twenty years selling for someone else, hoping to get start-up capital for their own enterprise. Five women had never attended school, with most women spending between six and nine years in school. The men were slightly better educated than the women. Ten men had never married, compared with two women. Eight women were single heads of households after divorce or death of a spouse, and one man was divorced. A few men had held low-paying jobs in factories or stores prior to launching their small business. Most of their wives did not have any earnings; a few conducted small-scale trade from home. A few women traders had previously worked in stores but preferred being their own boss to working under someone else's command. Some of their husbands did wage labor, but many were unemployed. Forty of the persons we interviewed had children, and almost half (twenty-one) kept one or more dependents in addition to their own children. Three women had children of school age who did not attend school, because they could not afford the expenses.

Ten vendors were born in Lusaka, ten had spent less than a year in the capital, and most of the rest had lived there between five and ten years, a few a bit longer. Their regional backgrounds reflect many parts of Zambia; twenty had come to Lusaka from the Copperbelt, and seven came from the Northern Province. There was only one person from the Eastern Province, for which Lusaka in the 1970s and 1980s served as a gateway to urban life.

The vendors we interviewed are part of Lusaka's large poor population. Except for two older and better-established traders who owned their homes, they lived in rented accommodation, most of them in two rooms together with their family and dependents. Ten vendors rented rooms in houses without electricity, and more than half purchased water for household use. More than half rented rooms in Lusaka's oldest and most run-down townships: Chibolya, John Laing, Misisi, John Howard, and Kanyama, fairly near downtown Lusaka.

Some vendors paid daily fees, on Los Angeles Road to a MMD cadre they called Euros and on and beyond Mumbwa Road to a MMD cadre they referred to as Jumbos. Some paid a monthly fee to the owner of the shop in front of which they worked. Shop owners sometimes phoned the City Council to have vendors removed from their premises. Most of the vendors complained of being "chased" by council police frequently, some every day, and many had had their goods confiscated. At times, they told us, the council police "eat" their goods and destroy their merchandise. Occasionally, vendors are brought to the Fast Track Court at the Civic Center. First-time offenders, according to a City Council official, are fined, but repeat offenders may go to prison. When the council police arrive, vendors try to run away, often leaving their goods behind.

In addition to paying for their stock, some of it purchased at the Soweto Market complex or at Indian- and Chinese-owned stores around Kamwala Market, vendors typically paid overnight storage fees and a transport fee for a wheelbarrow to haul their goods to and from the storage areas in the market complex. Some, especially vegetable and fruit vendors, who sourced their goods within the Soweto Market complex, bought their daily stock on credit, paying at the end of the day. During daytime trading, vendors pay for water, a lunch snack, and the use of toilets. Given the current attention to microfinance in development circles, including in Zambia, we were surprised that hardly any vendors knew about groups and organizations that might provide loans. Those who knew about two such organizations with offices near the Soweto Market complex were aware that they would not qualify for loans. Some microfinance institutions exclude vendors. Both FINCA (The Foundation for International Community Assistance), an American-based microcredit organization, and PULSE (PULSE Financial Services Limited), a microbanking institution originally established in Zambia by CARE International, insist that borrowers be authorized, operate from a fixed location, have several years of experience and some collateral (house, car, or stock), and operate on a group basis. There are interest rates as well. A few vendors engaged in *chilimba*, a rotating credit arrangement, with fellow traders and used *kaloba* loans (payment within a month with 50–100 percent interest) available in the townships. Working on the fringes of formal market systems, these vendors are further marginalized by a financial system they are unable to enter. In effect, vendors' spatial mobility makes them invisible to the institutional banking gaze.

Hardly any of these vendors kept accounts because, as they explained, they rarely "see" any profits. What they do earn is first and foremost destined for the household pot, their daily takings subject to household claims. They tightly balance their pursuit of vending with needs for rent, food, clothing, school fees, and transport. In most cases, the balance is tenuous and easily fraught, for instance, by the need to stop work to attend an overnight wake and a funeral, school fees for an additional dependent, increasing rental costs, among many others, against which there is no cushion because of the vendors' limited resources.

KASMALL BUSINESS

Do vendors make it? What are their prospects? Some had hope for the future. Others were disillusioned if not cynical. Consider twenty-three-year-old Jacob,[9] who with his older brother for a couple of years had worked along Mumbwa Road selling slippers, belts, socks, face towels, and men's underwear with the name Barack Obama woven into the elastic waistband. Not married, the brothers lived with their parents and ten siblings and dependents in a rented house in John Laing. Prior to this trade, Jacob had walked around the City Market selling cold drinks. The brothers started from small beginnings. Jacob said that they were "just trying" to see whether this trade might produce money for a different future and that he definitely did not intend to continue with only this "*kasmall*" business.[10]

Ronnie, a twenty-one-year-old unmarried man who shared two rented rooms with a friend in Misisi, had spent less than one year in Lusaka, arriving after school (grade eleven) from the Northern Province and initially staying with an uncle. We met him along Lumumba Road, where he sold DVDs, copies mostly, of popular Nigerian, Ghanaian, Indian, South African, and American productions. Ronnie had sold DVDs for approximately three months for a vendor of socks and belts along Lumumba Road, receiving a small wage, food, and transport money, as well as a daily bonus, depending on the level of his sales. Prior to this, he had walked around the Soweto Market complex selling plastic shopping bags. His uncle had provided start-up money. But Ronnie's real vocation is music. "I am a composer," he said, writing Zambian "traditional" songs. He told us that he had come to Lusaka to record music with a group for whom he already had done eight songs and one video. In short, Ronnie considered his job to be temporary, and his desires for the future did not relate to the street economy.

Twenty-six-year-old Chileshe, married with one child and living in rented quarters in John Laing, pursued a different strategy. We met him in the Munyaule Market, where he had been selling secondhand jeans for one year. For three years prior to that, he sold groceries along Los Angeles Road. When chased away, he traded for three months on the premises of the Soweto Market complex. When he heard about the MMD cadre, Jumbos, allocating stands in the Munyaule Market, he acquired one. He was bored inside the market, he said. Before he began vending, Chileshe had a factory job making detergent. He saved a bit from his wages, which he used as start-up capital. He made more money than many other vendors because every afternoon around 4 p.m., he walked to Freedom Way, where he sold groceries on the outskirts of the redeveloped City Centre Market, storing his groceries at a friend's stand. Late afternoon grocery sales attract office workers on their way to nearby bus stations for transport to their residential areas.

The case of forty-four-year-old Moono, a married woman from Kanyama who sold sweets and cigarettes by the stick opposite the Simoson Building is less upbeat. She began her trade one year previously when she "went broke" from her home-based charcoal trade. She lived with her husband and seven children in two rented rooms without electricity and water. Her husband worked as a zamcab driver, one of the hundreds of men who rent wheelbarrows for a daily fee (K4000) from "the garage" of a couple of wheelbarrow owners at the City Market to transport vendors' goods to their spots and customer purchases to cars or minibuses for resale in residential areas. An adult son, who had deserted his wife, sat nearby, resting. He, too, worked as a zamcab driver. Although Moono's business is indeed kasmall, requiring perhaps the least start-up capital of all the vending ventures we observed, sweets and cigarettes sell very readily as a constant stream of potential cus-tomers pass by. Still, Moono said, the business is "no good," so she has to keep on vending in order to feed her children.

Thirty-eight-year-old Chisanga's marriage had broken up thirteen years before, and three years later, she moved from Ndola on the Copperbelt to Lusaka. Five of her seven children lived with her in two rented rooms without electricity and water in Kanyama, together with five dependents. Chisanga never went to school. Neither did her children and dependents because, quite simply, there is no money for education expenses. She began selling green vegetables on the premises of the City Market in front of some wholesalers' stores. One week earlier, the anti-vending team from City Market had removed her from that location, so she had worked on Lumumba Road only for a short while. The council police had been there that very morning, chasing away vendors, she noted. Still, she said that busi-ness was better outside along the road than inside the market but that she would like to change her commodity from greens to dried fish in order to avoid spoilage.

At the opposite end of these kasmall businesses was the venture of a highly entrepreneurial, forty-nine-year-old, widowed woman, Mubanga, whom we met by accident when interviewing vendors in the open space in front of the shops in the New Soweto Market. In fact, we began inter-viewing a young man who sold salaula sportswear, *chitenge* (colorful printed cloth), and bed sheets in front of a shop. He was working for someone else, he explained, after quitting his job as a gardener for an expatriate household due to the low pay. Then the owner of the shop entered our conversation. She was the employer of the young man, owning a formal clothing shop and operating the vending enterprise in front of it. She had come to Lusaka from the Copperbelt seven years previously. Owning a house in Makeni, where she lived with several of her seven children and many dependents, she conducted "suitcase" trade, travelling by bus and always accompanied by a daughter, to Dar Es Salaam in Tanzania for qual-ity salaula, Lubumbashi in the Democratic Republic of Congo for chitenge, and Johannesburg in South Africa for Chinese clothing of better quality and style than the Chinese garments imported to Zambia. She had begun this business in Mufulira on the Copperbelt and had been trading for nearly thirty years. When she moved to Lusaka, she began vending in the Soweto Market complex under the power pylons, from where she had been relocated two years earlier. A well-respected entrepreneur, she was among the applicants who were allotted a formal shop in the New Soweto Market.

These cases demonstrate that most vendors seek to ensure household provisioning and that streets and public space serve as an important site and resource toward that goal. The survival function of the street economy helps explain its fluidity and mobility, with vendors coming and going, changing commodities, moving between indoor and outdoor spaces, and sometimes handling other jobs as well. This striking transience also helps to explain why Zambia's street economy displays very few organized groups and associations reported from elsewhere (Lindell 2010c).

THE STREET: OUTSIDE AND INSIDE

Why do vendors insist that selling along the streets is better than from a marketeer's stall within a designated market? And why do many vendors consider conducting their kasmall businesses on walkways in front of a shop to be better than renting it? To be sure, most vendors we interviewed lack capital to rent a shop or a stall in the new market, and, as we have noted, they are largely deprived of obtaining credit from microlending institutions. But there are other than economic reasons explaining vendors' trading preference. Streets everywhere are multifunctional spaces (Edensor 1998:206) representing "an environment of great complexity. Those who...exist, and operate within this complex acquire a subculture of their own, with the accompanying values, goals, expectations and savoir-vivre" (Mihalyi 1975:124). The streets are crowded with formal shops, some with storefronts and others with wall fences around them. Makeshift stands diversify the streetscape with a variety of activity spilling from one into the other. Altogether, open-air vending spaces along streets create a lively atmosphere as vendors go about their daily tasks, socialize with fellow traders, oversee a stand when another vendor has to go elsewhere. Customers come and go, women breastfeed infants, and small children play. In the low-income residential areas where most vendors live, much daily activity takes place outside the house: cooking, visiting, keeping an eye on children, sending a child on an errand, hair braiding, napping in the shade. Similar overlapping activities take place along streets and in the open space of formal markets, turning them into social spaces where vendors provide "ever present foci for the discussion and exchange of ideas, and the relay of information from and to all directions" (Mihalyi 1975:124).

Streets offer a rich ambiance with music from transistor radios and high-pitched calling out of the prices of salaula garments and shoes. Occasionally, there are political announcements transmitted by loudspeaker. The scene is colorful, the air filled with smells of fresh and cooked foods. Street vending is crowded, noisy, and also dusty and dirty with refuse lying around. Indeed, vendors along the streets must contend not only with dirt and dust but also with heavy traffic. Near the Soweto Market complex are two bus stations, and all kinds of vehicles pass by, including heavily loaded zamcabs, bicycles, cars, and long-distance trucks using Lumumba Road as the main north-south artery through Lusaka. Above all, the street is at the heart of everyday commerce for a vast segment of Lusaka's population, connecting them daily with the world beyond, regionally across all corners of Zambia, with neighboring countries, and with China, India, and the West, from where originate so many of the manufactured goods that the vendors sell. Yet, the unresolved disconnect between necessity, reality, and what is legally acceptable endangers street vending strategies as viable ways to livelihoods.

CONCLUSION: RECLAIMING THE STREET

The local effects of internationally endorsed development efforts play out across a reconfigured urban space. Freeing the market through foreign investments is accentuating inequality, sharpening long existing sociospatial polarizations, extending them by new dynamics that are particularly visible in urban areas. In effect, Lusaka's streets and designated markets have become a major stage in the struggle for economic access. Demonstrating how vending is bound up with much more than streets and markets, including all manner of concerns ranging from public health to safety, we found that the street constitutes a potentially volatile urban political geography that invites repressive action by the state. What is more, in a context of inefficient decentralization of power between the LGH Ministry and the City Council, rival groupings have turned streets and markets into a political tool. Today in markets and streets throughout Zambia, the political legacy with its cadre mentality is evident in the discourse about who gets access to vending space.

Our research on street vending, conducted during the impasse caused by the delay of the formal commissioning of the New Soweto Market in Lusaka, gives evidence of the vendors' main strategy for their livelihood: mobility. Displaced street vendors have turned the inside of the new market into the street, occupying open space in front of formal shops. One result is renewed tensions between marketeers, that is, the people with stands and shops, and vendors, who need to be highly mobile. Yet, during the impasse, even some shop owners did not occupy their shops but worked from the open space in front, or both, as in the case of Mrs. Mubanga. In the process of "interiorizing" the street, the social attributes that make street vending such a lively enterprise play out in this changed setting.

Street vendor mobility is an example of the limited power of the many traders who operate on the fringes of Lusaka's market system. Their occupation of locations with high pedestrian traffic and their reluctance to move beyond the CBD are tactics of resistance. Even then, their power is a two-edged sword, an improvisational tactic, in de Certeau's (1984) sense, enacted by vendors to escape normative regulatory strategies. Forced to change the location of their kasmall businesses in Lusaka's CBD, vendors are frequent targets for the clean-up exercises by regulatory authorities, whose main approach to dealing with them consists of confiscations, fines, and jail terms. In effect, regulatory agents "see" vendors (Scott 1998) only when vendors break the rules. The City Council, the LGH Ministry, and political parties view street vending largely as an economic and political nuisance (occasionally as a health issue) that needs to be contained, rather than a sociocultural practice conducted by fellow citizens who by their guts, persistence, and creativity are trying to make it in society. "Why," asked an itinerant, middle-aged vendor of secondhand trousers, who plied his trade by walking up and down at the intersection of Mumbwa and Lumumba Roads, "is an Eagle Eagle like me chased away all the time, fined, and taken to court? Why does the City Council not introduce a small fee, something like K5000, to license us to work so that our families can eat?"[11]

When the LGH minister predicted the end of street vending in Lusaka in June 2009, he did not approach Lumumba Road and the streets surrounding the market complex and its improvised interior streets to take a careful look. We did, and what we found was a changed battleground, where the boundary between market and street had been redrawn, placing the street in the middle of the New Soweto Market. In effect, by the mobility that defines them, vendors reclaimed the street within the new market, in this way disrupting the spatial regime of governing authorities.

On December 8, 2010, the president finally commissioned the New Soweto Market. Prior to the formal opening, vendors who still traded under the power pylons were moved into the market walkways. Many vendors who had sold their goods in front of stores in the new market did not vacate their spots. But growing numbers of vendors turned back to the streets, where they are likely to remain for a while (Times of Zambia 2010). In effect, the redrawing of boundaries continues as vendors once again seek to reclaim their streets.

Notes

1. Between mid-August and mid-October 2010, research assistant Diana Moonga and Karen Tranberg Hansen interviewed fifty vendors around the Soweto Market complex. Wilma S. Nchito facilitated formal contact with officials in the Lusaka City

Council, market managers, and other regulatory agents. Hansen prepared an initial draft, to which Nchito added specific insights.

2. In 2010, Zambia was ranked 150 of 169 countries on the Human Development Index (UNDP 2010), a slight improvement from 164 of 177 countries in 2003 yet a lower score than in 1970.

3. Part of this section draws on previous work: Hansen 2008a; Nchito 2011; Nchito and Hansen 2010.

4. The term *designated,* or *authorized,* refers to areas where urban retail is permitted under the Markets Act.

5. The term *cadre* stems from the socialist one-party state and the disciplinary, vigilante functions of its youth wing. It continues to be used for political involvement, often referring to thugs who beat opposition members at political rallies and rough up vendors, as in this case.

6. The association rented the plot from a businessman and then purchased it from his estate when he died. Strategically, the association involved COMESA, making the secretary general its patron and storing the title deed at the COMESA headquarters.

7. The EU market rehabilitation project was launched in the late 1990s, involving market upgrading and new markets in Lusaka and the Copperbelt, as well as a new governance model.

8. At the time of this study, one United States dollar equalled a little less than 5,000 *kwacha* (K).

9. All names are fictive; several allude to regional backgrounds.

10. *Ka* is a prefix, indicating small size. Everyday speech in Lusaka combines local language and English terms.

11. The Lusaka City Council issues licenses to peddlers and hawkers, yet these licensing regulations are not widely known or observed.

5

Taking the Street into the Market

The Politics of Space and
Work in Baguio City, Philippines

B. Lynne Milgram

The following *Baguio Midland Courier* newspaper article is typical of regular Philippine media accounts documenting the dramatic increase in street economy activities, the municipal government's vacillating policies regarding this arena of work, and vendors' advocacy to assert their rights to viable livelihoods (Palangchao 2008; Rillorta 2008):

> **Execs Backtrack; Allow Vendors Back in Market**
>
> Never mind case laws and ordinances.... The city council [Baguio City, Philippines] in its regular session on Monday approved a motion allowing unabated vending at the city market.... Going into overtime to accommodate hawkers who trooped to City Hall with the never-ending story that they'll starve if not given the chance to break existing anti-vending laws, [one] alderman... motioned "groups previously excluded from vending be allowed to sell pending a future market summit."... "This," the mayor said, "is on the condition that selling will be confined to specific sites in the market and certain guidelines should be followed." [Liporada 2008b]

The capitulation of the Baguio City government reported here represents one more reprieve among the many that city counselors have granted vendors since the early 1990s regarding when and where in the city they can sell. In this specific situation, street vendors who had moved their businesses from city sidewalks into the Baguio City Public Market protested the mayor's Administrative Order 115, which prohibits them from selling their goods in the public market aisles (City Government of Baguio 2008). Vendors argued that the mayor's directive contravened the Philippine government's 1997 Executive Order 452 mandating provincial and municipal governments to identify suitable selling spaces for all registered vendors, given ongoing rural to urban migration, the lack of formal sector jobs, and the recent contraction of the global economy, all of which have raised new livelihood challenges for the urban poor throughout the Philippines (Agoot 2008a; Gomez 2009; Republic of the Philippines 1997–2001). The mayor's Administrative Order 115 now joins a series of similarly unfulfilled proposals that municipal counselors have put forward over the past twenty years, each one failing to respond to the long-term subsistence needs of the city's growing population of street sellers. Because municipal elections occur every three years, shifts in administration and in government priorities mean that counselors have not been able to "implement a coherent policy [but] rather...one shot through with contradictions and paradoxes" (Seligmann 2004:95), as evidenced in this recent media report.

Street economy activities such as selling fresh produce, cooked food, manufactured goods, and grooming services occupy an edgy position. Although vendors generate income for their families and fulfill the consumption needs of urban residents and visitors, their presence on city streets simultaneously frustrates municipal government efforts to establish its vision of a clean, vendor-free, modern center (Liporada 2008a). The tension created by such urban dynamics is particularly evident in Baguio City, northern Luzon, Philippines, where a mushrooming street trade has given rise to ongoing disagreements and confrontations among street sellers, large retailers, and provincial and municipal governments regarding who has rights over and access to the city's streets for commerce (Agoot 2008b).

In this chapter,[1] I use Philippine women's street economy work in Baguio City to suggest that vendors, by expanding the spatial parameters of their trade to new business frontiers such as the aisles of the Baguio City Public Market, challenge taken-for-granted understandings of formal/informal sector work, urban public space, and legal/illegal practice. My research explores the work of women vendors in particular because Philippine women, consistent with their customary and historical roles as household financial managers and as the country's foremost public market traders, compose the majority of street vendors selling fresh produce, cooked food, and manufactured goods—a gendered occupation common throughout much of Southeast Asia (Leshkowich 2011; Lloyd-Evans 2008).

I came to street vendor studies through my research of women's entrepreneurial work buying and selling secondhand clothing in the Philippines, because women conduct part of these enterprises on village and city streets (Milgram 2004, 2008). My initial research on Baguio City street economies revealed that vendors, by pursing multiple channels to advocate for their rights to livelihood (letter writing, public protests), in 1996 obtained "maximum tolerance" for their businesses—municipal permission to sell in certain Baguio City street locations during particular times (Milgram 2009:118–119). Since the late 1990s, however, partially in response to the 1997 Asian financial crisis and to the 2007 global economic slowdown, the number of street vendors has increased substantially. Consequently, few if any downtown street sites remain vacant for new vendors to begin businesses or for established vendors to find better selling locations. I expand my inquiry here to explore the resultant situation, in which some vendors are redrawing the boundaries of their trade by moving it from the street into the wide aisles of the busy and centrally located Baguio City Public Market (Opiña 2009).

By simply crossing the street to relocate their trade, women vendors, in effect, transform the Baguio City Public Market aisles into new economic zones. What is particularly noteworthy is that these vendors establish permanent market-aisle stations in which to conduct business rather than work as ambulant or itinerant sellers, as identified in market studies analyzing similar shifts in trade (e.g., Yessenova 2006). Market-aisle vendors reconfigure and secure the space-use system in which they work by organizing collective associations, negotiating mutually beneficial selling arrangements with lease-holding storeowners, and exploiting loopholes in the municipal Market Code—the by-laws regulating retail and wholesale business within the public market. As vendors collaborate with market storeowners and gain the ear of city counselors such that the latter adapt selected municipal policies in their favor, both formal sector parties are complicit in enabling this conversion of space-use. I argue, then, that vendors' success in moving their businesses into Baguio City's public market demonstrates that such informal sector enterprises are so widespread, they are already integrated into mainstream urban daily life, provide essential services to urbanites, and contribute to urban economies. Indeed, that many of these market-aisle vendors have maintained their captured fixed-location operations for more than ten years highlights the need to add this new category of market player to the types of businesspeople we most often include in explorations of changing market dynamics (retailers, wholesalers, ambulant vendors).

In this chapter, I do not consider organized illegal businesses such as the drug trade and prostitution, although these are often street-based enterprises. To situate Baguio City's street economy activities, I begin by discussing the debates on formal/informal and legal/illegal work with regard to the use of urban public space. I then analyze the extent to which women vendors' actions can shape policies to achieve the warranted socioeconomic and political rights they demand.

RESITUATING INFORMALITY AND SPACE USE

Street economy practices across the urban Global South are customarily considered as operating within the informal economy—a term that generally refers to a heterogeneous group of activities and employment relationships that share a common characteristic, namely, that they "lie beyond or circumvent state regulation" and protection (Lindell 2010a:5; Castells and Portes 1989). As scholarship on the concept of informality argues, however, formal and informal activities, in practice, interconnect in multiple ways and the former are regulated through the context-specific rules, associations, and institutions that actors establish to achieve their ends, albeit within parameters that may be beyond prescriptive state systems (Hansen 2008a:217; Yessenova 2006:39). This positioning of informality is particularly relevant to understanding the current transformation of the wide aisles within the Baguio City Public Market. That permanent market storeowners currently engage in personalized business arrangements with market-aisle vendors demonstrates the "now widespread realization that the informal economy …is no longer restricted to the small-scale and survivalist activities of the poor, but is also a sphere of accumulation in which the non-poor operate" (Lindell 2010a:6; Smart and Smart 2005).

Until recently, research on informal economic activities, especially women's periodic work, overlooked street vending, perhaps because scholars assumed that such itinerant livelihoods would eventually disappear, absorbed into the expanding capitalist economy (Bromley, chapter 2, this volume). Because governments tend to regard street economies as disorderly, superfluous activities that clutter the urban environment and frustrate the "healthy functioning of the formal economy," they seek to leave behind such reminders of a traditional past in order to realize a future they deem appropriately modern (Brown 2006a:8; see also Holston 2002:248–249). Indeed, because vendors usually occupy sites with high pedestrian traffic flows, as in the Philippines, they are often seen as violating the "appropriate" use of urban public space and diminishing its socioeconomic value for more well-off urbanites (Cross and Morales 2007:19).

David Harvey's (2006) conceptualization of a tripartite, interdependent division of space and of the interplay among space, use, and value helps us understand how vendors transform space to confront the state's conflicting idea of appropriate use. Harvey (2006:271–277) argues that space is simultaneously absolute (e.g., fixed, individual property ownership), relative (includes exchange relations over time), and relational (a contextual frame defined by the myriad processes in which space is differentially embedded over time). He maintains that constructed spaces have material, conceptual, and lived dimensions and that we are situated in all three frameworks simultaneously, though not necessarily equally. Harvey's approach highlights the ways in which different actors negotiate ties grounded in the exchange of values to represent their urban public space activities as suitable and justified. Baguio City vendors, for example, validate their claim to so-called illegal spaces in public areas by paying legally regulated rental fees to municipal collectors or by making individualized agreements with lease-holding market storeowners. In both situations, they convert absolute into relative and relational space, creating a tension among space/use/ value categories that enables the political struggle they require to realize their aims (Harvey 2006:279). Indeed, as Harvey (2006:293) suggests, "it is only when relationality connects to the absolute spaces and times of social and material life that politics come alive" to foster transformative livelihood possibilities (see also Daniere and Douglass 2009).

RETHINKING LEGAL AND ILLEGAL PRACTICE

The disjuncture between state laws, market logics, and the working lives of those engaged in street economies and how they perceive their work demonstrates the variable notions of legality and illegality. State discourses tend to uphold rigid definitions of legal and illegal actions as governments implicitly label formal activities as licit and informal ones as illicit, often meshing informal activities with criminal engagement (organized corruption, gangs, violence) without questioning the size or intent of such associations. As people struggle to make a living across work sectors, however, their activities may emerge as simultaneously formal, informal, legal, and illegal (Abraham and van Schendel 2005:4–5). Indeed, current scholarship argues that licit and illicit activities coexist in social and economic life and are together imbricated in state processes since states themselves do not always uphold the law (Heyman and Smart 1999:10–11). Recent studies additionally demonstrate that government officials charged with enforcing state laws often have a complicated relationship with informal sector activities. Whereas some officials regulate businesses according to state definitions of what is legally permitted, others may accept bribes or may establish friendly concessionary relationships with selected traders (Ribeiro 2009:321). Such circumstances capture the Baguio City situation. Here, both fixed-location and ambulant street and market-aisle vendors pay daily rental fees to the Office of the City Treasurer at the same time as police periodically chase some vendors from their rented locations or receive "gifts" from other sellers to overlook their trade (Olson 2008). Infractions to Baguio City street and market vending laws emerge as simultaneously encouraged, tolerated, and punished (Laking 2008; Liporada 2008b).

Despite the policing efforts of local-to-national law enforcers, the scale of street economies continues to grow as the sophistication and knowledge of vendors increase (see Bhowmik 2005; Cross and Morales 2007; Kusakabe 2006; Mitullah 2004). I suggest, then, as other alternative economy studies similarly evidence, that research needs to explore a distinction between what states consider to be legitimate or "legal" and what people involved in so-called marginal trade consider to be legitimate or "licit" (Abraham and van Schendel 2005:4). Street and market-aisle vending are illegal because they defy the rules of formal political authority, but these actions are acceptable or licit in the eyes of participants because these enable them to earn an integral living using their personal labor, resources, and ingenuity.

Most street and market-aisle vendors thus emerge as "ant traders"—individuals who engage in formally unsanctioned trade in in-between spaces with small quantities of goods—"but they do not represent global syndicates of organized crime" (Abraham and van Schendel 2005:4; Morales 2007). By questioning the state's often rigid, oppositional positioning of what constitutes legal or illegal practice, we can more perceptively assess local rationales for alternative and often marginal enterprises that continue to persist over time and space. Josiah Heyman and Alan Smart (1999:11) perceptively situate the co-existence of such "multiple ideas of legitimacy and morality" when they point out that "legality and illegality are thus simultaneously black and white, and shades of gray."

Within this context, I analyze Baguio City street economies by exploring the extent to which street vendors can operationalize new opportunities when they move their businesses into the commercial gray zone of the public market aisles. With my research assistants, I collected data from 2009 to mid-2011. During this time, we conducted sixty-seven interviews with women market-aisle vendors ranging in age from twenty-one to seventy-two, but the majority were mid-twenties to sixty-five years of age.

Because I had worked with some of these women when they were ambulant street vendors, I was able to conduct more informed follow-up interviews with them in their new market-aisle sites. We also interviewed six men who periodically assisted their wives in market-aisle sales, and in each produce section of the market, we interviewed permanent storeowners (thirty-seven in total) to understand their attitude toward the aisle vendors in their section. I conducted interviews with market administrators and with Baguio City government counselors, including following their Facebook pages and Internet blogs, and I consulted the Baguio City Hall Records Office to document the municipal government policies regulating street and market-aisle vending. Since market-aisle vendors, like most street vendors, sell seven days a week, I, with my assistant, had ample opportunity to casually and repeatedly talk with and observe vendors to augment our formal interviews. Although sellers' street economy enterprises remain constrained by state regulation, their ongoing advocacy is earning them fruitful livelihood concessions, as the following account of Baguio City market-aisle vendors demonstrates.

LOCATING STREET AND MARKET-AISLE VENDING IN BAGUIO CITY

In the early twentieth century, the American colonial government in the Philippines established Baguio City as its mountain summer resort to escape the hotter lowland temperatures. Built to accommodate 25,000, today Baguio City supports a population of 250,000. The city is the government, education, and administration center for the five mountain or Cordillera provinces in northern Luzon. Baguio City's cool upland climate ensures its ongoing attraction as a summer vacation destination for lowland visitors, and its extensive Baguio City Public Market, offering wholesale and retail sales of fresh produce, manufactured goods, and crafts, supports businesses throughout the region. Baguio City is home to more than fifteen colleges and universities, which, along with the city's government services, retail stores, and three new shopping malls, provide the customer base that those starting new businesses seek. Most entrepreneurs, however, must negotiate individualized strategies to realize the potential of this urban market. Indeed, since the 1986 restoration of democratic government in the Philippines, successive national leaders have failed to institute economic and political reforms that effectively "act on behalf of the public interest" (Hutchcroft and Rocamora 2012:98). Instead, state policies continue to put forward anti-poverty programs that rarely come to fruition and to support projects that tend to benefit favored corporate interests

(Balisacan 1995). Although the Philippine government's structural adjust-ment polices have succeeded in opening up economic sectors to increased competition, national leaders to date have not constructed the basic politi-cal and economic foundations that can provide more people with viable work opportunities (Hutchcroft and Rocamora 2012:97–98; Lucas 2009).

Not surprisingly, the municipal government estimates that the number of Baguio City street vendors is approximately three thousand five hundred, but the unofficial estimate more realistically places the range between five and seven thousand sellers (City Government of Baguio 2009:4). In ear-lier research, I identified that vendors sell fresh produce, cooked food, and manufactured goods (DVDs, CDs, cell phone and grooming acces-sories, secondhand clothing) throughout the streets of Baguio City's Central Business District. I also highlighted that in 1996, through their collective action, vendors gained the status of "maximum tolerance"—municipal government–sanctioned permission to conduct business in par-ticular street locations between 4:00 and 8:00 a.m., 12:00 and 1:00 p.m., and after 5:00 p.m., paying a daily rent of ten pesos ($US.25)[2] (Milgram 2009:116). Vendors, however, must continually advocate to maintain this status because changes in city government leadership or pressure from large-scale retailers mean that sellers periodically lose this hard-won right for extended periods of time (Agoot 2010). The dearth of downtown street selling sites has now reached a tipping point, such that many vendors are claiming in-between locations in the spacious Baguio City Public Market. The city market, situated in the heart of the Central Business District, was founded in 1909 along with Baguio City itself. As the market expanded to fulfill the consumption needs of the city's growing population, buildings were constructed with wide aisles that could accommodate vehicular traffic for the delivery of goods. Unlike the narrow aisles that commonly separate businesses in public market buildings, in the Baguio City Public Market, the generous aisles between the rows of product displays in each section almost invite itinerant vendors to set up their enterprises (figure 5.1).

The laws for conducting business in the market are outlined in the 1952 Market Code that has been incorporated into Baguio City Tax Ordinance 2000–2001. Most Market Code guidelines apply to permanent storeowners (both retail and wholesale) and stipulate that only those holding a lease to their store premises can legally sell their goods throughout the day within the market. Wholesalers and farmers from outside the market who bring their produce to sell directly to permanent market storeowners pay a "market-entry fee" of ten to twenty pesos depending upon the volume of their goods, but they must leave the market after making their deliveries

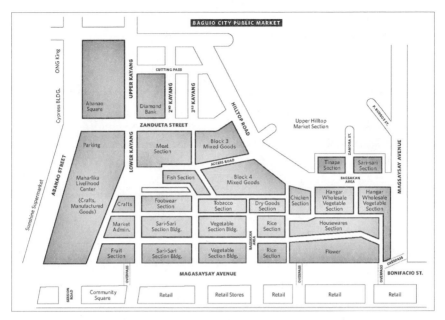

FIGURE 5.1

Map of the Baguio City Public Market buildings. Map: B. Lynne Milgram.

(City Government of Baguio 2000–2001:50). Clauses in the document acknowledge the rights of "traveling vendors and peddlers" and that vendors can sell in "authorized locations" but not in "designated passage ways or alleys"; however, the code does not identify specific market locations for such commerce (City Government of Baguio 2000–2001:50–52). In an effort to clarify this dilemma, the manager of one of the market's banking cooperatives notes, "What is banned is selling in unauthorized areas.... In fact, under Tax Ordinance 2000–2001, peddlers can sell anywhere in the city provided they pay an annual tax of one hundred pesos plus other business fees...[thus] it is unjustified for the city to confiscate the goods of peddlers" (Niñal 2008:1).

Although vendors can apply for this annual one-hundred-peso Mayor's Permit to conduct business (City Government of Baguio 2000–2001:47), they explain that their efforts to do so have been repeatedly thwarted by municipal officials. The ongoing disagreements about appropriate market development among the three bodies responsible for market reform— the Office of the City Treasurer; the Committee for Marketing, Trade, and Commerce; and the Market Superintendent—mean that no one has heeded the cooperative manager's advice or updated the applicable sections of the 1952 Market Code. Debates over "acceptable" alternative vending practices within the Baguio City Public Market thus continue (Liporada 2008b; Opiña 2008).

To regulate the commerce that persists in the public market's unofficial economic zones, the Market Superintendent has enabled market-aisle sellers to conduct business during the same three daily periods (early morning, noon, and evening) that city street vendors holding maximum tolerance status can sell and to pay their daily ten-peso rental fee to do so. In practice, however, market-aisle vendors sell throughout the day, and this situation leaves them vulnerable to periodic clearances by market patrols.

Although the Baguio City Public Market aisles are under the jurisdiction of the Market Superintendent, vendors approach permanent storeowners for informal permission to sell in front of the latter's businesses. Since vendors' products differ from the goods that storeowners sell, these businesses do not compete with each other. Whereas some storeowners readily grant vendors permission for their aisle-location trade, others do so only after negotiating special agreements; still others, such as the storeowners in the Vegetable Section Proper, prohibit itinerant vendors from selling in their area. A tour of aisle vendors' enterprises in these newly created economic zones reveals the innovative options vendors have created for consumers and the dilemmas they have raised for storeowners.

At a main market entry junction where four aisles merge, eight to ten women sell a variety of goods that include cooked rice cakes, dried lowland fish, and different types of vegetables and fruits. In the Sari-Sari Section (Philippine crafts and processed snack foods), approximately forty women belonging to the long established Baguio Women's Vegetable Vendors Association (BWVVA) sell upland Baguio vegetables (cabbage, cauliflower, broccoli, green beans) that they purchase in the Hanger Wholesale Vegetable Section (figure 5.2). The BWVVA's location near main market entry points provides shoppers with a convenient opportunity to purchase Baguio vegetables without having to walk to the wholesale section at the back of the market. In the Rice Section, two separate vendor associations, with twenty and seventeen members, respectively, sell lowland vegetables (string beans, eggplant, greens) that they purchase from wholesalers who bring their produce each day to a designated delivery area on Hilltop Road, an upper market section (figure 5.3). In a main aisle sandwiched between the Hanger Wholesale Vegetable Section and the Housewares Section, fifteen sellers offer either homemade peanut butter or fresh fish—women purchase the latter product daily from their contacts in the neighboring lowlands (figures 5.4, 5.5). In an open-air area in front of the Chicken

FIGURE 5.2
Women in the Baguio Women's Vegetable Vendors Association sell upland vegetables in the aisle of the Sari-Sari Section. Photo: B. Lynne Milgram, Baguio City, Philippines, 2010.

FIGURE 5.3
Women belonging to the Rice Section Vegetable Vendors Association, sell lowland vegetables with some of their husbands in the aisle of the Rice Section. Photo: B. Lynne Milgram, Baguio City, Philippines, 2010.

81

Figure 5.4

A woman sells homemade peanut butter and vegetables in the aisle between the Hanger Wholesale Vegetable Section and the Housewares Section. Photo: B. Lynne Milgram, Baguio City, Philippines, 2010.

Section, twelve women have set up umbrellas to protect the fresh fish they purchase from lowland wholesalers who also deliver fish daily to the permanent stores in the Fish Section. Indeed, at any unoccupied passageway

FIGURE 5.5

Baguio City Public Market. Women sell fresh fish in the aisle between the Hanger Wholesale Vegetable Section and the Housewares Section of the market. Photo: B. Lynne Milgram, Baguio City, Philippines, 2010.

leading from city streets into the market, vendor groups sell upland or lowland fruits and vegetables and a variety of cooked foods. On 3rd Kayang Street and along Hilltop Road where storeowners sell lowland vegetables, approximately fifty to sixty secondhand clothing vendors conduct brisk businesses throughout the day. The best place to purchase particular produce, then, is not always in the market section named for that product, as the following case studies demonstrate.

RICE SECTION VEGETABLE VENDORS ASSOCIATION

Helen Sigura,[3] a widow, sixty years old with eight children, was among the first women to sell lowland vegetables in the Rice Section in mid-2008. Before moving into the Baguio City Public Market, Helen, like her fellow women ambulant vendors, sold fresh produce along the city streets bordering the market. The ongoing risk of periodic police raids on vendors' street trade prompted Helen and some of her fellow sellers to use their husbands' personal connections in the market—the men's work as rice porters—to secure vending sites within the spacious aisles of the Rice Section (see figure 5.3).

The first women to relocate to the Rice Section encouraged their older children and relatives to claim selling spots until the approximately twenty places available were filled. Helen and two of her daughters occupy three of these sites. As the municipal government has only limited resources with which to control other-than-formally-authorized vending activities within and outside the Baguio City Public Market, early attempts to prevent vendors from selling in the market aisles largely failed (Palangchao 2008). "These new vendors in our area are like flies," one Rice Section storeowner explains. "Shortly after you swish them away, they are back again selling." Aisle vendors in the Rice Section currently pay the customary ten-peso rental fee to conduct business during the specified times. One permanent storeowner described what happens when market officers patrol the Rice Section in non-selling hours, which I myself often witnessed: "Vendors disperse in a wave. Women quickly hide their products with cooperating storeowners and sweep their stations so clean, you would not know they had been selling here only a few moments ago."

The Rice Section aisle vendors sell lowland vegetables that are usually combined for customary Filipino dishes such as pinakbet (eggplant, squash, beans, and tomatoes), organizing this produce into what they term "vegetable sets." This means that shoppers can purchase all the ingredients they need for specific recipes in one location. The vendors in Helen's section display their produce in shallow rattan baskets mounted on plastic boxes. By raising their vegetables off the floor, vendors explain, their goods are more accessible to shoppers, and this type of presentation speaks of permanency and care, setting them apart from the ground-level product displays used by aisle vegetable vendors at the opposite end of the Rice Section. "Such small transformations of space," vendors explain, "make a significant difference to our livelihood viability." For some families, selling vegetables in the Rice Section has become more lucrative than transporting rice, so some men assist their wives in business rather than work as rice porters.

The Rice Section vegetable vendors purchase their produce each morning from lowland traders who sell their goods in the wholesale area in the upper Hilltop Section. Vendors store the stock that remains at the end of the day in the permanent shops where they have negotiated agreements with the owners. Vendors work with a rotating capital of approximately two thousand pesos, paying one-half the cost of their order upon purchase and the remainder at the end of the day when dealers visit vendors' selling stations to make their collections. Any remaining balance that vendors owe is carried over to the next day, so many vendors maintain a revolving debt to wholesalers in order to take home daily earnings of three hundred to five hundred pesos. The proliferation of new vendors selling lowland vegetables in the Rice Section means that lowland wholesalers do not leave the Hilltop Section once they deliver their produce as they did in the past. Instead, they park their trucks on the roads until their 5:00 p.m. collection, causing added congestion to this area. Not surprisingly, the permanent Hilltop Section retailers complain not only that the trucks hamper shoppers' access to their stores but also that they are losing sales because shoppers are spared the uphill walk to Hilltop (only five to seven minutes) and can more conveniently find the same lowland vegetables in the easily accessible, ground-level Rice Section.

After Rice Section storeowners' similar attempts to remove the aisle vendors failed, one permanent trader summed up the section's attitude when she stated, "As long as these peddlers' products do not compete with our goods, we will give their aisle sales a chance." Indeed, some permanent storeowners have transformed their tolerance of aisle vendors' activities into complicity. After the vegetable vendors established their enterprises, Carole Vanga, for example, a permanent rice dealer, claimed a middle-aisle spot opposite her two-meter wide store in which to stack her 50-kilogram sacks, or *cavans*, of rice. "By maintaining such open storage," Carole explains, "it is more convenient for me to distribute the cavans of rice to shoppers rather than fetch the heavy sacks from the storage area behind my store." Carole pays the standard ten-peso rent for this additional aisle space and, like other aisle vendors, quickly clears her area in non-selling hours when market patrols approach. Carole is periodically fined for her aisle encroachment—a one-thousand-peso fine that she can afford—but she explains, "When this occurs, I just pay the fine. For me, the penalty is worth the convenience of this extra aisle space."

In a similar initiative, Elizabeth Monteban, a permanent rice dealer in business for thirty years and with her daughter Paulina in the neighboring stall, explains that after the arrival of the vegetable vendors, she and her daughter extended the length of their two-meter-wide stores by one meter into the aisle in order to sell spices and condiments commonly used together in Filipino dishes (fish sauce, vinegar, and soya sauce). After they created this new commercial zone—becoming simultaneously store and a market-aisle vendors—Elizabeth and Paulina each started to make the ten-peso rental payments to the Market Superintendent. Elizabeth explains, "It is convenient for shoppers to purchase these ingredients from us after they buy fish or meat in the adjacent market areas. In addition, if people linger in our area to buy vegetables from the aisle vendors, our rice sales could increase. I also expanded my store, as have other dealers, by constructing overhead shelves from which I hang large carrying bags. And I pay ten pesos to the market collector for this second upper extension area."

Each day, collectors from the Market Superintendent's office visit the Rice Section and collect the ten-peso rental fee from the so-called illegal vegetable vendors in the middle of the aisle; from Carole, the permanent storeowner occupying the middle-aisle storage location; and from the permanent legal storeowners who have extended their retail premises into the airspace above their stores and into the same central aisle location occupied by the illegal vegetable vendors. The permanent retailers, however, do not risk periodic raids on their store extensions.

Mary Tayad, president of the Rice Section storeowners, explains that it became evident that the aisle vegetable vendors were determined to defend their enterprises, so, given that she employs some of their spouses as porters, in 2009 she encouraged the vendors to join the Baguio Market Vendors Multipurpose Cooperative (BMVMC), an organization she founded in 1997. Mary explains that the cooperative's banking services provide vendors with loans on fairer terms than those they customarily receive from moneylenders, who charge high interest rates, usually 10 percent per month. To accommodate aisle vendors' irregular incomes, the cooperative decreased the share capital that vendors must contribute—from four thousand to two thousand pesos—before they can borrow association funds, albeit in smaller amounts. Since the initiative's inception in 2009, many aisle vendors have paid their share capital and have taken cooperative loans.

Within the first year of operation, the Rice Section vegetable sellers also organized themselves into a formal collective—the Rice Section Vegetable Vendors Association (RSVVA)—and organized their documents to register with the Securities Employment Commission (SEC) in April 2010. To do so, they secured the assistance of Patricia Esteban, president of the Baguio Women's Vegetable Vendors Association (BWVVA), a group that has been selling upland Baguio vegetables in the aisles of the Sari-Sari Section since approximately 2000 and was the first market-aisle vendor group to register its association with SEC, in 2003. Patricia, with two years of college education and income from her husband's work as a night security guard, has successfully navigated the SEC bureaucracy to facilitate her group's status, as well as that of other vendor groups.

What results in the Rice Section of the Baguio City Public Market is a paradoxical situation in which formerly ambulant vendors occupy illegal selling spaces in market aisles they share with permanent storeowners and for which they pay a daily rent to the Office of the City Treasurer via Public

Market collectors. They have registered their vendor association with SEC and are paid-up members of the Baguio Market Vendors Multipurpose Cooperative at the same time as the Market Code categorizes them as "traveling peddlers" (City Government of Baguio 2000–2001:50). Such circumstances of market-aisle trade suggest that distinctions between formal/informal or legal/illegal work emerge more as elastic gradients than as discrete categories.

SELLING PEANUT BUTTER AND FRESH FISH

Like the vegetable vendors in the Rice Section, the women selling homemade peanut butter and fresh fish in the walkway between the Hanger Wholesale Vegetable Section and the Housewares Section have established innovative and fluid spatial trade relations with permanent storeowners. Dominga Batton, for example, forty-eight years old with six children, has been selling her homemade peanut butter in this location since 1999. To augment her husband's periodic wages from contract wage labor, Dominga obtained permission from a Hanger Wholesale Vegetable Section storeowner to set up her display of goods opposite the latter's store (see figure 5.4).

Baguio City is renowned for its fresh strawberries, strawberry jam, and peanut butter, of which the latter two products, especially popular with tourists, are widely available in the Sari-Sari Section of the market. Ironically, the commercial peanut butter sold in the Sari-Sari Section is not made in Baguio City, but in neighboring lowland areas where peanuts are grown more widely. Dominga's peanut butter, like that of her five companion vendors, however, originates in homemade recipes. Local Baguio City residents know that they will find the freshest product in this busy side-aisle destination. Dominga also displays one or two baskets of vegetables that change throughout the week, but these vegetables belong to the permanent store in front of which she has her peanut butter business. In this arrangement, Dominga agrees to sell the wholesale dealer's vegetables, but she does not earn income for this work. Instead, the vegetable dealer gives Dominga some of the day's extra produce, allows her to store her unsold peanut butter jars in the store overnight, and when Dominga is late setting up her display or is ill, sells Dominga's peanut butter for her without taking a commission.

In 2004, seven women from the neighboring lowland province of La Union and members of a fresh fish cooperative secured permission from other Hanger Wholesale Vegetable Section storeowners to display their goods in the same aisle location as that occupied by Dominga and her fellow vendors. Although these women have moved to Baguio City, they continue to purchase their fish from cooperative members who drive each morning (a one-hour trip) to Baguio City (see figure 5.5). Indeed, shoppers can purchase the same products in the Fish Section for similar prices through economies of scale, but many consumers believe that they obtain a bargain by buying produce directly from small-scale sellers in such alternative aisle locations. In an arrangement similar to that of Dominga, the aisle-based fish vendors also sell vegetables belonging to their partner storeowners, and in return, they can store overnight in the vegetable store any fish not sold during the day.

This practice of extending one's display of goods into market aisles through a second seller is a common strategy that fresh produce vendors throughout the market employ at the busiest daily selling times, paying their ten-peso rent to do so. In key locations such as along Lower Kayang and Zuandeta Streets, permanent storeowners organize relatives or employees to set up middle-aisle displays of selected goods that capitalize on shoppers' attraction to sleuthing out a bargain (see also Seligmann 2004:205). Indeed, a recent *Baguio Midland Courier* reporter comments on the increase in such practices: "Everywhere in the market there seems to be a vendor.... Because the city government tolerated the proliferation of the so-called side walk vendors...the legal vendors abandoned their stalls and installed their trades along the market streets, side by side with the illegal vendors" (Evangelista 2010). Such marketing strategies resonate with those of Lusaka's displaced street sellers and permanent market traders who sold their goods in the same open spaces of the New Soweto Market when the formal opening of this building was delayed (Hansen and Nchito, chapter 4, this volume).

Like other market-aisle vendors, the women selling peanut butter and fresh fish in the Housewares and Hanger Wholesale Vegetable Sections explain that their ten-peso rent receipts represent their "physical and moral right" to continue their businesses. To maintain the group's claim to its aisle selling sites, peanut butter vendor Dominga organized her selling companions into a location-based collective—the Hanger-Housewares Aisle Vendors Association—and obtained assistance from Patricia Esteban, BWVVA president, to organize the required papers for SEC registration. However, because some of the relocated fish sellers have not yet officially confirmed their Baguio City residency, the group's SEC registration application remains in process.

In addition to the vendor groups who sell in regular market aisle locations and hold SEC status, the Baguio City Public Market passageways accommodate ambulant sellers who work independently or with two to

FIGURE 5.6

A woman sells cooked food on a roadway within the city market. Photo: B. Lynne Milgram, Baguio City, Philippines, 2010.

three partners. A substantial number of women, for example, sell coffee, cold fruit drinks, and a variety of homemade snacks and meals (noodles, fried bananas, cooked rice cakes) to storeowners and visitors. Other ambulant vendors carry one basket of a specific product they believe is always in demand, such as seasonal fruit, fresh chili, salt, and boiled and roasted peanuts (figure 5.6). One usually finds these vendors moving from one aisle location to the other, depending upon the schedule of market patrols. In May 2010, the Committee for Marketing, Trade, and Commerce mounted a town hall meeting urging vendors to "professionalize" in order to work in partnership with the city (Baguio Midland Courier 2010). Many of these independent vendors, following the model of the already established vendor organizations, have begun to form location-based associations to collectively advocate for their cause, but this process is not always a smooth one. Patricia Esteban, for example, has repeatedly approached a neighboring group of mixed-product vendors to join the BWVVA, but these independent sellers maintain that they prefer to form their own collective. As these women have not yet agreed on their group's organizational structure, however, they lack a collective voice, leaving their positions tenuous amid the government's ongoing market regulation. Sarah Turner (chapter 8, this volume) similarly highlights the heterogeneity among Hanoi's street vendors by identifying differences between the rights and advantages fixed-stall sellers enjoy and the constraints itinerant vendors face (see also Porter et al. 2010).

CONCLUSION

Local-to-national governments often place limitations on urban informal sector livelihoods such as street and market-aisle vending because these activities run counter to mainstream discourses and images of "appropriate" urban development (Cross and Karides 2007). In Baguio City, such a socioeconomic and political positioning means that vendors' voices are commonly excluded from broader government agendas, which privilege instead the needs of well-off urbanites whose interests realize the city's vision of modernity. Baguio City vendors have therefore developed strategies to reconfigure restrictions on their trade by capturing in-between spaces in which to operate their enterprises, establishing location- or product-based vendor associations, and negotiating reciprocal business agreements with permanent storeowners. What emerges as particularly noteworthy in the Baguio City Public Market is the high degree of vendor cooperation. Unlike the Maya vendors described by Walter Little (chapter 6, this volume) who have had limited success in collectively organizing into stable associations, Baguio City's market-aisle vendors have not only established such organizations but also registered their collectives with the Securities and Employment Commission, thereby leveraging more official channels to lobby for their demands.

The relationship between the Baguio City municipal government and the informal market-aisle vendors is not solely one of antagonism or resistance, but rather one of negotiation allowing sellers considerable agency. As we have seen with the Baguio City government's see-saw pattern of policy implementation, many restrictive vending by-laws are rescinded shortly after their introduction, often enabling vendor organizations to drive the strategic decisions of the state. Baguio City Public Market aisle sellers' actions highlight that traders' informal practices operate in a "parallel and intersecting system of law" with that of government structures as vendors intentionally and directly interact with the state, even if they do not pay taxes or buy business licenses to sell (Gonzalez 2009:259). Vendors' actions—opening new socioeconomic spheres within old ones—are not in opposition to development or modernity, as they are repeatedly positioned. Rather, market-aisle vendors' initiatives fashion an interdependent or gradient space that conflates dichotomies such as formal/informal or legal/ illegal work. Indeed, the Baguio City government contributes to collapsing such dichotomies because its repeated tolerance of informal vendor activities is, itself, a form of regulation akin to "enforcement discretion" (Gonzalez 2009:259).

Although I argue that women vendors' work-based activism is grounded in and "speaks to broadly shared experiences of exploitation" and exclusion (Mills 2008:93), the Baguio City situation also makes evident that particular market-aisle vendor groups may have an advantage in securing their captured work spaces, depending on members' class (education, income) and the strength of their social networks. The SEC-registered vegetable vendors in the Rice Section who are also members of the Market Vendors Multipurpose Cooperative and the members of the Baguio Women's Vegetable Vendors Association who are led by an experienced administrative president are, both, well situated to defend their livelihoods. Conversely, the more loosely organized Hanger-Housewares Aisle Vendors Association, the independent ambulant cooked food and fresh produce vendors, and the BWVVA's neighboring independent vendors who have not self-organized face more challenging obstacles to secure their trade.

In stark evidence today, the Baguio City government's policies regarding vendors' initiatives in the Public Market aisles fluctuate between tolerance and harassment, interspersed with officials' condoning of so-called illegal commerce via their receipt of legal rental payments. Women vendors learn how to best use "market space and its expectations to take advantage of the contradictions that lie within it in order to defend their livelihoods" (Seligmann 2004:203). The fact that these vendors have established long-term businesses despite the ongoing risks to their trade evidences that they have devised "solutions to seemingly intractable social problems" (Gonzalez 2009:260). By innovatively refashioning absolute market space into dynamic relational sites, Baguio City women vendors have managed to assert their place as legitimate and visible actors in arenas of public power that have largely excluded them from the privileges of modern citizenship and rights to livelihood.

Notes

1. Field research for this chapter was conducted in the Philippines during several periods from 2003 to 2012, with the majority of the interview data reported here collected from 2009 to mid-2011. Financial support for this research has been provided by the Social Sciences and Humanities Research Council of Canada (SSHRC), Standard Research Grants (2000–2003, 2004–2007, and 2008–2011) and by OCAD University Faculty Research grants. I thank my research assistants, who have kept me informed of street economy events during this time. In the Philippines, I am affiliated with the Cordillera Studies Center, University of the Philippines Baguio. I thank my colleagues at CSC for their ongoing support of my research. I also thank the anonymous volume reviewers for their helpful comments, and to the many people in the Philippines who answered my questions about street and market trade, I owe a debt of gratitude.

2. The exchange rate I use here is $US1.00 = 50 Philippine pesos.

3. All names of people and street vendor associations are pseudonyms.

6

Maya Street Vendors' Political Alliances and Economic Strategies in the Tourism Spectacle of Antigua, Guatemala

Walter E. Little

Every day, the colonial city of Antigua operates as a spectacle because its primary function is to entertain by taking tourists into colonial pasts with Maya "others." This chapter frames Guy Debord's (2005) concept of spectacle—that which obscures capitalist economic relations—in terms of the human economic subjects of the spectacle, those who are the objects of touristic representations.

URBAN TOURISM SPECTACLES: MAYAS AND SPANISH COLONIAL ARCHITECTURE

The focus on spectacle as event has been widely discussed in tourism studies (Edensor 2001) and in terms of the cultural industries' (mass media, advertising, and entertainment) representations and tourists' consumptive practices (Gotham 2002, 2005). By contrast, my aim is to situate Maya handicraft vendors' political and economic practices in dialogue with Debord's thesis to explore how vendors challenge global, national, and local representational hegemonies that incorporate Mayas as adornment to tourism sites and at the same time obscure their labor. Maya street vendors, I argue, are in a distinct position to disrupt the spectacle and use it to their economic and political advantage since they are well represented in the tourism literature.

The Antigua tourism spectacle is a combination of effects that gives the impression that "it monopolizes the majority of time spent outside the production process" (Debord 2005:2). Antigua is spectacular: Spanish colonial architecture in various stages of restoration and ruin, Mayas who speak and dress distinctively from the non-Maya Ladinos and visiting tourists, and tourism conveniences and services that range from humble home stays with local families to grungy backpacker hostels to elegant five-star resorts. It is a place where American, European, Japanese, and other tourists are removed from their everyday lives as they walk cobblestone streets and mingle with splendidly dressed Maya vendors. Gotham (2002:1737), writing about New Orleans, argues, "Tourism has decentred and localised consumption, replacing work with entertainment and lifestyle as the pivotal facets of sociocultural life." He (Gotham 2002:1738) adds that within such touristic spaces, the representation of the place and inhabitants, Antigua and Mayas in my case study here, makes it difficult for tourists to distinguish between what is illusion and what is real. Like Bruner (2005), I take issue with this division because it assumes that both tourists and the subjects of their interest behave according to the entertainment logic of the spectacle and because the real relations of production (or the economic activities that support the spectacle) are so obscured that tourists cannot see them.

For Maya street vendors, the contexts in which they sell are all too real as they try to make sales and dodge police, who will impound merchandise and fine them. In particular, I am concerned with how Maya vendors use dominant tourism representations and tourists' expectations to make a living and challenge local political authority. My observations are based on a more than twenty-year ethnographic engagement with Antigua as a tourism destination and with the people who populate it. Drawing on archival research and participant observation of Antigueños and Maya vendors, I have listened to local debates about how to represent the city, who has the right to be in it, and what place street vending holds. Within the context of Antigua as tourism spectacle and Mayas themselves as spectacles, Maya street vendors devise ways to organize that are not obviously related to labor or culture but do fall within tourists' and Antigua's non-Maya political leaders' prescribed expectations. In the following sections, I discuss the ways Antigua is imagined and recognized as a national, Latin American, and world heritage. I then discuss the various and often conflicting concepts of space, local politics, and the place of urban entrepreneurialism by looking at ideologies of urban space, the politics of public space use, and vendors' strategies for recuperating entrepreneurial places.

IMAGINING ANTIGUA AS HERITAGE

Antigua has long been recognized as an important national heritage site, beginning more than a century ago when well-heeled residents from Guatemala City came to relax amid the quiet streets and crumbling colonial buildings. By the 1930s, it was a fixture on the international tourism circuit. Cruise ships docked at Puerto Barrios on the Caribbean coast and Puerto San José on the Pacific coast, and Clark Tours operators then drove tourists into the highlands to experience Maya culture and architectural remnants of Spanish colonialism that characterized many communities. Antigua was always on the itinerary. After the 1976 earthquake wracked the highlands, however, Antigua stood alone among Guatemalan cities as the place to tour Spanish colonial architecture. The uniqueness of Antigua was fortified in 1979 when UNESCO designated it as a World Heritage site. In contrast with other World Heritage sites, which offer pages of description and arguments rationalizing their importance, the UNESCO review statement (April 10, 1979) says merely that it is a "fundamental site, a well understood history, an appropriate inscription." Such an ambiguous definition allows Antigueños, Maya vendors, and the tourism industry, in general, creative freedom in imaging and promoting Antigua as a place worth seeing. This also has contributed to tensions among the stakeholders in Guatemalan tourism, within Antigua itself and beyond (Little 2004a).

One of Debord's (2005:12) key points is that in the separation of use value from exchange value, there is a "general acceptance of the illusions of modern commodity consumption. The real consumer has become a consumer of illusions. The commodity is this materialized illusion, and the spectacle is its general expression." This, in part, occurs through processes of representation in which "the spectacle is money one can only look at, because in it all use has already been exchanged for the totality of abstract representation" (2005:12). Later, he continues that the use of commodities matters less than "through recognition of their value as commodities.... Waves of enthusiasm for particular products are propagated by all the communications media" (2005:19). In the case of Antigua, those products are Spanish colonial architecture and Mayas dressed in their traditional clothing (*traje*) and performing non-modern weaving on backstrap looms, tending fields with hoes, and selling hand-loomed textiles, and rough-hewn wood carvings. All of these are well represented in the tourism literature, including guidebooks, brochures and pamphlets, news media coverage, and the Internet. Long before traveling to Antigua, tourists have a good idea as to what and whom they will see.

In Antigua, these representational processes have slowly evolved over

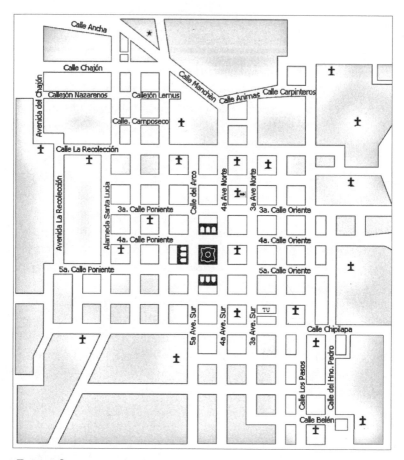

FIGURE 6.1

La Antigua, Guatemala: the central historic district. Map: Walter E. Little.

the course of several decades, though more intensely since the 1930s with increasing global interest in ethnic tourism. Similar representations, tourists, expatriate artists, and even anthropologists can be found populating Guatemala (Little 2008b), Mexico (Berger and Wood 2010), and Indonesia (Bruner 2005; Vickers 1989). Representations of Antigua expanded from identifying it as a quiet place for wealthy residents from Guatemala City who visited on weekends, to identifying it as a unique place to see exotic Maya Indians and bustling marketplaces where tourists could visit the past (Anderson 1984) by walking among the city's Spanish colonial houses, churches, and plazas (figure 6.1). The representational shift to Mayas and colonial architecture took place as a result of dictator Jorge Ubico's national development strategies from 1931 to 1944 (Little 2004a, 2008b) and the growth of international tourism, beginning post World War I (Fussell 1980) and accelerating after World War II as greater numbers of Americans and Europeans travelled abroad (MacCannell 1976).

Over the past eighty years, Antigua has been represented in the local, national, and international tourism literature as a stuck-in-time Spanish colonial city populated by Mayas, primarily, Maya women. Women Maya street vendors are central in these representational practices, namely, because they are so public. They are the subjects of postcards sold locally; they adorn locally, nationally, and internationally produced maps and tourism brochures and guidebooks; and their images are used as stock photos to accompany positive and negative articles about Antigua in national periodicals. Representations of Maya women serve to give the illusion that the association between Mayas and Spanish colonial architecture is natural and symbiotic. Such representations portray Mayas as adornment and as a form of in situ entertainment for tourists. The phenomenon of indigenous women being significant to tourism is far from distinctive, as Seligman (chapter 7, this volume) clearly illustrates. Representations rarely show Mayas working, other than the occasional marketplace scene or a Maya woman weaving. Instead, smiling Maya women street vendors pose like decorations before the Spanish colonial buildings, as if to beckon foreign tourists to relax in the exotic tranquility of Antigua.

According to Debord (2005:18), "the city spectacle needs to preserve those [old urban] districts as tourist attractions." Antigua certainly fits this description, but therein lies the tension between the representations—the illusion that it is a place of leisure—and actual encounters among tourists, Mayas, and Ladinos—many going about their business irrespective of tourists. I take up these physical encounters in subsequent sections, but I want to emphasize here that the representational practices of both businesspersons (local, national, and, international) and government officials have created value that is not tied to use value. It is not even tied to exchange value. Instead, it is a value that derives from the representation of Mayas and Spanish colonial buildings as being linked, for tourists' visual consumption. These representations create value, but not on the bases of Mayas working and being productive. They are just there to be consumed visually.

CONCEPTS OF SPACE, LOCAL POLITICS, AND URBAN ENTREPRENEURIAL SPACES

Debord (2005:55–56) argues, "As urbanism destroys the cities, it recreates a pseudocountryside devoid both of the natural relations of the traditional countryside and of the direct (and directly challenged) social relations of the historical city." What UNESCO urban World Heritage sites and the tourism industry offer tourists are "direct...social relations." Problematic, however, are the social relations that tourists encounter as city officials, Maya street vendors, and Ladino residents try to live in a World Heritage site that is widely promoted as a tourism destination by the national government and the global tourism industry. Like other scholars conducting research in heritage-designated cities, such as Salvador da Bahia (Collins 2007, 2008), Havana (Matthew Hill 2007), and Cusco (Michael Hill 2007; Seligmann, chapter 7, this volume), I find that the often idyllic media and touristic representations are out of sync with the realities of living, working, and doing business in these cities. In Antigua, this incongruence plays out in the ways that local residents and workers—Mayas, Ladinos, and expatriates—try to accommodate touristic representational renderings of the city and reconcile these with local historical and cultural concepts of urban space. Touristic and local concepts of urban space are, in turn, negotiated in the ways the people live and work in the city.

Ideologies of Urban Space

Given that I have written elsewhere about Ladinos' and Mayas' ideological differences regarding urban space (Little 2004a, 2008a, 2009), I treat them briefly here. Ladinos, especially those who have been in political power, have tended to conceptualize urban space in terms of order, cleanliness, and efficiency and as an indication of economic, political, and social health. What is conceived as chaotic—Maya-occupied marketplaces—is relegated to the edges of the city. The extreme position would be the modernist city experiment of Brasilia, described by Holston (1989), in which the disorderly street, filled with direct and challenging social relations of historic Latin American and European cities, is replaced with orderly streets devoid of social messiness. City officials—the mayor and city council, urban planners, and municipal police—struggle to maintain order in this far-from-modernist city. Tourists, Maya street vendors, and even Ladinos who do business, relax, and consume in the historic center disrupt the ideology of order. Zoning laws are broken by tax-paying "legitimate" businesses that spill onto the streets and hang unauthorized signs. Anti-littering laws are violated as tourists from the capital and neighboring Central American countries clog the fragile cobblestone streets with cars and discard food wrappers and plastic drink bottles in the Central Plaza and in Catholic church courtyards throughout the city. Of course, this order-disorder tension underlies each of the chapters in this volume, with local authorities attributing disorder to street vendors.

Traditional Mayas' concepts of urban space have little in common with those of Ladinos, except that power—cosmological, economic, and political—should be concentrated in the city center. However, because power is in, and should be focused in, the *ruk'u'x tinamït* (literally, "the heart of the city" in the Kaqchikel Maya language), the perfect place to be—to socialize, relax, and conduct economic and political business—is the city center. For Maya street vendors, it is no mystery that banks, which are located primarily around or within a block of the Central Plaza, command a great deal of economic power, but these are not places of intense social interaction and the economic interactions are impersonal. Instead, the plaza without the periodic marketplace (moved more than a century ago out of the plaza) and the street vendors is *b'ison* (sad) and *tz'iran* (quiet, without activity or excitement). Indeed, for the Maya vendors I have conversed with for more than twenty years, an ideal expression of economic, political, and social power is the periodic marketplace, centrally located in the city plaza. In fact, there are also cosmologically powerful links on both Catholic and Maya ritual holidays. At least once per year, the day of and days around the town patron saint's day, Mayas' community celebrations fuse economic, political, and social relations. These are boisterous affairs that include the intermingling of religious, political, and economic events. Vendors maintain a strong presence in these activities. Antigua has not had these patron saint celebrations for decades. Most Maya-dominated towns retain weekly periodic marketplaces, complete with the messiness of politics, economic exchanges, religious practice, and everyday socializing. The intense, face-to-face, economic and social relations of the periodic marketplace, as well as those of street vendors (ambulatory and stationary), epitomize Mayas' view of a vibrant and even chaotic ruk'u'x tinamït as evidence of power and urban health.

It is within these two poles of ideology that tourists visiting Antigua meet the Mayas and Ladinos who operate tourism-related businesses. There is little agreement among these parties as to which ideological perspective of urban space is preferable. Most of those working in the tourism industry try to use each to attract customers and gain an advantage over their competitors. In my interviews and conversations with tourists, most want to see and interact with Mayas, albeit on their terms and not those of Mayas, to experience quiet streets and rustic Spanish colonial architecture by day, have access to a lively night scene, and sleep in accommodations that match or better the service and technological conveniences of their home countries. These contradictory ideologies, representations, and practices become manifested in what can be considered "Maya Antigua" or "Maya Colonial."

Politics of Public Space Use

These ideologies of space use and the contradictory practices of tourists and tourism businesspersons (including Maya street vendors) play out in urban street politics. City administrations going back to the early 1990s embraced strategies to remove artisan marketplaces, as well as stationary and ambulatory vendors located on public sidewalks and plazas (Little 2004b). Actions included seizing merchandise, fining vendors, and incarcerating, and relocating vendors into authorized zones, often far from the city center, all of which intensified in the years following 2001 (Little 2008a, 2009).

The city's officials and police forces are reluctant to remove street vendors in the presence of tourists, unless the vendors are clearly nuisances. Citywide sweeps to confiscate merchandise and expel vendors tend to happen during tourism lulls, but street vendors are prey to random seizures by police scouring the city for lone vendors outside tourists' gazes. Following the September 11, 2001, attacks on the World Trade Center and the Pentagon, a dramatic drop in tourism, globally (Bonham, Edmonds, Mak 2006) as well as in Guatemala, gave municipal authorities a window to more aggressively remove vendors. In our interviews with street vendors during this time, most said that with so few tourists, it was not worth the effort to go to Antigua; sales were so meager, they could not recover the costs of travel, lodging, and meals. Vendors did not suffer alone in this economic downturn. Restaurants, hotels, travel agencies, and Spanish-language instruction schools shuttered their doors. With anxieties about terrorism subsiding and tourism on the rise, many street vendors have subsequently returned, especially under the administration of the current mayor, Dr. Adolfo Vivar Marroquín, who has been much less aggressive toward street vendors than his predecessor, César Antonio Siliézar Portillo. Such ebbs and flows have long been part of life for vendors in Antigua because tourism slows not only in relation to global fears of terrorism and economic recessions but also in reaction to political and social violence, which continually plague Guatemala (see Carmack 1986; Little and Smith 2009).

Over the past fifteen years that I have attended handicraft vendor meetings and city council sessions, vendors have slowly changed the ways they conceptually frame their arguments about why they have the right to sell in Antigua. Vendors throughout the 1990s and 2000s used identity strategically, drawing on whichever identity they thought would help them economically and politically (Little 2004a, 2008a). In the early 2000s, street vendors shifted their political and economic tactics and organized themselves into vendor and artisan associations. As with other organized, contemporary political-economic organizations, like the new social movements described in the social science and humanities literature, worker-based identities are not necessarily the most salient around which vendors have organized (Jackson and Warren 2005; Little 2004b; Nash 2007). Vendors from 2002 to 2008 did organize around worker identities, putting aside community, linguistic, and ethnic differences to form the Ambulatory Vendors Association of Antigua, Guatemala, and become members of CORAGUA (Comite Representativo de Artesanos del Altiplano de Guatemala), FENVEMEGUA (Frente Nacional Vendedores Mercados de Guatemala), and CGTG (Central de Trabajadores de Guatemala). These artisan, labor, and vendor organizations backed street vendors when they made appeals to the city officials to allow street vending and when they directly confronted those same city administrators and police officers for reselling seized vendor merchandise. In the opinion of most vendors, these years of political organization and confrontation with the city's officials yielded very little, namely, a weekend marketplace located two blocks from the Central Plaza and too small to accommodate all vendors. Besides, most long-term street vendors have resisted selling in one of the officially designated marketplaces due to the high overhead, their inability to compete with the marketplace vendors, and many tourists' refusal to enter marketplaces, out of fear.

In recent years, vendors have used ethnic and worker identities less often in order to argue to city officials and police that they have a place in the local economy. They also have used less frequently what can be considered rational arguments about why they should be allowed to sell in Antigua, including these positions: they help the local economy by drawing tourists ,who spend most of their money in hotels, restaurants, and Spanish-language classes; they clean up trash left by tourists; and they improve tourists' safety by keeping a protective eye out for thieves. They have dropped appeals to establish joint vendor-municipality regulatory policies and a permit-to-vend fee structure because these strategies consistently failed with the past four city administrations, despite strong support from the above-mentioned worker organizations, human rights organizations, the governor, and national congress members. By contrast, other street vendors and service workers—candy and fruit cart sellers, photographers, shoe-shine men and boys, for example—have secured rights to vend on the street and in the Central Plaza, the most coveted place to sell in the city. What distinguishes the street workers who can be found throughout the city is their lack of overt Maya ethnic characteristics. This is not to claim that Mayas do not work in these occupations. The former street workers, however, do not display their ethnicity as handicraft vendors do, because their clientele is primarily local Ladinos, rather than foreign tourists.

Handicraft vendors now claim that they are national patrimony, when defending their economic place in the city to police and political officials, but have not stopped claiming that they are Maya and artisans as well. This represents a semantic shift in how they represent themselves as productive contributors to the economy; vendors claim that they have historical precedence because they are part of a continuous line of Maya vendors who have sold goods there. That vendors would come to this position is not surprising. I have heard them jokingly claim that they themselves are "Maya tours," mocking a Shimano bicycle of that name (Little 2008c). Shimano is one of a number of companies, in this case, a Japanese transnational corporation, that incorporate representations of Mayas into product marketing schemes, in effect, making Mayas the product of consumption and a national and global spectacle.

Some vendors, since they were babies accompanying their grandmothers, mothers, and older sisters, have experienced tourists' continual interest in and fascination with them. What have changed and intensified over the past few years are the popular media, tourism industry promotions, and travel-related blogs and other online representations about Antigua that associate Mayas and colonial architecture with each other. As more and more vendors purchase computers, going online in their homes, in schools, and in Internet cafés, they are gaining a greater knowledge of how central they are in the representations of Antigua. They are aware that they are part of the spectacle of Antigua, that they themselves are spectacle. As economic actors, they are connecting their concepts of livelihood to the spectacle of "Maya Antigua" in ways that are reconfiguring their sense of value. Here, value is shifting in their self-conceptualizations away from the use value or exchange value of the products they sell.

Instead, the objects they sell have sign value due to what these symbolize to tourists—mementos of the vacation, gifts for friends and relatives, embodiments of social relations with Mayas, and material statements of solidarity with Mayas' political struggles. Hence, production processes, use values, and exchange values tend to be hidden or, with some tourists, ignored. At the same time, a self-awareness of their own intrinsic value from within the space of the spectacle has intensified for Maya vendors. Some tell police and city officials, "We are so important to Antigua that we should be paid to be here." There is a growing shift in attitude from servility to self-assuredness in their dealings with officials that is detectable in statements like "If we're not here, tourists won't come" and "Look at the tourism promotion—INGUAT uses us, guidebooks use us."[1]

The self-awareness of being represented in the mass media and the way this can relate to economic value for the subjects of the representations are not recognized in Debord's theory of the spectacle, nor in sociological studies that have drawn on his theory, focusing on sign value (Gotham 2002) and consumption (Gotham and Krier 2008). Part of this may be the result of the particular ethnographic contexts in which the phenomenon of the spectacle has been explored. Urban heritage sites are not subject to urban planning in quite the same ways as cities where, as Debord (2005:53) claims, "urbanism—'city planning'—is capitalism's method for taking over the natural and human environment. Following its logical development toward total domination, capitalism now can and must refashion the totality of space into its own particular decor." Certainly, places like Antigua have their own décor, but they are not fashioned only from contemporary forms of capitalism based on sign value (mass media representations) and consumption. Instead, heritage cities are fashioned out of histories of memories and long-standing economic, political, and social relationships and are populated not by paid actors but by living persons who have come to symbolize Antigua. This has, as Gotham (2005:226) argues, entailed a theory of "urban spectacles that highlights both progressive and resistant characteristics, and oppressive and negative attributes." Unlike what Gotham describes, heritage cities like Salvador da Bahia (Collins 2007), Havana (Matthew Hill 2007), Cusco (Michael Hill 2007), and Antigua are not museums or historic sites that are staffed by workers and trained actors playing fictitious roles (Bruner 2005). No matter how much pressure is applied by the national government, UNESCO, or international tourism companies, residents do not have to behave appropriately. The tensions among the representations of Antigua; the expectations and consumption of Antigua by international tourists; the maintenance of Antigua by local (municipal), national (INGUAT and historical conservators), and global (UNESCO rates and reviews heritage sites, removing those sites that do not comply) regulatory bodies; and the people who live and work in Antigua allow for new political, economic, and social spaces that can open or restrict opportunities for locals.

Recuperating Entrepreneurial Spaces

Most entrepreneurial spaces that have opened for Maya street vendors cannot be considered new. Vendors follow the same routes from hotel to hotel, church courtyard to church courtyard, Spanish school to Spanish school; they crisscross the Central Plaza to ply the same handwoven merchandise they have sold for at least the past eighty years, since ethnic tourism and handicrafts first attracted tourists. What have changed, however, are the magnitude of representations of Mayas in Antigua,[2] the numbers of tourists and their consumption expectations, and Mayas' greater understanding of what their place in the imagination of Antigua is. This has contributed to changing attitudes about how to treat Maya street vendors. Most local resistance to them still comes from the municipal government and some businesspersons, but the current administration has elected to ignore the street vendors' handicraft sales, and many tourism-oriented businesspersons have symbiotic economic relationships with street vendors, permitting them to make sales in the lobbies of hotels, restaurants, and Spanish-language schools. More owners of these businesses have come to terms with the mutual economic benefits they and vendors can potentially enjoy when they increase the opportunities for tourists to mingle with Maya vendors.

Maya women, especially, have been able to capitalize on these arrangements because, in contrast to men, they perform their public and political ethnic identities (see Butler 1990) in ways that are more recognizable to foreign tourists. Although the male street vendors speak the Maya languages of their respective hometown and linguistic community, few wear the traje typical of their town or region, for example, a few older men from Santa Catarina Palopó. Younger vendors from that town and from Sololá and the surrounding region abandoned their regionally distinct clothing. They explained to me that tourists think that they are acting, "dressing up just to sell," so they all stopped wearing traje generations ago. These same tourists, however, do go to vendors' towns of origin expecting to see men dressed in the community's garb. Because women are represented in and are the predominant subjects of tourism (Little 2004a), traje, caring for children, and weaving are recognized as part of their identity.

One of Debord's (2005) major concerns is how processes of representation relate to the spectacle and, in turn, how the reconfigured economy is comprehended. He (2005:18) claims, "Wherever representation becomes independent, the spectacle regenerates itself." Additionally, he (2005:58) argues that the "preservation [of culture is] a dead object for spectacular contemplation [that is a] defense of class power." Indeed, within the context of Maya handicraft vendors in Antigua, I would argue that Debord's observations about the spectacle apply to representations of Maya vendors and the Spanish colonial architecture. The Internet and the tourism industry do much to facilitate the regeneration of the spectacle and preserve social, political, and economic hierarchies that are historically rooted in the colonial period.

Lived-in heritage cities in comparison with living heritage museums like Colonial Williamsburg (Handler and Gable 1997) and New Salem (Bruner 2005) are represented in very similar ways, with the preservation of social hierarchies clearly marked and performed, especially with respect to occupations like street vending in Antigua. As powerful as Debord's argument is—that the spectacle obscures economic processes and that representational practices are forces that can reaffirm particular economic and political identities—the residents of heritage cities add social and economic dimensions that are not anticipated in the theory of the spectacle, in living history museums themselves, or in the expectations of tourists going to heritage cities. At the most basic level, this disjuncture between representation and lived experience can be unsettling to those who share the same social and physical spaces, as do Ladinos, Mayas, and foreign and national tourists. It is in this political context that Maya street vendors find ways to reinterpret the meanings of the social and economic spaces to reclaim urban entrepreneurial places.

Countless representations of Antigua by the mass media (print and television), on the Internet, and in tourism promotions put Mayas in the city and only serve to construct an imagined space that challenges existing ideologies of public space and the use of space for economic and political means. Just as this configuration of representation, consumption, and social interactions has contributed to changes in Maya street vendors' assessments of their own worth and their strategies for contesting municipal government restrictions on vending, it has also resulted in changes in Maya street vendors' conceptualizations of urban entrepreneurial spaces. What is significant about this shift in self-conceptualization is that it gives vendors a rationality for reclaiming places they were expelled from in the 1990s, including public parks and plazas, Spanish Colonial church ruins, sidewalks, and streets (Little 2004a). From the mid-1990s until 2008 when the current mayor was elected, vendors had been subjected to forcible removal from all public places in the city, as well as merchandise seizures and fines. The negative political responses to the vendors were similar to those experienced by street vendors and workers in the informal sector around the world (Bromley 2000; Donovan 2008; Middleton 2003; Stoller 2002; Swanson 2007; Timothy 1997; in this volume, the chapters by Lindell, Scheld, Seligmann, and Turner).

After more than a decade of social and political actions similar to those used by street vendors elsewhere (Cross 1998; Cross and Morales

2007; Hansen 2004; Lindell 2010b) that yielded few successes (Little 2008a, 2004b), Maya street vendors' political organizations began to fracture, and greater numbers of street vendors returned to work without participating in the larger street vendor and worker organizations described earlier. In fact, during summer 2008, several vendors explained their frustration about not having recovered the public places in which they had sold their goods the prior decade, despite their unification and support from vendor and labor organizations. They decided that paying dues to these organizations made little economic sense. They claimed that without any clear legal mechanisms on their side, most city politicians and businesspersons would not support their causes. Rather than retreat to their hometowns, they reassessed their places in what can be considered the touristic imaginary of Antigua. It was not that vendors had just come to the realization they played a major part in how the city is represented. This they knew. Rather, they began to use it as a strategy to re-insert themselves into places where they had previously sold. Hence, their attitude shifted to treat the city as "Maya Antigua" or "Maya Colonial," where they are the spectacle. To tourists in their presence, they are more public in their protests that they will not be fined, expelled, or intimidated by the city police. The police still issue tickets, but vendors reported fewer and fewer incidents of their merchandise being seized in each of the years I spoke with them, in the summer of 2008, 2009, and 2010. None knew of any street vendors being arrested, something that was commonly done in the previous administration.

USING AND DISRUPTING THE SPECTACLE

Careful not to draw the ire of tourists, police tended to pull back from public confrontations with vendors. In fact, the places where Maya street vendors returned were those that had the heaviest tourist traffic, such as the Central Plaza and the Calle del Arco between the Central Plaza and La Merced Church three blocks away. Another well-tread route that tourists and street vendors use runs along 4ta Calle Oriente, on which are located hotels, shops, and restaurants that cater to tourists. It is the main through-way to exit the city and is regularly clogged with traffic. Street vendors also sell along routes usually originating in the Central Plaza and linked to the numerous Spanish-language schools, colonial churches and buildings, and hotels that are scattered throughout the city. The farther that vendors are away from the Central Plaza, Calle del Arco, and 4ta Calle Oriente, the greater the risk of being fined and even having their merchandise confiscated by the police, which usually occurs when they are walking between the places tourists frequent.

FIGURE 6.2

Calle del Arco on the weekend. Photo: Walter E. Little.

The ways that Maya street vendors take advantage of their being part of the tourism spectacle of Antigua, especially in the Plaza–Calle del Arco corridor, relates, largely, to the density of tourists. On weekdays, this street is full of automobile traffic, at which time vendors concentrate in the Central Plaza, at La Merced Church, and in front of a few select tourism-oriented businesses on Calle del Arco. The automobile traffic and parked cars alone make it difficult for them and tourists to walk this route, and there is little space to make sales pitches and show merchandise. Instead, vendors position themselves where they are visible to tourists. Female vendors, especially, commented to me that they are "adornments to the city" who "help attract tourists." On weekends, however, Calle del Arco is blocked to automobile traffic, allowing vendors and tourists to amble between the plaza and La Merced (figure 6.2).

Selling on Calle del Arco and in the plaza presents vendors with the same problems they and street vendors of all products have always faced, namely, convincing passersby to purchase their goods. Just as vendors are increasingly confident about their rights to sell in Antigua, particularly in

FIGURE 6.3

A vendor from San Antonio Aguas Calientes holds a tapete (su't). *Photo: Walter E. Little.*

places where architectural coloniality is strongest, tourists expect them to be there. Tourists anticipate a wide range of interactions with Maya vendors, all of which they want on their terms, not those of the vendors. Some tourists clearly engage vendors with the sole purpose of purchasing something. Others prefer to just look at the vendors, at most, taking photos of them. Others, particularly those with better Spanish skills and those who are studying Spanish, seek out vendors to engage in conversations. Vendors try their best to make sales pitches and cater to tourists' expectations. Like the police, vendors try to avoid confrontations with tourists since they are well aware that it would be seen by other tourists, who would then comment to yet other tourists about their "bad behavior." Vendors do their best to regulate their behavior and be what tourists expect. In-your-face selling tactics tend not to work, so vendors take slower, soft-selling approaches: draping merchandise where it can be easily seen and conversing about everything but what they hope to sell (figure 6.3).

Sometimes these tactics, based on how vendors think tourists will react, are not always economically successful. Although most tourists are eager to meet Mayas in the flesh, many have explained to me that they are not always looking to buy something. "Besides," said one who captures what many others said, "I don't like to feel pressured by vendors. There are so

FIGURE 6.4
Street vendors selling to a group of Spanish students/tourists. Photo: Walter E. Little.

many of them, and, yes, I know some are really poor, but that doesn't give them the right to get in my face or make me feel guilty that they're poor just to get me to buy something." Vendors' miscalculations can lead to contentious interactions when tourists feel pressured to buy or, simply, culturally and linguistically misunderstand vendors' behavior.

Street vendors argue that the advantage of being recognized as fixtures (I contend, spectacles) of Antigua and selling near prominent colonial buildings and plazas (figure 6.4) is that they have access to a great flow of potential customers. The tourists interested in Mayas are largely the only consumers these vendors will have. In the years of city-wide expulsions of street vendors, especially from 2000 to 2008, vendors complained about the difficulty of making a viable living, not just because of fines and confiscated merchandise, as mentioned earlier, but because they were alienated from their clients.

Where Maya street vendors are most successful in using their being spectacles in the spectacle, as well as disrupting the spectacle itself, is with the authorities. Street vendors use dominant touristic representations and tourists' expectations to challenge local authority. On past occasions when they were threatened by police, particularly in the Central Plaza or along Calle del Arco on the weekends, they would cease selling and quietly leave. Now, they challenge the officers and say, "We are the attraction" and "Tourists look for us," in order to draw attention to the police pressure to leave. If the tourists can understand Spanish, vendors will try to make them part of the scenario and turn them against the police. This has a dual effect. First, from the perspective of the police, the Maya street vendors are too much of a hassle to deal with. In fact, the police officers I spoke with in October 2009, June to August 2010, and June and July 2011 said that unless the vendors are bothering tourists or doing something that is illegal, they would let them go with a quiet warning.

In October 2009 after years of trying, I was able to interview the city police captain about policies related to Maya street vendors. First, he explained that the years of expelling vendors were fruitless and had a tendency to backfire on the public relations front. He said that the city was concerned with more important matters, like "controlling the rise of violent crime" and "cultivating better relations with Antigüenos, because they feel [the police] are only interested in tourists and vendors." The municipal police force had been relocated only a few short months before my interview with the police chief. The force was reformulated from the municipal tourism police, which had been created just for tourists rather than for the general protection of Antigua's citizens and workers.

Second, from the perspective of tourists, when Maya vendors used them to usurp police authority, the vendors, in fact, risked disrupting the ways in which tourists imagined them. Being placed in a scenario that brings the social control and even social and ethnic hierarchies into view has a tendency to make tourists nervous, especially since tourists do not recognize Mayas as not being part of the city. Some even call them Antigüenos, which does not sit well with the Ladino families who own property and, in many instances, have lived in the city for generations. These encounters of police, vendors, and tourists awaken tourists to social problems and divisions they had not considered in Antigua, even if they were aware of Guatemala's long history of ethnic division and outright conflict. Greater awareness of local politics leads them to question vendors about why they are not allowed to sell in public places and makes them wonder why not, when so many representations include Mayas in the colonial cityscape of Antigua.

WHAT ABOUT MAYA MEN?

Male vendors do not fit well into the touristic imagination of Antigua as mutually constituted by Mayas and colonial architecture. Few wear traje,

FIGURE 6.5

A vendor from Santa Catarina Palopó. Photo: Walter E. Little.

for instance, and when they do, like the vendor in figure 6.5, they have to explain themselves. The same tourism literature that powerfully locates Maya women in the colonial landscape tends to obscure, if not outright omit, Maya men. The overt ethnic signs that make Maya women recognizable to tourists are lacking in Maya men: it is highly unlikely that men will find a place to weave or will wear traje. In a few communities, men do continue this practice. The associations between male vendors and architecture and between male vendors and tourism in Antigua are so weak that tourists often failed to identify them as Maya, categorizing them as Ladinos or generically as Guatemalans.[3] Men in traje, like the man with his family

FIGURE 6.6

A family from Sololá, not vendors. Photo: Walter E. Little.

in figure 6.6, are considered outsiders, Mayas from the pueblos, in town for some official business, but not vendors. In fact, some of my Maya male Kaqchikel friends, including some who were vendors, helped me administer surveys in which tourists were asked how to identify Mayas and whether they could recognize or distinguish a man in Antigua as Maya. Not only did the tourists have difficulty making this distinction, but also not one person identified the man giving the survey as Maya—even when he spoke Kaqchikel Maya.

Because of the overt Maya ethnic characteristics embedded in the imagination of Antigua, Maya men in terms of ethnicity are largely invisible, especially as vendors. The fact remains that Maya men compose between a quarter and a third of the total number of street vendors in Antigua. Some, unlike the women, do not make claims to the police that they are the "tourist attraction," which makes them more vulnerable to being fined and arrested and less likely to make sales to tourists. Because such claims would fall on deaf ears to both police and tourists, their selling strategies are to position themselves in places with large numbers of tourists, like the Central Plaza, Calle del Arco, and 4ta Calle Oriente, or near major hotels, like the Casa Santo Domingo, a large luxury hotel. Their selling technique is primarily limited to holding out a small selection of their merchandise for passing tourists to see but not saying anything. One said to me, "As long as we don't make problems around tourists, the police usually leave us alone."

CONCLUSION

Urban heritage sites challenge capitalism's effects on urbanism and tourism, or perhaps the kinds of urbanism and tourism that are imagined. They are living cities. Maya street vendors are not playing scripted roles or conforming to the imagined place created in the tourism literature. At the same time, Mayas have gained greater awareness of how important and central they are to the imagined Antigua, and Ladinos, too, are keenly aware of this.

Debord (2005:54) claims, "Urbanism's petrification of life can be described…as a total predominance of a 'peaceful coexistence within space' over 'the restless becoming that takes place in the progression of time.'" UNESCO World Heritage cities, such as Antigua, contest this conceptualization. In many ways, they are enigmatic, represented as unchanging and stuck in the past but populated with residents very much in the present, and are regulated by the state and global organizations that focus on cultural and architectural aesthetics over the changing attitudes and desires of the residents themselves. The touristic imagination of Antigua is certainly that of peaceful coexistence. This powerful illusion fades when tourists experience the city, because they find themselves in a city that has deep ethnic divisions; business conflicts, as handicraft vendors, souvenir shops, restaurants, and Spanish-language schools compete for clientele; and a local population with a limited tolerance for playing its part in the touristic illusion. Antigua may be imagined as the past, but it is lived in the present and concerned with the future, inverting Debord's conceptualization.

The causal relationship between Maya street vendors of handicrafts and the representations of Antigua and the consumption of tourists can certainly be challenged. Over the past twenty years, there have been profound political changes—the end of a thirty-six-year war in 1996, the rise of Maya cultural activism (Warren 1998), and a turn to what Hale (2006) calls neoliberal multiculturalism—from which it is difficult to draw causal relationships in order to explain changes in street vendor and Ladino political strategies and attitudes in Antigua.[4] For many Maya vendors, representations of Mayas in Spanish colonial Antigua and tourists' consumption patterns are far more immediate and have been more immediate than the end of the war, Maya social movements, and neoliberal multiculturalism.

These examples highlight how Maya handicraft vendors act in and act on Antigua, as both spectacle and working city. In fact, through their flexible participation as spectacles within the spectacle that is Antigua, they are finding more successful ways to sell and to stay in a city where officials have been expelling them for several generations.

Notes

1. Instituto Guatemalteco de Turismo (Guatemalan Tourism Board).

2. A Google search (November 3, 2010) with the terms "Antigua" and "Maya" yielded 2.6 million website hits and 313,000 photos; "Antigua Maya" yielded 3,000 website hits and 535 photos.

3. Based on surveys conducted over fifteen years: first, a survey of 245 tourists in 1998 and, then, an additional 785 surveys with student assistants in 2005, 2006, and 2007.

4. This, in part, is the offering of cultural concessions (rights to speak one's indigenous language and dress in ethnically distinct clothes, among others) in order for the hegemonic Ladino elites to co-opt and control Mayas without making structural changes that allow greater political participation and economic equity.

7

The Politics of Urban Space among
Street Vendors of Cusco, Peru

Linda J. Seligmann

In 2010, I returned to Cusco after five years away to changes that directly affect Cusco's complex street economies. Gone was the congestion of hawkers lining the streets emanating from the San Pedro Central Market that I documented in 2004 (Seligmann 2004). A deliberate policy of formalization had displaced most vendors from the streets. Although street economies have not vanished, where the circuits of exchange transpire has shifted, and the "warehousing" of vendors indoors has made it far more difficult to locate them. Almost seven years since its inception, with few exceptions, the formalization process in Cusco has not been undone and has had major impacts on the economic and political organizational capacity of vendors, especially with respect to their ability to use space to their advantage.[1]

In contrast to most of the chapters in this volume, I discuss the effects of displacement on the vendors even as they strive to continue performing their occupations. I also take up the question of how neoliberal policies and ideologies and tourism are interacting to affect their daily lives (Harvey 2005). Peru's free trade agreements have encouraged a giddy celebratory climate amidst a 10 percent annual growth rate. Tourism, at the same time, has reached levels no one could quite imagine (Steel 2009). Over one and a half million tourists visited Cusco in 2009, more than three times its resident population, and the same was true in 2010. This represented a 15.5 percent increase in tourism from 2007 and includes national and international tourists (DIRCETUR 2011). Cusco was designated a UNESCO World Heritage site in 1983, and in 2007, Machu Picchu was voted as one of New Open World Corporation's New Seven Wonders of the World (New Seven Wonders 2007). The population of the city of Cusco has doubled in twenty years, now reaching approximately 510,000, and the population of the Cusco region is 1,274,742 (INEI 2008).

Tourism and neoliberalism have contradictory and specific impacts on different populations (Babb 2011; Freeman 2007; Gilbert 2004; Jackson and Warren 2005:553). Here, I compare and contrast the ways that vendors of agricultural products, on the one hand, and artisan vendors, on the other, have been affected by these forces, and I trace their creative and pragmatic struggles to make a living in these conditions (Comaroff and Comaroff 2009; Little 2004a).[2] I then examine their political engagement, arguing that the commodities they sell, their clienteles, and their distinctive ways of relying on flexibility together determine the conduct of their respective daily operations and their degree of participation in political mobilization. A copious body of literature addresses how street vendors' lives are shaped by informality. However, far less attention has been paid to the consequences of the ubiquitous trend toward systematic formalization that has accompanied policies of neoliberalism and the concomitant expansion of tourism as a central engine of economic development and growth.

THE MEANINGS OF WORK IN THE CONTEXT OF SPATIAL RESTRUCTURING AND FORMALIZATION

The activities of vendors transpire in and across physical spaces that may systematically create or reinforce boundaries, hierarchies, and networks that, in turn, structure material flows, discourse, and actors themselves (Brown 2006b). Spatial relationships carry meaning and produce meaning (Gupta and Ferguson 1997; Low 1996). The displacement of vendors has upended how vending occurs across the urban topography of Cusco and has disrupted social networks that vendors have depended on for many years to facilitate their livelihood. At the end of 2004 (and, in some cases, as early as 2001), Cusco's mayor announced his "market rehabilitation" plan and gave vendors the choice of giving up their vending operations or paying a license to move into one of at least six new alternative edifices constructed for the sole purpose of housing street vendors. Many vendors without permanent stalls in already established markets agreed to move, if they could afford it, but they faced new challenges. The buildings to which they were moved are located far from the traditional touristic center of town and range in size from one to four stories. Their scale is immense. Most of the vendors appreciate what they call "the security" and "the tranquility" of being inside. They are happy about the extended shelf life of their agricultural products—they no longer have to store their products daily in rented storage space or take these home with them—and they are proud of having bathrooms and even showers (when water is available).

However, they also speak of the negative consequences of the formalization process and physical move. Many had chosen their vending site by assessing the amount of street traffic and the relative proximity to where they lived. Their homes, in well-established *pueblos jovenes* (shanty towns) where they have extensive social networks and feel a sense of community that has extended over close to three generations, are at a greater distance from the markets where they now must work. This makes it harder for them to combine household and labor activities, including child care, and also makes political organizing and information sharing more difficult. Information sharing is further constrained because the flow of people and interaction with other vendors is segmented, discontinuous, and disrupted. In street vending, the flow of people is correlated closely to access to the flow of information about market conditions, social dynamics, and economic and political policies. The congestion that urban authorities decry as a scourge creates the conditions for vendors, clients, and wholesalers to exchange vital information. It also allows vendors access to more information in order to figure out market dynamics such as the going rate of informal loans and possible profit margins of particular products. No less important are the support systems they came to take for granted for helping one another to watch their stalls or children if they needed to run an errand.

Vendors also bore the economic costs of the move—they accrued debt as a result of the high price for licenses. The municipal government has controlled vendors' access to credit. Although those who moved indoors became more "credit worthy" in the eyes of lenders, the primary lender was the municipal bank, and for vendors, the annual interest rate has ranged between 18 and 22.5 percent. Because of the dispersal of vendors, access to loan sharks, whose interest rates are not so different from those of the municipal bank, is far more limited. The comfortable conditions they are now working in have come at a cost since the vendors must pay for the required services of watchmen and janitors.

AGRICULTURAL VENDORS, FLEXIBILITY, AND THE LOCUS OF MARKETS

Flexibility is constitutive of neoliberalism (Harvey 2005). For corporations and investors, flexibility means being able to move operations to avoid having to pay higher wages and tariffs, comply with environmental regulations, or deal with political instability. For Quechua people in the Andean highlands, flexibility carries other meanings and practices. For centuries, they have deployed their understanding of spatial relationships in order to expand their control over multiple production zones, diversify their resource base, and ensure social reproduction. Flexibility is a key component of their economic and social practices but has different goals from the relentless profit seeking that characterizes neoliberal capitalist enterprises (Mayer 2002; Seligmann 1995). Vendors, too, depend heavily on flexibility as a survival tactic. Many of them come from indigenous backgrounds and have adapted their understanding of how to control space, originally crafted in the countryside, to their needs in the marketplace. They have also used it to fight back against governmental regulations and actions that directly threaten their livelihoods (Seligmann 2000). Their ability to locate themselves in the path of prospective clients and move and hide to avoid the authorities, their reliance on kinship ties to access products and to strategize about the diversity of their products for sale, these are examples of their uses of flexibility. Their physical displacement to high rises (known as "commercial centers") and warehouses has markedly constrained their successful use of flexibility, especially among agricultural vendors. Even though the "new markets" where they are now located sport "streets" inside, complete with street signs, the vendors themselves are no longer in movement, and it is less possible for them to use the resource of space to their advantage. Unlike in the past, when they were often "the eyes and ears of the street," now they cannot even see the nonfabricated streets outside. These constraints have also affected their ability to mobilize politically, as I discuss below (figure 7.1).

The relocation of the principal wholesale market, which had been strategically and informally located along the railroad tracks of Avenida del Ejército, has confronted vendors with additional challenges. Vendors, until 2005, would make a quick trip from the markets or pueblos jovenes ringing the city above to obtain their goods from enormous lorries. Peasants from the countryside also had easy access to this market, permitting them to engage in transactions with both wholesalers and retailers. This sprawling market has vanished entirely as part of a government initiative to construct a highway that will go to a new international airport in Chinchero, a highly ranked tourist destination just outside Cusco that is known for its fine weavers and textiles (figures 7.2 and 7.3). The primary wholesalers' market, Vino Canchón, has moved outside the city to San Jerónimo, a half-hour cab ride for retailers. Some of the agricultural products amassed at

FIGURE 7.1

The warehouse to which vendors were moved during the formalization process. Photo: Linda J. Seligmann.

the new wholesale market come from producers in the Cusco region, but the market increasingly attracts products from as far away as Chile and Arequipa, which are supplying hotels and restaurants in Cusco and the Sacred Valley of Urubamba. In this context, social networks, loyalty to particular wholesalers and producers, and the advances and credit available to retail vendors are now much harder for vendors to maintain.

The locus of Cusco residents' everyday activities has also shifted with the rise in tourism. Cusco has always had a tourist center, but with the eviction of vendors and the expansion of urban infrastructure, a process of segregation is underway. Increasingly, the city's day-to-day activities, other than tourism, are taking place far from the center. Cusco's first mall, yet another kind of competition to vendors, is destined to be built next to the Universidad Nacional de San Antonio Abad del Cusco, which is located at some distance from the center. Eight "Mega" and "Maxi" supermarkets also now exist in the city. The supermarkets are often more convenient to residents, including middle- and lower-class residents, than are the vending warehouses. Whether to permit construction of the mall has been a fiercely contentious issue for Cusqueños. These new vending sites mostly allow advantages to accrue to wholesalers, who can control market share

FIGURE 7.2
The main informal wholesale market, Avenida del Ejército, before the formalization and displacement of vendors. Photo: Linda J. Seligmann.

FIGURE 7.3
The same wholesale market after the vendors were moved in 2005 to Vino Canchón wholesale market. Photo: Linda J. Seligmann.

and obtain the information they need with greater speed and at a much greater scale than retail vendors, even when retail vendors organize among themselves to collectively obtain and redistribute products.

One producers' market, Huancaro, a huge sprawling outdoor affair established by Cusco's regional government in conjunction with an NGO, is held Saturdays east-southeast of Cusco's center and stands as a stunning contrast to existing warehouse and wholesale operations and transactions. Huancaro is called a *feria* (fair) rather than a *mercado* (market), and many of the former informal vendors from various parts of the city now sell their wares here. Also present are many vendors who openly identify as *cholas* (indigenous) in their tall, white, stovepipe hats (Babb 1998; Seligmann 1989, 2000, 2004; Weismantel 2001). Hundreds of producers and wholesalers occupy the carefully marked, chalk grids within a huge rectangular area. Not a single tourist was there, and only a few mestizo clients. The preponderance of producers and the apparent familiarity and trust engendered by enduring social relationships in this market contrast sharply with the lack of control over information and knowledge between buyer and seller in the Vino Canchón wholesalers' market and in many of the warehouse markets.

How are vendors making a go of it, given their dislocation and these new constraints on their operations? They continue to try collaborating with neighbors and relatives in order to strategically capture flows and to organize the usual operations they undertake—producing and gathering up goods, distributing them, processing them, and selling them. Despite policing efforts to keep vendors far away and inside, some still spill over into side streets in the center of town. In addition to their daily operations in warehouse settings, they have taken to traveling farther to frequent periodic Saturday and Sunday markets, often leaving a relative to run the warehouse stall. Vendors have always done this, but well-established vendors now find themselves having to participate to a much greater extent in activating these networks at a time when they expected that they would no longer need to. Those in the middle or near the end of their vending careers are expending far more labor in their operations. They find it exhausting to coordinate these variables, and they can rely less on their fellow vendors since relationships of trust are more brittle. They often do not know who has come to occupy the stall next to them. I asked Luisa, a vendor of fruit who used to sell outside the Central Market but is now inside the warehouse Molino II, what she thought about her new surroundings and the changes over the preceding five years. She put it succinctly:

There may be more sales, but for me, my life, my economy, is not any better. Rather, it's the institutions rather than vendors who have benefited. Everything has gone up in price. There's too much competition, too many people.... It's far for me to get fruit from Vino Canchón.... There's more discord among vendors.... I go to other markets outside so that I can have a social life. There's more work, and sometimes I earn more that way.

Another vendor noted:

Sales are okay. They've gone down.... It's very hard work.... Before, we sold a lot, but now few people buy. There used to be a union.... But since Carlos Valencia [the mayor who started the displacement of vendors], it's very difficult. Too many municipal agents, too expensive to get a permanent stall. Before, you would take out a loan to build your house. Now we are nothing if we don't have a stall or are not registered in an association.

ARTISAN VENDORS

The biggest boom in vending is in artisanry. Artisanry—ceramics, weavings, knitted clothing, jewelry, stuffed animals—has always characterized Cusco, sometimes produced by individuals but more often by cottage industries and factories. Many artisan sellers and producers once occupied the arcades of Cusco's major plazas. Tourists, literally, had to step over them. In accordance with the Master Plan of Cusco enacted by the municipality in conjunction with UNESCO (2003), artisan vendors, like agricultural vendors, have now been displaced to an enormous warehouse structure called the Centro de Artesanías Wanchaq. They were removed to "protect the authenticity of Cusco and its plazas and arcades as a World Heritage site." Instead of wandering the arcades, tourists are now transported in buses to the warehouse, with its neo-Inca murals, to purchase "indigenous" goods. Outside, the warehouse sports the ancient Inca admonition "Ama Suwa, Ama Qella, Ama Llulla" (Do Not Steal, Do Not Be Lazy, Do Not Lie) in enormous letters. The vendors work inside at well-numbered stalls, and each aisle is named with a Quechua street sign. They are celebrated as producers, but many of the seemingly indigenous goods they sell are imported from China, Arequipa, or Tacna, with pieces of cloth imported and then sewn together in cottage industries (figure 7.4). Further, approximately 40 percent of the stalls are rented by other vendors, or employees are operating them.[3]

FIGURE 7.4

The interior of Wanchaq, the artisan vendors' warehouse market. Many of the goods hail from China. Photo: Linda J. Seligmann.

In addition to the operations described above, many artisan vendors who own stalls in Wanchaq strategize to sell their wares in the courtyards of restaurants and sometimes of hotels (Bromley and Mackie 2009). This is often a symbiotic relationship between artisans and business owners because artisan goods may attract more tourists to the site. Permanent stores also sell artisanry, and periodic fairs, many of which are regulated by the municipality, are dedicated to "artesanía." Artisan vendors have always been savvy and creative. They are quick to come up with innovative designs and products, many of which are quite practical and will appeal to tourists (see Little 2004a). Markets, in general, attract tourists, and the many periodic fairs that take place outside Cusco are now part of popular tourist circuits.

One consequence of the increase in tourism and the focus on indigeneity is the proliferation of fiestas, promoted from above by government agencies such as DIRCETUR (Dirección Regional de Comercio Exterior y Turismo) and the National Institute of Culture and from below by residents, including the vendors. In Cusco, fiestas had regularly taken place about once a month in concordance with saint days and the agricultural calendar. These occasions are a fine opportunity for vendors to sell their wares to tourists and nationals alike. Fiestas are now being celebrated about every two weeks, thus attracting greater numbers of tourists and creating more opportunities for vendors to make sales. And the vendors include not only artisans but also purveyors of snacks and agricultural products. On these occasions, the municipal agents make no efforts to control the illicit occupation of spaces by itinerant vendors.

Cusco's municipality provided me with the registration information of so-called "formal" artisan operations, excluding the many informal operations. Even so, there were 349 registered (many with the same last name). If one includes unregistered operations, the number would at least double. True, the demand for artisan products has increased with the surge in tourism, yet it is difficult for so many vendors to make much and if they have a profit margin at all, it is very narrow. The artisan vendors I interviewed who had worked in the business for a long time noted that they initially benefited from tourism but that this is no longer the case because there are too many vendors and they are increasingly dependent on intermediaries, wholesalers and exporters who control prices. Teodoro Qiuispe, who makes leather goods, commented, "We are at the apogee of tourism because of the multiplicity of artisans. With competition, it is difficult. And quality. People won't pay for high quality. Others who are learning make things any way they want and sell better."

PERCEPTIONS AND INTERACTIVE DISCOURSE BETWEEN TOURISTS AND VENDORS

Pride in indigeneity as a product is everywhere in Cusco. It is impossible to dissociate economic from cultural ventures (Brown 2003). Vendors take this into account as they make decisions about what indigenous products to sell and how to perform indigeneity (Comaroff and Comaroff 2009). Several artisans explained that they now make it a practice, when selling to tourists who doubt the authenticity of their products, to set small pieces of their yarn or leather on fire, because synthetic yarn will burn, as will plastic, but alpaca fiber and leather will not.

The cultural discourse surrounding participants in Cusco's street economies reveals a complex grammar of indigeneity at work. Tourists who flock to Cusco to admire indigenous culture but purchase little are known by vendors as *wakcha turistas* (orphan tourists), a critical commentary on their lack of purchasing power (or obversely, the superabundance of vendors). More metaphorically, the longings and desires of tourists are understood by some vendors as indicating the tourists' loss of roots or rootedness and attachment and their wish to recoup it through tourism and the consumption of indigeneity that accompanies it. Vendors seriously and explicitly discuss the centrality of "identity" to their marketing strategies. There is also an intriguing juxtaposition between the term *campesinos metálicos* (metallic peasants), given to peasants who convert their agricultural and pasture land into sites where they may provision tourists (camp sites or small stores for selling things), and the attribution *waqcha turistas*, given to miserly or spiritually poor tourists. *Sácamefotos*, or "take pictures of me" women and children (figure 7.5), wander Cusco dressed in indigenous costume accompanied by baby lambs or alpacas, and the labels "indígena" and "Inca" are sprinkled liberally on signs and commodities (Maxwell and Ypeij 2009; Simon 2009). The sácamefotos project the image of exotic, essentialized, endearing, and impoverished others. Viewed as "indigenous" by tourists and municipal authorities alike, they are given ample leeway to market themselves for photos at tourist venues, whereas itinerant vendors who are not garbed in "native" dress are prohibited from occupying the same sites. Many sácamefotos do quite well for themselves, making up to $14.70 per day (S./2.72 = $1.00). To put this in perspective, artisan vendors clear roughly $73.52 per week, working eleven hours per day. Most of the sácamefotos work only on the weekends; their outfits are homemade; and they contribute their earnings to the household, which is almost always located in the countryside up to several hours from Cusco and which still farms agricultural lands.

DIRCETUR, the bureaucratic arm of the national government that controls formal artisan operations specifically targeted at tourism and export, has entered into battles over what it means to claim indigenous identity and how it is presented in selling particular commodities. Its policy has been to support those individuals, locales, and operations whose products it deems "directly produced" and "organically traditional." DIRCETUR personnel distinguish between traditional products and those "imposed" or copied (the latter is increasingly difficult to discern). Vendors themselves have taken up this discourse and have cannily decided to sell a mix of homemade products and those they purchase from others.

The intensity and expansion of tourism have affected gendered identities and relationships. Marisol de la Cadena (1991) argued that in Quechua highland communities and in Peruvian society in general, indigenous women were "more Indian" and more subordinate as carriers of indigeneity. Their status and earning capacity have changed now that their "indigeneity" articulates so fully with touristic and export markets. These changes raise questions about who controls these meanings and how the centrality of indigeneity to tourism and to those who are selling or offering it is

FIGURE 7.5

A girl dressed as a sácamefoto, *making the rounds during the Fiesta for the Virgin of Carmen. Photo: Linda J. Seligmann.*

viewed by Cusco's residents. Does it make a difference when culture rather than any other commodity is circulating for sale?

Cusco's residents recognize that exotic vendors serve as a key magnet for tourists to visit Cusco and the surrounding areas. Walter Little (2004a) reports a similar phenomenon among Maya women vendors. But the vendors are nevertheless treated as second-class citizens and discriminated against precisely because they are perceived as "indigenous" or "Indian" (Michael Hill 2007; Meisch 2002; Montoya 2009; Silverman 2002). The very picturesque and entrepreneurial identity they cultivate to make a living within the tourist industry becomes a mode of survival that requires them to appear colorfully poor and indigenous (Little 2004b).[4]

Performativity is ever more central to processes of production, exchange, and consumption among artisan vendors. These processes are partly shaped by organizations and agencies that have invested in tourism, such as NGOs, branches of regional and municipal government, and foreign venture capital. Women and children seem to be most able to take full advantage of these processes. Although an anthropologist or a tourist might query whether these displays are "authentic," the principal goal of vendors is to take advantage of these desires and sell their wares (Little 2004b). Some are doing well, but the majority of revenues from tourism go to major hotel chains and restaurant owners, foreign capital, and the Cusco municipality. Cusco has always been characterized by its touristic veneer, but it has now become an iconic tourist city, in part, a consequence of powerful, top-down planning measures (Fainstein and Judd 1999; Silverman 2002; Steel 2009; Van den Berghe and Flores Ochoa 2000).

Artisan vendors are extremely stratified. They run the gamut from small-scale producers of goods to vendors of purchased items including mass-produced textiles from China that appear to be indigenous and products from factories in Puno and Juliaca that look quite rustic. Some own their stalls; others rent them or work for other artisans; and still others wander the streets selling their images or wares. At the high end are stores carrying alpaca design fashions, most of which come from factories in Arequipa but some of which are produced by small-scale cottage industries. DIRCETUR and nongovernmental organizations are involved in the latter enterprises. Increasingly, they sponsor fashion show contests to encourage weavers who often control alpaca herds to create products and then sell their designs to factories, which then refine them and sell them to boutiques in Peru and for export. Take the following newspaper article with the headline "Cusco Artisans Negotiate with Foreign Businesses":

> With a parade of collections of alpaca clothing called "Show Room and Wheel of Commerce," textile artisans from the provinces of Espinar, Quispicanchis, Canchis, and Cusco, assisted by the Swiss designer Eva Michaela Frohli, displayed their creations and negotiated with Lima, Arequipa, Puno and Cusco businesses. The activity, which proposes to encourage competition

> among alpaca producers in order to generate a productive com-
> modity chain of alpaca wool and its transformation, was orga-
> nized by the regional government of Cusco and the export
> business Raymisa, which is carrying out its project Alpaca Cusco
> in the courtyard of the hotel Casa Andina. [Sicuani Noticias
> 2010]

Saturnina and her husband exemplify yet another kind of artisan operation. They have a small workshop in their two-story adobe home in Wimpillay, a dusty shanty town. There, they design and produce high-end alpaca sweaters. Saturnina had worked in a textile factory and learned many techniques there. Their home houses a sewing machine and ten looms, five of which are in operation at a time. Her husband makes the designs, and she and a group of women produce the end product. The women who help her are paid by the piece. With some backing from an NGO and the municipal government, they, along with other direct producers, were selected in a competition to display and sell their wares to tourists in a large room next to a major church on the central plaza.

Artisan vendors are alert to the dangers of freezing their identities and make efforts to keep them flexible, creatively and strategically adjusting to the next fashion statement of indigeneity through the commodities they sell, the dress they don, and the acts, including linguistic acts, they perform. They have also successfully shifted the locus of their operations away from Cusco, the center, to the various trajectories that tourists take to ceremonial centers in the surrounding area, for Cusco is surrounded by at least forty well-known archaeological sites (Anderson 2008; Simon 2009). As vendors have resorted to situating themselves along tourist circuits, battles have developed between vendors and the state. At issue are visions of how these circuits and archaeological sites should be maintained and how entrepreneurial activity should be regulated.

Although a critical component of maintaining Cusco as an attractive tourist site has been the formalization of vendors, at the most local level, informality has been shrewdly incorporated into the official governance structure by putting a manager in charge of informal markets. In my conversations with him, he stressed how saturated vending operations were. He acknowledged that despite efforts to formalize vendors, which he called "at best, a palliative," close to 88 percent of them in one market were still not paying taxes and enforcement was weak. He estimated that currently there were close to fifteen thousand informal vendors in Cusco, a growth of 80 percent.

Some vendors have been migrating to sell their wares in Brazil, Argentina, Chile, and Paraguay. Taking the skills they learned from their parents, they are using them to expand their operations in a more far-flung radius that is less evidently saturated by vendors. Consequently, their political presence in Cusco is weak, they have less commitment to investing in political actions that could bring about local transformations, and they have less knowledge of how everyday street politics could conceivably work to vendors' advantage.

At the same time that powerful forces are at work to suppress vending from both the city center and now the periphery, tourism is a key activity that intensely brings together contradictory ideologies that are manifested in the efforts of vendors to make a living. Vendors have succeeded time and again in reoccupying the city center. This tactic is now less effective because of artisan vendors' precarious access to a basic bread basket in the off-season and the greater competition and individualism among them. Although the celebration of Incanismo and the seeming dynamism of Cusco as an urban center prevail in the public imagination, as Michael Hill (2007:438–439) remarks, "a fundamental dimension of Cusqueño criticisms of the neoliberal state, including its 'modernization through tourism' paradigm, is the daily experience of poverty and need that have only increased, despite the promises of neoliberalism and despite the growth of the tourist industry."

THE POLITICAL ENGAGEMENT OF AGRICULTURAL AND ARTISAN VENDORS

Are there notable differences in how formalization and tourism have affected the political engagement of artisan and agricultural vendors, respectively? I argue that despite the potential for artisan vendors to wreak havoc on the tourism industry in Cusco, they are more reluctant than agricultural vendors to participate in political mobilization and in the social movements that have been on the rise in Cusco.

Agricultural vendors have a history of belonging to and supporting guilds, unions, parties, and confederations, they have an equally impressive history of political participation in strikes and demonstrations, and they have skills honed from their collaboration in land seizures in rural areas and in urban pueblos jovenes. Politicians court them with rhetorical promises and deals because they are an attractive political bloc that can make a critical difference in election outcomes. However, these promises rarely materialize after elections. Agricultural vendors could also be counted on to play a major role in political mobilizations, many times opposing repressive regimes, specific economic policies, or regressive tax measures. Because many of them facilitated the flow of goods among regions with weak infrastructure, their participation periodically brought commerce to a halt. Their history, as well as their provisioning of basic subsistence goods to a regular, loyal clientele, gives them the capacity to take the risk and the motivation to pursue political agendas that extend beyond their particular self-interest. Many of them have also been vendors for a much longer time than those who have entered into touristic ventures. Nevertheless, although they continue to participate in political demonstrations or actions, it is far more difficult for them to organize because of their displacement and formalization. Their social networks in the workplaces where they are now located are tenuous, and the burden of debt they are carrying because of the purchase of their stalls creates greater risks for them. As memories of their prior social networks, which are more difficult for them to actively maintain, fade away, a different kind of temporality is taking hold (Connerton 2009). In the past, they set their own "time," socializing, eating, sleeping, and working in and near the streets. The discipline of industrial time is becoming the norm as agricultural vendors close up shop indoors and go home. Further, until the displacement of the vendors occurred, the visual image of vendors occupying the city's center and clogging its streets was iconic of illegitimacy. Contained within structures, they are now far easier to control. The additional expanse of the streets theoretically should permit protesters to occupy the streets more easily, but it is also far easier for the forces of law and order to target them. Women vendors in particular, who have always used their bodies as a weapon of protest, are no longer "in" the streets. In short, the selective upgrading of the city and the new patterns of spatial segregation that have accompanied the growth of tourism have affected their political engagement. Taking agricultural vendors off the street and "formalizing" them has turned out to be a form of social control and depoliticization. It has fixated them, creating obstacles that make it more difficult for them to organize politically and build and facilitate relationships of trust. Agricultural vendors themselves acknowledge that their political clout has weakened, attributing this to a variety of reasons, among them, their obligation to pay off loans, their lack of faith in political leaders and parties, and their need to make a living. Roxana put it succinctly when I asked her whether vendors were engaged politically: "Before, they thought of the people. Today, they only think about their pocketbooks."

Artisan vendors have even less of a cushion economically than agricultural vendors. Their entire livelihood depends on tourism, and their primary clients are tourists, who come and go. The risk of losing a client, a tourist who "happens" to want to purchase from them, is greater than that experienced by agricultural vendors. In addition, many of the products they sell are imported. Gender and indigeneity are significant tools in their ability to make a livelihood. However, they are reluctant to essentialize their donning of indigeneity as a key component of their participation in social movements because they prefer to maintain a high degree of flexibility in their embrace of indigeneity for purposes of making a living (Little 2004b). Despite their heavy dependence on tourism economically, were they to decide to participate in protests, work stoppages, and more sustained social movements, they could do great damage to all the hotels, transport companies, restaurants, and various branches of government that are heavily invested in the foreign exchange that tourism brings. Yet, it is precisely their dependence on tourism and the unpredictability of their clientele that make them a weak force in social movements. This is compounded by their reluctance to embrace a collective indigenous identity that could put in jeopardy a major source of their economic livelihood. The following comment exemplifies the almost unanimous rejection of political engagement on the part of artisan vendors: "The strikes affect us gravely. It shouldn't be that way. They should find another way to make their complaints that doesn't affect us. Cusco lives from tourism. The tourists come for a limited amount of time."

Ironically, artisan vendors are less compelled to take political action due to their desire to maintain flexibility, whereas agricultural vendors are constrained because they no longer have as much flexibility. Their lack of flexibility and their formalization, as I have described here, have been two dramatic physical consequences of neoliberalism and tourism in Cusco. Thus, for related but very different reasons, both agricultural and artisan vendors find themselves less able or willing to join social movements.

THE FORCES OF DECENTRALIZATION AND REGIONALIZATION

The political engagement of vendors has also been affected by changes in Cusco's governance structure and that of Peru, in general. Most development and budgetary decisions benefited Lima, the capital and economic and political center of Peru, at the expense of other regions. This began to change with a program of decentralization coinciding with the privatization of key industries and natural resources. According to a formula developed in a series of laws passed in recent years, local and regional governments became entitled to a higher percentage of taxes originating from the exploitation of "their own" natural resources. Both globalization and neoliberalism indirectly acted as forces favoring decentralization since most transnational and foreign direct investment went to the oil- and gas-rich regions in the Amazon and to mining in the Andean highlands of Peru. Despite regional control over revenues, local populations have not benefited from them. The Cusco region received two million dollars every day from mining and gas royalties in 2010, but poverty increased outside Cusco proper (Villar Campos 2010). Poverty rates in 2008 were at 58.4 percent, extreme poverty was 29 percent, and child malnutrition 31.7 percent (INEI 2008). In addition, Peru's governance structure frequently pits one region against another when both are opposing centralization. At issue are how environmental degradation directly affects people's health and livelihood, who controls natural resources, such as water, and who has the right to the revenues from the extraction of natural gas, water, and oil. How do vendors view these political and economic conditions, and do their views matter to political outcomes?

June Nash (2007) and Anthony Bebbington (2009:10), in different ways, make the point that people may participate in political actions as "affinity blocs" about issues that do not narrowly and directly concern their self-interest in economic terms. These issues more amply involve questions of morality, legitimacy, and basic quality of life. Emergent social movements in Peru have appeared in recent years, partly catalyzed by the locus of extractive resources—minerals and natural gas—found in both highland and lowland regions—and the need for water for both agriculture and urbanization. Movement participants have also been learning from indigenous movements in other parts of the Andes, such as CONAIE in Ecuador (see Becker 2011; Pallares 2002) and MAS in Bolivia (Lazar 2008; Olivera 2004; Postero 2007). Because foreign investment and tourism are central concerns of the Peruvian government, these social movements represent serious threats to investment prospects.

Protests in 2008 and 2009 took place in the Cusco region against a natural gas project, Camisea, promoted by the government, which decided to sell gas to Mexico at a lower price than to Peruvians themselves and to sell gas to Lima at a lower price than to provincial inhabitants (Cornejo 2010). A second set of uprisings, in 2009, protested the central government's decision to assert control over the extraction of natural resources in the Amazonian lowlands, where it had allowed multinational corporations to explore for oil without consulting the indigenous population, although this is required by ILO 169. When the national police were sent in to break up the blockade and protests, at least thirty-four people were killed and more than one hundred wounded in the clashes that took place (Griffith 2010;

FIGURE 7.6

Some of the few vendors marching in Camisea and Bagua Massacre protests. Photo: Linda J. Seligmann.

Janicke 2009; Montoya 2009). This debacle became known as "The Bagua Massacres." In protests against the Camisea Natural Gas project and commemoration of the Bagua massacres in Cusco, the agricultural and artisan vendors who marched were few in number, especially in comparison with political mobilizations in years past (figure 7.6).

Yet, their willingness to take political risks may be growing. Many more vendors joined in the 2010 uprisings catalyzed by the Majes-Siguas II Project, a multimillion-dollar mega–irrigation project that will take water from small-scale agricultural producers in the Cusco region and divert it to Arequipa for agroindustry. A Spanish-Peruvian partnership was awarded the project. The entire city of Cusco came to a halt in September 2010. Almost all agricultural and artisan vendors shut down operations. Allying themselves with students and the urban working poor (including those who identify as middle class), they took to the streets in a forty-eight-hour strike. Among other actions, they toppled and set fire to a statue of Victor Raul Haya de la Torre, founder of the APRA party, to which Alán García, president at the time, belonged. Tourists were stranded, and approximately $240,000 per day in tourism revenues were lost (Ramón 2010). The central government cynically viewed these actions as an effort to rally the masses prior to municipal and regional elections. Yet, the concerns that catalyzed them were profound and complex, condensed in the vendors' bitter commentary that all politicians were *"rateros"* (thieves) and that the prior government, for whom many vendors had voted, "just pushed the people to one side."

Lowland and highland indigenous groups and the urban poor found common ground in their struggles against state efforts to privatize their land or territory and to effectively diminish or destroy their ability to make a living, including eroding their access to agricultural lands. Three major electoral outcomes also entailed greater political activism among vendors. In the municipal and regional elections in October 2010, residents in the Cusco region, including most vendors, overwhelmingly voted in a regional government whose platform, at least nominally, was leftist, progressive, and, most specifically, nationalistic and decentralized. And in the presidential elections, 80 percent of Cusqueños voted in Ollanta Humala, a leftist and nationalist president (ONPE 2011). One artisan vendor put it this way to me:

> The government should have a mission to defend the interests of people who have received less income. The prior government has been inclined to defend the powerful families and people and have ignored the poorest people. We have protested against that government so that the economic returns in Peru are more equitably distributed, and this is why we elected Ollanta.... Ollanta is defending working against corruption. I think that those who govern should think about the growth of Peru, about nationalism, rather than their own future. There are many monopolies.

Throughout this chapter, I stress that the access vendors have to different kinds of space and the structure and locus of commodity chains are critical to vendors. The Bagua case, the Camisea pipeline debacle, and the Majes II project have started to knit together highland, lowland, and urban concerns that, interestingly, follow transport and commerce corridors for both agricultural and artisan goods, including imports from China that travel via Lima and Arequipa or from Chile through Tacna. A front that included a growing number of vendors emerged, contesting state definitions of "the meaning of order, the control of public space, and access to public and private goods" (Bayat 2004:90–91).

CONCLUSION

Cusco's dependence on tourism and the erosion of people's agricultural livelihood base offer possibilities for vendors to channel their concerns through their political engagement. Cusco's agricultural and artisan vendors, especially women, through their everyday practices, recognize that the policies of Cusco's municipality, its regional government, and the Peruvian state affect their living standards and prevent them from being able to provide for their families and maintain their dignity. They know that tourism brings revenues and that Peru depends on foreign exchange. Artisan vendors, especially, realize that they actively contribute to the circulation of popular culture and images that make Cusco an attractive tourist destination.

All vendors have experienced increasing segmentation and stratification. Agricultural vendors suffer from a disjuncture between their roles and functions as urban purveyors of agricultural products to Cusco residents, on the one hand, and their increasingly tenuous links to the countryside, on the other. The discrepancy in scale between the expanding sector of wholesalers, factory operations, and foreign capital and the sector of retail vendors, in already saturated markets, places obstacles in the way of their political engagement. Speculation in real estate, rehabilitation (displacement) policies that demand conformity to bureaucratic rationality, the desire to implement local notions of modernity about how best to attract tourists, and the regulation of entrepreneurial activities have pushed Cusco's vendors further to the margins. Most have not benefited economically in any substantial way from formalization, although a burgeoning market in stall operations will prove lucrative to some vendors.

Even though vendors sometimes participate politically in street demonstrations, hunger marches, and road blockades, it is unlikely they could sustain these for long, and artisan vendors have little interest in supporting strikes. Fewer of them have an economic cushion in the form of savings to fall back on, the heterogeneity among them is pronounced, and the forces of law and order are mounted against them. In different ways, agricultural and artisan vendors embody the contradictory consequences of neoliberalism and tourism, and they struggle with these consequences in their daily efforts to make a living.

Notes

1. Funding for this project was made possible, in part, by the Ruth Landes Memorial Research Fund. Many thanks to Karen Tranberg Hansen, Walter Little, and

B. Lynne Milgram for organizing the seminar at the School for Advanced Research in Santa Fe, New Mexico, and to my research assistant Daniel Guevara for his significant contributions to this chapter. I have also benefited from the sustained intellectual engagement and pointed editorial suggestions of the SAR seminar participants. I am most indebted to the vendors in Cusco who continue to share their insights and experiences with me. My research is based on participant observation and interviews with vendors in the warehouses and markets in Cusco and with those at agricultural fairs, satellite markets in pueblos jovenes, the wholesale market just outside Cusco, along the tourist circuits radiating outward from Cusco, and in hotel and restaurant courtyards. I also interviewed public officials who supervise aspects of market operations.

2. This estimate derives from interviews with artisan vendors in Wanchaq. Interviews with courtyard vendors organized into "Associations" revealed similar patterns.

3. Rodrigo Montoya (2009:52, 57) gives examples of these contradictory perceptions. Pablo Kuczynsky, a former prime minister and a candidate for the 2011 presidential election, commented that "those born at more than 3,000 meters above sea level, had diminished brain capacity." In a similar vein, a former minister of defense and parliament member, in a debate over Cusco's future cultural patrimony, announced that there was "no need to consult with the llamas and alpacas and that Cusqueños should just be content with their Machu Picchu." The use of disparaging and racist labels for persons who appear indigenous makes it a double-edged sword to embody indigeneity as a commodity. Yet, the fact that people can make money from being indigenous may also threaten those whose remarks are so denigrating.

4. Montoya (2009:59) argues that rather than directly eliminate communities and their territories in order to expand the extraction of resources, the central government, through decentralization, privatization, individualism, the invocation of tourism, and competition, successfully eroded collective rights and indigenous control of territories. He concludes, "President García insists that these decrees are not against communities...but there is not a single element in any of his decrees that strengthens community rights.... Without communities, the space will be freed up for businesses." Vendors realize that their precarious rights to spaces where they can sell, the erosion of arable agricultural lands and access to water, and their lack of control over how regional profits are reinvested in Cusco, in similar fashion, jeopardize their livelihoods.

8

Appropriate Space?

An Everyday Politics of Street Vendor Negotiations in Hanoi, Vietnam

Sarah Turner

In 2008, the People's Committee of Hanoi, capital of the Socialist Republic of Vietnam, introduced a decision "promulgating regulation on management of street-selling activities in Hanoi." Consequently, since July 2008, street vending has been banned from sixty-two selected streets and forty-eight public spaces in the city's urban core (figure 8.1; People's Committee of Hanoi 2008; Vietnam News 2008). The vast majority of street vendors targeted are from the neighboring countryside, which is experiencing urban encroachment at a rapid pace. Many inhabitants are being pushed off their land and consider street vending one of their few remaining livelihood options. Also pursuing a living via vending are long-time Hanoi residents, who feel fully entitled to their small slice of public space. Thus, despite the ban, vendors still ply these urban streets. This chapter takes up their story, investigating the everyday politics and negotiations regarding access to space among itinerant and fixed-stall street vendors in Hanoi. Drawing on a conceptual framework bringing together Henri Lefebvre's triad of perceived, conceived, and lived space with literatures on everyday politics and covert resistance, I want to better understand how street vendors make a living in a politically socialist yet increasingly neoliberal economic context. By carefully organizing spatial routines, building upon social capital, and negotiating power relations with state officials, Hanoi's street vendors continue to defend their lived spaces and "counter-spaces."

Modernization efforts often pit street vendors against state visions for city development, leaving vendors with few rights and limited options for physical relocation (Bromley 2000; Brown 2006c). Scholarship across the Global South documents the measures that street vendors use to organize street space as their "weapon," including maintaining an ongoing physical presence in the face of developers' plans (Cross 2000; Seligmann 2004). In Hanoi, traders deal with the 2008 ban—and others previously implemented—with their own "take" on what forms of legislation and control are fair and reasonable. Because overt protest and resistance to restrictions on their livelihoods are usually considered futile in this semi-authoritarian, socialist state, many individuals use subtle, under-the-radar approaches to either comply with the law in a manner that suits them or work around regulations and their enforcement. I examine these approaches by drawing on the works of Ben Kerkvliet (2005, 2009) on everyday politics and James C. Scott (1976, 1985, 1990) on everyday forms of resistance. Furthermore, I analyze what Henri Lefebvre (1991) would term the conceived spaces of a city bent on modernization and the means by which its poorest inhabitants, who appear—to the state at least—to be standing in the way, draw together perceived and lived spaces to enact survival mechanisms in this complex social environment.

In socialist Vietnam, open protest is still rare. Yet, since the 1990s, in part due to Đổi mới (economic renovation), officially introduced in 1986 and pursued via numerous reforms, interplays between state and society have become more ambiguous (DiGregorio 1994). Lisa Drummond and Nguyen Thi Lien (2008:178) have noted that the limited and decreasing public space in Hanoi, coupled with a high degree of state surveillance and intervention, leaves little room for discussion, let alone dissent: "While the government structure reaches out and down to the street and neighborhood level, interaction is mainly in the form of delivery of top-down directives and allocation of responsibility for participation in government campaigns. Bottom-up delivery of desires, opinions, and complaints is rarely effective unless or until there is a crisis." Indeed, something of a crisis regarding land seizures in peri-urban zones around Hanoi, where many itinerant street vendors originate, occurred in 2012, with far more numerous and widely reported protests than in recent years. Nevertheless, the government still clamped down quickly on these outpourings of public discontent (BBC 2012).

Previous research on street vending in Hanoi has produced important insights into how vendors make a livelihood (DiGregorio 1994; Drummond 1993; Higgs 2003; Jensen and Peppard 2003; Koh 2008; Li 1996; Mitchell

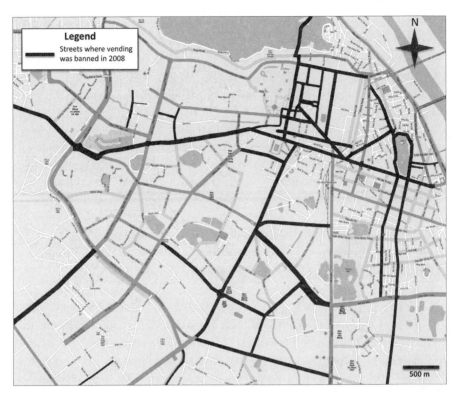

FIGURE 8.1

Areas declared off-limits for vending following the 2008 Hanoi street vending ban. Map: Sarah Turner.

2008). However, the everyday politics and resistance tactics of street vendors to the 2008 street trading legislation and the government's most recent modernization drive, as well as how these actions shape specific social spaces, have yet to be analyzed, aside from initial findings in Turner and Schoenberger 2011. As such, in the following chapter, I ask, What does Hanoi's modernity drive mean for those whose livelihoods depend on street vending? How do the everyday politics of street vendors play out on Hanoi's streets? And how do these actions form specific lived and social spaces? This analysis builds upon semistructured interviews undertaken in 2009 with forty street traders, thirty-eight of whom were women (we did not sample to exclude men; rather, street vendors in Hanoi are overwhelmingly women). Both long-term resident and migrant vendors, aged from their late twenties to seventies, were interviewed. The sampling strategy was based on locating vendors operating on or within two street blocks of a banned street. These interviews were completed with the help of two research assistants, one Vietnamese and one Canadian, and build upon my observations of street vendor livelihoods and trading tactics throughout the city since 1999.[1]

Before turning to explore these vendors' livelihoods, I outline the conceptual framework for this analysis. Then I interpret the situation for street vendors in Hanoi, putting the conceptual tools of social space, everyday politics, and everyday resistance to task. I examine how perceived and lived spaces are intertwined through the experiences of street vendor practice, focusing on vendors' differing motivations to trade, the hierarchies that exist between fixed-stall and itinerant vendors, and their everyday politics and resistance measures. I conclude by arguing that a complex range of street vendor survival tactics is at play on the streets of Hanoi. These tactics highlight the heterogeneous nature of vendor infrapolitics in their defense of lived spaces and the creation of new ones.

SOCIAL SPACE, EVERYDAY POLITICS, AND RESISTANCE

Henri Lefebvre's conceptualization of social space is useful to this investigation (notwithstanding concerns from human geographers, for example, Dear 1997; Merrifield 1997; Unwin 2000). Simplistically put—since his work is "not reducible to a simple set of parameters" (Unwin 2000:13)—Lefebvre (1991) adopted the concepts of conceived, perceived, and lived space as a conceptual triad of "moments" to argue that space is an ongoing production of spatial relations. Briefly, conceived space, also known as representations of space, is "tied to the relations of production and to the 'order' which those relations impose, and hence to knowledge, to signs, to codes, and to 'frontal' relations" (Lefebvre 1991:33). Conceived space is that imagined or envisioned by planners, bureaucrats, architects, and officials, with governmental and institutional discourses and their products, such as decrees, maps, and development plans, being fundamental (Elden 2001). Lefebvre (1991) considers this the dominant space in society because the state—responsible for the cultivation of this space—can influence the population as a whole to accept a particular interpretation of the meaning of a space. Hence, these "representations of space" are intimately tied to ideology and societal power relations (Merrifield 2006). The clearest example relevant to our case here is the 2008 People's Committee of Hanoi decision prohibiting street vending on specific streets and locales. This imposes an image of what "should be" over perceived space. The landscape becomes dominated by what state planners and municipal authority officials argue to be its correct usage and form.

Perceived space (also known as spatial practice) includes "production and reproduction, and the particular locations and spatial sets characteristic of each social formation" (Lefebvre 1991:33). In other words, perceived space relates to the physical framework of a place or the routes, networks, and concrete features that constrain daily activities (Merrifield 2006). It is both the "medium and outcome of human activity, behavior, and experience" (Lefebvre 1991:66). In Hanoi, this includes the narrow lanes that street vendors use in their everyday routines to hide from authorities and the wider avenues that they often avoid. Such spatial practices structure vendors' daily lives.

Lived space or representational space is the everyday space in which people live and operate, including the meaning we give to such space. It is "space as directly lived through its associated images and symbols, and hence the space of 'inhabitants' and 'users'" (Lefebvre 1991:39). This space is the dominated space—the space that "the conceived, ordered hegemonic space will intervene in, codify, rationalize and ultimately attempt to usurp" (Merrifield 1993:523). It includes "complex symbolisms, sometimes coded, sometimes not, linked to the clandestine or underground side of social life" (Lefebvre 1991:33). This representational space is rooted in the histories of specific groups and in those of individual members (Soja 1996). For street vendors, their narratives reveal the everyday practices of making a livelihood on Hanoi's streets and the tensions and everyday politics that emerge to produce meaning in these representational spaces.

Although Lefebvre remained vague regarding how various components of space interact and connect in dynamic ways, he stressed that the production of social space inevitably includes unequal power relations and social control (Stillerman 2006). He argued that under capitalism, conceived space is dominant, overpowering perceived and lived space. Conceived space becomes central to the production of abstract space. Abstract space is "space represented by elite social groups as homogenous, instrumental, and ahistorical in order to facilitate the exercise of state power and the free flow of capital" (McCann 1999:164). Nevertheless, Lefebvre sees the possibilities for emerging new spaces—a differential space—to serve as resistance to the forces of homogenization present in abstract space. While abstract space seeks to deny the possibilities of differential space, class and social struggle "prevents abstract space from taking over the whole planet and papering over all differences" (Lefebvre 1991:55; see also Merrifield 1993:524). Interestingly, Lefebvre turned his attention specifically to modern-day "socialist space" in Cuba, Moscow, and Beijing, asking, "How is the total space of a 'socialist' society to be conceived of? How is it to be appropriated?" (Lefebvre 1991:54). He argued that there are probably two possible ways forward: one opts for accelerated growth with state socialism, aiming to "do no more than perfect capitalist strategies of growth" (Lefebvre 1991:55); the other is founded on small- and medium-sized businesses and like-sized towns. It is increasingly apparent that Hanoi's authorities, with the central state's blessing, are pursuing the former.

Everyday Politics and Resistance

It is useful at this stage to consider the concepts of everyday politics and everyday resistance in order to unravel how street vendors might push toward a differential space. Ben Kerkvliet's (2009) work on everyday politics helps us explore the daily realities for Hanoi's street vendors and the relationships between them and the broader political system of which they are a part, including Hanoi's municipal authorities, the police, and the Vietnam state. Kerkvliet (2009:232) defines "everyday politics" as involving "people embracing, complying with, adjusting, and contesting norms and rules regarding authority over, production of, or allocation of resources and doing so in quiet, mundane, and subtle expressions and acts that are rarely organized or direct.... Key to everyday politics' differences from official and advocacy politics is [that] it involves little or no organization, is usually low profile and private behavior, and is done by people who probably do not regard their actions as political." Kerkvliet (2009:233) divides everyday politics into four further categorizations, namely, "support, compliance, modifications and evasions, and resistance." As we will see, street vendors in Hanoi are a composite group of actors whose actions stretch across this range.

Although there are numerous works on overt and collective action and resistance, ranging from protests and riots to transnational social movements, few examine more subversive forms of daily resistance. This latter school of thought is perhaps best represented by the writing of James C. Scott (1976, 1985, 1990) and, again, Ben Kerkvliet (2005). In a socialist country such as Vietnam, these authors help us to interpret the actions of non-elite individuals who are wanting to improve their lot or just survive on a day-to-day basis, wishing to be "left alone" by the long arm of the state.

Everyday forms of resistance include how "peasants (and others) who are subjected to social and cultural subordination create continuous, mundane and hidden ways of resisting oppression (inequality, hierarchy)—in effect, through avoidance, ridicule and acts of petty revenge" (Bernstein and Byres 2001:33). Similarly, Kerkvliet (2009:233) defines resistance, framed within his four approaches to everyday politics, as "what people do that shows disgust, anger, indignation or opposition to what they regard as unjust, unfair, illegal claims on them by people in higher, more powerful class and status positions or institutions. Stated positively, through their resistance, subordinate people struggle to affirm their claims to what they believe they are entitled to based on values and rights recognized by a significant proportion of other people similar to them." Kerkvliet (2009:234) proposes that "the concept of everyday resistance...travels well when studying political behavior and views of people in other sectors of society, not just peasants, who are in relatively weak and subordinate positions—office secretaries, factory workers, clerks, street vendors, and so on." Drawing on such a framework, I argue that people in a subordinate position maintain some degree of decision-making power and agency. Unlike Gramsci's (1971) approach to hegemony and naturalization of elite domination, Scott and Kerkvliet argue that the subordinated are aware of their position in society and vis-à-vis the state and, through their everyday actions, work around and cautiously attempt to deflate the dominant ideology or hegemonic discourse. The results of such everyday procedures are often deemed more effective than other, more drastic, organized actions might be.

THE CONCEIVED SPACES OF HANOI

On August 1, 2008, the Vietnam state expanded the official area of Hanoi city from 920 to 3,345 square kilometers, resulting in an overnight expansion of the city's population from approximately 3.5 to 6.23 million inhabitants (Prime Minister of Vietnam 2008; Vietnam News 2009a). Because Vietnam is a socialist state, this occurred with little public input. The government aims to create an economic superhub, rapidly modernizing the country's capital and generating a metropolis more populous than Singapore or Kuala Lumpur and rivaling Ho Chi Minh City (Straits Times 2008). The following year, the general secretary of the Communist Party of Vietnam, Nông Đức Mạnh, urged Hanoi authorities to "focus on developing a more modern and civilized capital city" (Vietnam News 2009b). Hanoi and its hinterlands are transforming at breakneck pace. Not only are the city limits expanding, engulfing peri-urban regions and opening them up to private investment for high-rise office and apartment towers, but also internal neighborhoods are being razed in order to widen streets and create new transport throughways while city markets are being renovated or demolished entirely.[2] A sharp increase in unregulated and illegal building activities has also occurred, and land prices have skyrocketed.[3] Guiding the city's development is the Hanoi Capital Construction Master

Plan to 2030 and Vision to 2050, aiming to make Hanoi the world's "first sustainable city" (Turner 2009; VietnamNet 2009). Such growth has not been without its downside, and intra-urban social disparities have been rising (Van Horen 2005), as well as mounting discontent over land seizures, noted earlier.

Before the 2008 ban, approximately 5,600 vegetable and 5,900 fruit vendors worked in greater Hanoi (using the 2004 city limits). These figures include mobile street vendors, fixed vendors selling on pavements, and vendors trading in informal markets (M4P 2007). Legislation regarding street vendor trade and its enforcement has oscillated over the past twenty-five years. Before this time, stricter socialist period rule had attempted to eliminate street vending and small-scale trade activities that were not merged into cooperatives, albeit with haphazard enforcement and limited success. In 1984, city authorities specifically declared that pavements were only for walking on and that other activities would be charged a fee (Koh 2008). Following a series of traffic and order legislations, in 1991 a nationwide traffic and pavement order campaign was implemented in Hanoi (Decree 135/CT). Drummond (1993) details how police would subsequently "swoop down" on inner city areas, demanding fines from street vendors, who relied on word-of-mouth warnings that police were nearby. The 1995 nationwide Decree 36/CP similarly attempted to clear pavements and improve transport flows (Leshkowich 2005). Again, over time, street vendors returned, and Hanoi ward officials complained that enforcing such regulations was impossible. Five months after Decree 36/CP, some leniency was provided for vendor trading along fifty-seven specific Hanoi streets, and retirees were permitted to sell lottery tickets on pavements (Koh 2008). Eight years later, Decree 15/2003 was enacted by Hanoi authorities to "re-establish order" on the streets and to "build up civilized lifestyle" in preparation for hosting the December 2003 Southeast Asia Games (Cohen 2003; Koh 2008). Although this nine-month campaign was characterized by stiffer fines and the confiscation of trade tools (baskets, scales), enforcement remained uneven because ward officials were accustomed by then to a steady flow of pay offs (Cohen 2003; Jensen and Peppard 2003). A similar crackdown occurred prior to the 2006 APEC summit held in Hanoi (Koh 2008; see also Lindell, Hedman, and Verboomen, chapter 10, this volume). The 2008 street vendor ban is a specific effort by Hanoi's municipal government to create a dominant conceived space by defining "the appropriate meaning of, and suitable activities that can take place within, abstract space" (McCann 1999:169).

Importantly, the 2008 ban is implemented and enforced, like many

Vietnamese state policies, at the lowest level of local urban administration—the ward (*phường*). Here, ward officials often adjust state policies to local conditions, and the conceived space of the state regime is mediated to fit the interests of local officials and sometimes the concerns and needs of residents. This hybridization of state-society relations—or the interactions between conceived and lived spaces—means that ward officials are occasionally lenient due to the socioeconomic situation of residents in their jurisdiction but also act to uphold their own informal interests, such as partaking in corrupt actions (Koh 2004b, 2006). Often, these elements blend, such as when a ward official tasked to clear street vendors from sidewalks decides to turn a blind eye, citing "local economic conditions" for why state policy has not been enforced and concurrently taking bribes (Koh 2004a). At specific holiday periods, however, as discussed below, ward officials often receive instructions to take a stricter approach to vending before the usual negotiations soon reappear. Vendors are well aware of this temporal adjustment. As Lindell (2010a:17) notes regarding informal workers in the Global South more broadly, "the various—and apparently contradictory—modalities of power used by the state [vis-à-vis informality] may coexist and be combined. They may also change over time and be deployed selectively upon particular groups of informals." With this in mind, let us examine the ways in which Hanoi's vendors regard, negotiate, and transform conceived space.

STREET VENDOR LIVELIHOODS: MOTIVATIONS AND TRADER HIERARCHIES

In response to state-conceived and state-constructed spaces, street vendor livelihood tactics in Hanoi draw upon spatial routines and social networks—embedded in perceived space—to protect existing lived spaces as much as possible (see Stillerman 2006).[4] Yet, during interviews with such vendors, a number of differences quickly became apparent between itinerant street traders, on the one hand, and city residents operating small, "fixed" pavement stalls, on the other, highlighting a lack of uniformity across lived spaces. The majority of itinerant traders are from peri-urban areas, particularly those merged in 2008 to form the Hanoi Capital Region.[5] These vendors commonly rent a room shared with other street vendors, returning to their village to visit family on a monthly basis. Alternatively, fixed street traders often see vending as a means to supplement their household income, establishing a small stall in front of their house or nearby.

Correspondingly, the most pronounced demarcation regarding motivations to vend and the infrapolitics of street trading is by vendor type.

Given this divide, it is interesting to note that all vendor interviewees typically earned 35,000 VND ($US2.00 in 2009) a day, equating roughly to ten million VND ($US570.00) a year, depending on the number of days worked, other commitments, and access to products. These findings correlate with previous surveys of street vendors in the city (M4P 2007).

Seventy percent of itinerant traders interviewed stated that their main motivation to trade on Hanoi's streets is the need to gain funds for their children's school fees. Because đổi mới has instigated user-pay services, school fees can reach as high as one to two million VND ($US60.00–$120.00) each month. Street vendors consider this a crippling financial burden as many vendors have two or more school-aged children. Hoa,[6] an itinerant fruit vendor from Hưng Yên province, was grim in her prognosis of the direct impacts of the street ban on rural children's education, noting, "If the government were to actually practice the ban strictly, then the people in the countryside will die, and no children from the countryside will have a chance to get a complete education."

Second to school fees, a core motivation for trading is the loss of livelihood means in peri-urban areas. Hoa's continuing comments echoed many street vendors' assessments of the factors pushing them to the city, "Despite all the challenges of being a street vendor, I come to Hanoi to sell because my house is in a town that's recently been added to the city, so now there are urbanization policies in place. The government has taken the land and sold it to builders, so there's no more land to cultivate.... There are families with five to ten people, all of whom have mouths that wait for food brought by the one member who sells in the streets of Hanoi."

For one-third of interviewees, both itinerant and fixed, street vending is their only source of income to meet their family's basic needs. Vendor Nhu highlighted the precariousness of these livelihoods when he noted, "My savings are very small and are just enough to pay for food and my room on days that it rains and I can't sell."

Fixed-stall street vendors tend to be long-term Hanoi residents selling to make some extra cash, often to supplement pensions. For a number of elderly Hanoi residents, operating a teashop or selling fruit for family altars helps them pass the time, "get out of the house," and stay active in old age. Often, fixed street vendors have previously worked in state-owned factories or enterprises, finding themselves unemployed when the subsidized period ended in the late 1980s, albeit with a small pension. These traders generally have higher levels of training and education than itinerant street vendors, and by and large, their motivations for becoming a street vendor are radically different from itinerant traders'. The only overlapping "push factor" we found is illness or death of the family's main breadwinner, often the vendor's husband.

Fixed vendors overwhelmingly view itinerant vendors as "outsiders," making disparaging comments about them and their lowly position in the social hierarchy. Ha, a fixed trader selling tea, candy, and cigarettes, stressed these social distinctions:

> Hanoi is getting crowded because people are coming from the countryside more. No Hanoi resident does the itinerant trading, because they all have a stable place to sell from. The reason for the ban is to reduce the number of people coming from the countryside and to control the security of the population and the environment. The [itinerant] street vendors take up a lot of space, and it is overpopulated already.

In comparison, itinerant street vendors express resentment toward the often favorable treatment received by Hanoi resident traders from local officials, commenting that fixed traders monopolize the best trading opportunities. Van, selling convenience items itinerantly from a carrying pole, bluntly explained the social distinction: "The fixed street vendors think that the temporary or wandering street vendors are nothing in comparison with themselves." Although many itinerant street vendors interviewed had been in Hanoi for upwards of fifteen years, they nevertheless continue to feel excluded by Hanoians. The impacts of this social hierarchy become even more pronounced when we examine vendor interactions with the authorities.

EVERYDAY POLITICS OF HANOI STREET VENDING

In urban Hanoi, there are at least five branches of the state apparatus related to surveillance, crowd control, security, and policing. These include the *Đội tự quản* (ward-level "self-management security/team"), *Công an* (public security), *Cảnh sát giao thông* (traffic police), *Thanh tra giao thông* (inspector), and *Cảnh sát cơ động* (mobile police, or "fast response" team). It is the Công an who have the right to fine street vendors. Hence, although the Đội tự quản will often be seen participating in raids and chasing after vendors alongside the Công an (whom most vendors simply call "the police"), Đội tự quản cannot (theoretically) fine vendors.

This division of responsibility and authority among state officials plays into the hands of street vendors and limits the extent to which the state apparatus can control vending behavior, thereby extending the degree to which vendors can defend and reconstruct their lived spaces. For example,

Hien, a migrant itinerant street vendor, explained, "When the ban was first launched, I thought I could be caught by any type of police. But then I found out that the traffic police couldn't harm me and have no authority when it comes to street vendors. They will even purchase goods from me. The only type of police that I have to worry about is the Công an and Đội tự quản, and when I see these police, I run." Other branches of the policing apparatus even support street vendors economically by purchasing food and goods while in uniform, and government officials in general are sought-after customers. Paradoxically, Ha locates her tea stall near government offices because the "government officials are reliable customers with money in their pockets."

Despite the codification of fines and permissible street vending activities outlined in the 2008 legislation, the behavior of Công an officials remains erratic and lacks coordination. One Hanoi resident, Ly, a fixed vendor, explained, "Some days the police [Công an] take your goods, and the next day the same person will walk by, smile at you, and not do anything. For example, yesterday they confiscated my goods and fined me, but today they are smiling at me like nothing happened." In 2009, when fined by the Công an, vendors were paying in the vicinity of 75,000 VND ($US4.50) to have their goods released—a fine twice their average daily profit. The process by which this fine is paid varies. Sometimes the transaction is conducted "on the spot," but at other times, vendors must report to the local Công an station to pay and attempt to collect their confiscated goods (if not already eaten or stolen by officials). Fines vary among neighborhoods and between fixed and itinerant sellers. For instance, Huong, selling fruit from a carrying pole, noted that she pays between 25,000 and 75,000 VND each time she is fined. Another itinerant vendor, Lan, added, "Every police station has a different fee that ranges from 20,000–75,000 VND, and so the fee that street vendors pay is dependent on which officials catch them." In particular, she remarked that "the Hàng Đào police station [Công an] near Đồng Xuân market is the most expensive. As for the cheapest, that's harder to say since it depends more on the feelings of the policeman at the time."

An, an itinerant trader selling pineapples and pomelos (citrus fruit), explained that if she is able to settle the fine on the spot, then she usually has to pay only 40,000 VND. Yet, if the police decide to take her goods to the station, she can recover them only in the late afternoon, when they will have spoiled, and has to pay 75,000 VND. She added, "When the police confiscate my goods, they almost always eat the pieces of pineapple that are already cut. With the pomelo, I count how many pieces there are before the police take it, and I put it in a bag that I tie tight to prevent them from taking it." Frequently, officials also confiscate traders' implements, such as baskets, bicycles, stools, cups, or teapots, and in a few cases sell these items back to their owners "below market price."

Itinerant Traders' Resistance: Spatial and Temporal Tricks of the Trade

Part of the everyday, covert resistance measures used by itinerant street vendors includes understanding and interpreting the spatial practices and surveillance gaps of the Công an. One such gap occurs along the borderlines where two wards meet. Itinerant street vendors operating here have the advantage that if they are chased by police, they can quickly cross the ward boundary to escape capture, because police are unable to fine street vendors outside their jurisdiction. Itinerant traders also become acutely aware of which streets are less targeted by police. An itinerant trader selling pineapples explained, "I move around, but I never enter the Old Quarter and especially avoid Hàng Đào street since I have been caught by police whenever I enter that street." These comments were echoed by Yen, an itinerant trader selling rice cakes, who never goes near the Old Quarter: "I am sure to be caught by the police, because the police do their work there more seriously. Those streets have a lot of police."

Not surprisingly, in response to police spatial practices, those of vendors have been modified. Routes chosen by itinerant street vendors have shifted to small streets and alleys that are relatively more appealing for police avoidance than larger, busier roads. Also bound up in this decision making are the different tools of itinerant trade, namely, baskets, baskets suspended from a bamboo carrying pole, or bicycles. Huong, a woman selling fruit, explained that a shoulder pole, though heavy, gives her the flexibility to navigate her goods down narrow alleys directly to the homes of her customers and to move quickly if she hears mobile Công an units approaching. Bicycles are viewed as advantageous because they allow the seller to move large quantities, but also risky because they are far more expensive to replace if confiscated (figure 8.2).

Temporal tactics are also key to vendor livelihood survival, and traders are quick to learn police routines and rhythms. For example, Hanh operates her fixed stall with tea and snacks one lane away from a banned street. Her stall nevertheless remains a target for police, and she knows to locate it on the pavement only on Sundays, when local police are off duty. On other days, she locates herself inside the doorway of a friend with whom she has made financial arrangements to use this space. Hanh explained that she would prefer to sell on the pavement: "I can earn more money since people sit down for tea more casually. My customers also prefer outside

FIGURE 8.2

An itinerant bread vendor selling from her bicycle, Hanoi. Photo: Sarah Turner, Hanoi, VN, 2011.

because it gives them more space." But she negotiates her temporal restrictions to make do as best she can (figure 8.3). During weekdays, an important window of opportunity occurs around noon—lunch break for the Công an. This window allows traders to enter areas that are usually highly monitored, like the Old Quarter. Indeed, eleven itinerant street vendors we interviewed were actively selling on banned streets, using the police lunch break to their advantage.

As well as daily temporal routines, the police presence routinely increases around important national holidays, and the chances of street vendors being fined and their goods confiscated rise accordingly. Police control is more intense during Tết (the Vietnamese New Year period) and, as Ly noted, "other times of the year when the government wants the police to work strictly" or, indeed, police want extra cash. Vendor Lien interpreted these escalations of surveillance in cyclical terms, explaining, "Usually, I get fined one time each month. During a big event like Tết, Christmas, International New Year, or when an international state leader comes to Hanoi, at those occasions I will be fined about four times."

Itinerant traders negotiate state directives either clandestinely through spatial and temporal avoidance tactics or via covert resistance measures in

FIGURE 8.3

A Hanoi resident fixed-stall tea seller and her customers, negotiating their rights to pavement "time." Photo: Sarah Turner, Hanoi, VN, 2011.

efforts to defend and expand their lived spaces. The infrapolitics of fixed traders, discussed next, also include compliance and overt adjustments in their negotiations with local-level state officials.

Fixed Trader Negotiations: Social Capital, Bribes, and Identity Management

Prior to the most recent street vending legislation, Koh (2004a) reported that police active at the ward level found it difficult to fine local traders with whom they had a long-term relationship and met on a daily basis. Officials explained, "It is unrealistic to impose fines because offenders reject the summons by claiming they have no money.... People expect ward officials to 'look the other way' [*bỏ qua*] or be sympathetic [*thông cảm*].... Basic-level officials cannot follow the law strictly when implementing policies, because they risk losing votes and their 'authority'" (Koh 2004a:221). Similar, as well as novel, tactics are being advanced since the 2008 ban, with fixed-stall vendors negotiating their "right" to vend via bribes and payments or through what I call "identity management" techniques as they play upon specific identities to uphold their right to trade.

For others, simple avoidance techniques, through the support of neighbors and customers via important social capital ties, help them escape the wrath of police.

Camaraderie and a degree of solidarity among vendors and customers play an essential role in vendor livelihoods and in defending existing lived spaces. The majority of street vendors interviewed, both itinerant and fixed, said that informing one another verbally of a police presence was critical to avoiding fines. One fixed street vendor, Thao, a retired factory worker now selling tea, explained that since the 2008 ban, she must react quickly whenever police approach. Thao obtains help from both customers and traders selling lottery tickets nearby to move her goods to a nearby shop doorway, out of "harm's way" on the pavement. Solidarity is also shared among itinerant traders, and since many rent rooms with others in the same vocation, they exchange precise information on police enforcement that can be used for avoidance tactics, reflecting the important role of social capital within their everyday politics.

The spatial tactics of Hanoi's resident, fixed-stall operators highlight nuanced negotiations between conceived and lived space as vendors claim their right to trade. Fixed-stall operators are far more likely to broker an arrangement with local ward officials than are itinerant traders. Trang, a fixed-stall tea trader, explained that in her local ward, "the head of the local police station is an older policeman who has decided not to confiscate the goods from the local street vendors." "Instead," noted Dao, another trader, "we have to pay an annual *thuế môn bài* [business tax/excise tax]" of about 100,000 VND ($US5.70). Trang and Dao believe that this is because the fixed traders are all local residents, reflecting the mediation of state-society relations noted by Koh (2006). In this same area, police confiscate goods from itinerant traders, who now tend to avoid the area; resident vendors thus benefit further, through the exclusion of potential competition.

Sometimes, as part of their negotiated relationships to settle upon bribes or "taxes" with local police or to avoid such payments, a number of fixed-stall traders use "identity management" techniques to secure a trading spot. For instance, Linh exploits her status and partial identity as a war veteran to openly resist Công an officials while operating her tea stall. She does not hide her disapproval of the new street vending ban and related police activities, perceiving them to be "daily robbery.... The police take any means available to get money. The street vendors are forced to pay the police money, and in some wards, they pay a monthly fee just to sit on the streets." She explained that she is not frightened to shout at the police, "I had to give my blood in the war for you to have the life you have today!

Why don't you understand my situation? Why do you take my things?" Well aware of her elevated status as a war veteran, she explains, "Among the street vendors who sell here, I am the only one who can shout at the police because I am a veteran. The others don't dare to shout, because if they did, they would be arrested. In my case, if I shout, they can only hate me. They cannot arrest me."

In other cases, long-term fixed-stall operators understand when to move aside or retreat from view when police come by. Be, a woman selling on the same street corner for more than a decade, explained, "We know the police will not catch us. We simply move aside to show our respect to the police." In particular, Be noted the importance of demonstrating that she does not look down on the law and police: "We must pretend to be afraid, to show respect." Such quotidian acts manipulate the mechanisms of state discipline and conceived space so as to "conform to them only in order to evade them" (de Certeau 1984:xiv).

CONCLUSIONS: COUNTER-SPACES

"The rationality of the state, of its techniques, plans and programmes, provokes opposition" (Lefebvre 1991:23). As Vietnam's capital city rapidly modernizes, vendors are targeted by the state apparatus as old-fashioned, obsolete, and a traffic hazard. Yet, they remain a favorite source of daily necessities for a large proportion of the urban population, and for many traders themselves—especially, rural migrants—vending remains a core livelihood strategy. Prior to the 2008 ban on street selling and ever since, vendors have faced erratic behavior from ward-level officials. The ban's implementation is fractured due to enforcers' limited geographical jurisdiction and disjointed surveillance, both grounded in temporal routines and/or in interpersonal relationships. To survive, street vendors move within these different fissures on a daily basis. Taking note of the spatial practices and jurisdictions of specific officials and the timing of their operations, itinerant vendors carve a niche both spatially and temporally to continue their work with the least possible harassment. In comparison, fixed street vendors more often engage in direct power struggles and negotiations at the local level, paying bribes and/or leveraging their personal identity as individuals who are elderly, retired, educated, war veterans, well-connected, and so on. Police are less threatening to residents and more easily dismissed. Here, we witness the fashioning of discrete public and private transcripts (Scott 1990). On the one hand, street vendors publicly appear submissive to local police and try to hurriedly move aside or out of sight. On the other hand, interviewees frequently express their distaste and disrespect for these uniformed officials, uncovering covert or, at times, more overt resistance tactics.

Political and cultural conflicts over the use of space on Hanoi's streets and pavements are ongoing as the state works to reshape all space as abstract—that space which facilitates the state's exercise of power and the flow of capital (McCann 1999)—via its management and control of citizens. The municipal authorities, strongly supported by the central state in its quest for modernity, conceive this urban space so as to privilege the wealthy, especially those owning motorized transportation, with pavements becoming legitimate parking lots for thousands of motorbikes rather than vendor sites and pedestrian right-of-ways. The state's plans to preside over lived space through its modernization drive—including, among other strategies, its city planning rules, urban renewal projects, encouragement of high-rise development, and large residential gated communities—have resulted in a range of (usually) covert resistance strategies from the "other," those marginalized groups who are constantly made to feel out of place. Through reappropriation and struggle, these groups create "counterspaces" in an attempt to preserve their livelihoods and a livable environment (Lefebvre 1991:381; Stillerman 2006). These differential spaces, as Stewart (1995:615) notes, "endure or arise on the margins of the homogenized realm, through resistances to the agendas of land developers, urban planners, and the State."

It is important to remember, though, that when operating in the current political climate of socialist Vietnam, those opposing the formation of abstract space are not necessarily going to mount all-out "counterattacks" (Lefebvre 1991:373) overtly and directly challenging the state. Here we have a situation quite different from that noted by Mitchell (1995) regarding riots in Berkeley in 1991 and by McCann (1999) regarding radicalized street protests in Lexington, Kentucky in 1994, where the authors examine the restructuring of public space as "spaces for representation" by marginal groups (Mitchell 1995:115), and likewise the recent Occupy Movement (see Bromley, chapter 2, this volume). In Hanoi, as noted in the introduction, a high degree of state surveillance and intervention leaves little room for discussion, let alone dissent, and new spaces must be produced through subtle means and judicious negotiations.

Hanoi's street vendors are responding to the abstract space of the central and local municipal governments by drawing on a range of careful, everyday tactics to defend existing lived spaces and create new ones (Stillerman 2006). Itinerant traders utilize their understandings of officials' spatial and temporal routines in order to circumnavigate the rule of law. They also draw on spatial practices that reinforce their identity, such as maintaining regular routes for customers, formulating daily interactions, and maintaining social capital ties and networks within neighborhoods and vendor communities. Fixed-stall operators attempt to preserve existing living spaces and also create new spaces, drawing on place-based identities and forging alliances. These lived spaces that vendors seek to create are necessarily selective and at times contradictory in the face of the power of abstract space. These multi-use, lived spaces are a political and ideological challenge—albeit frequently a covert one—to the urban spaces conceived under socialist rule and (carefully sanctioned) free market capitalism. This results in an ongoing conflict between lived and abstract spaces, between actual use and regulation.

Within a political system in which the state continues to have a strong hand in organizing social space and people's livelihoods, especially on Hanoi's streets, these interviews have shown that the picture, though not that bright, is not entirely bleak either. The simultaneous defense of lived spaces and the creation of new ones are allowing subordinated actors to contest abstract space, reconstruct lived spaces, and create counter-space. Hanoi's street vendors are actors with agency and resourcefulness, reflecting a spatial politics with which marginalized groups seek to build and maintain livelihoods and represent themselves in specific ways, be it to officials or customers. A combination of ingenious everyday politics, including carefully designed covert and overt resistance tactics, might just enable vendors to continue to appropriate and rove these streets a little longer.

Notes

1. My thanks to Karen Tranberg Hansen, Walter Little, and B. Lynne Milgram for organizing the seminar at the School for Advanced Research in Santa Fe, New Mexico, and to the participants for their suggestions on this chapter. This research was funded by the Social Science and Humanities Research Council, Canada.

2. The municipal People's Committee has renovated a number of city markets, including Chợ Mơ and Chợ Hàng Da, and the 19/12 Market, active since the 1940s, has been closed to make way for an office complex (Vietnam News 2008). Renovated markets have comparatively high fees, so relocation is not an option for street vendors, in comparison with the cases made by Milgram (chapter 5, this volume) and Seligmann (chapter 7, this volume).

3. All land in Vietnam is owned by the state. Individuals cannot buy or sell land but, since the 1993 Land Law of Vietnam, can "exchange, transfer, lease, inherit and mortgage the rights for land use." As such, land has gained a commercial value, one that is rapidly rising in Hanoi.

4. Although I use the word "tactic" loosely here, it could be considered to relate to de Certeau's (1984:xix) more specific term, referring to an action that does not have the formal legitimacy of a "strategy" and that belongs to the less powerful "other."

5. The prime minister's Decision 490/QD-TTg (2008) created the "Hanoi Capital Region" or "Hanoi Metropolitan Area." The decision merges Hanoi with communes from seven surrounding provinces, and Hà Tây province has been fully merged with Hanoi.

6. Pseudonyms are used throughout.

9

Veiled Racism in the Street Economy of Dakar's Chinatown in Senegal

Suzanne Scheld and Lydia Siu

Between 2000 and 2005, a Chinatown emerged in Dakar, the capital of Senegal. In 2000, there was a handful of shops along the Boulevard Général Charles de Gaulle, a street that is also commonly called Allées du Centenaire. By 2005, there were over one hundred shops on the boulevard and a number of others in Gare Petersen, a separate neighborhood approximately one kilometer from Centenaire.

Since Chinese businesses opened on the boulevard, scores of Senegalese street vendors have moved into the neighborhood. The vendors sell inexpensive clothing and shoes that they source from Chinese merchants in the neighborhood and display on makeshift tables in front of the Chinese shops. Some of the displays are so large that it is difficult to walk on the sidewalks and to access the Chinese shops.

Considering how close Chinese and Senegalese vendors are to each other in the market, there appears to be a high level of cooperation among the entrepreneurs. Chinese and Senegalese vendors are friendly toward each other and help each other set up their goods. In private, however, the situation is quite different. Our conversations with Chinese shopkeepers reveal that many have disparaging views of Senegalese street vendors—views that are often cast in racialized terms. Some Senegalese street vendors have equally negative, xenophobic views of Chinese traders. But Senegalese street vendors benefit from Chinese trading; therefore, many more Senegalese express positive views of shopkeepers rather than negative views. The positive views are often cast in terms of *teranga,* a local idiom that refers to the notion of welcoming foreigners and embracing cultural differences.

In this chapter, we explore expressions of racism and anti-racism in Centenaire in relationship to the practices, social relations, and networks among actors in this emerging site of Dakar's street economy. Street economies are often thought of as small-scale, local phenomena, but Centenaire contradicts this assumption. These sites are embedded in global processes and foster diverse social networks with global reach. In particular, expressions in Centenaire's street economy reach international audiences. When researchers highlight street economies, they often focus on the voices of organized vendors critiquing governments and demanding rights to a decent livelihood (Brown 2006c; Lindell 2010a). But citizens' ordinary expressions are also important to consider. In the case of Centenaire, citizens expressing racism and anti-racism are going global. This chapter highlights these expressions and their links to transnational networks. The focus on ordinary voices demonstrates that street economies are composed of global and local processes and therefore are not merely small-scale phenomena.

THE BOUNDARIES OF STREET ECONOMIES

The boundaries of a street economy are challenging to define for at least three reasons. First, the mobility of vendors. Ambulant vendors are often unlicensed and do not have fixed locations for their work. Other unlicensed vendors may routinely work in particular public spaces until authorities push them out. In these cases, vendors insert themselves in open spaces that are less regulated, or they wait to return until authorities relax their efforts to regulate space. All of these circumstances make it challenging to precisely account for the number of people who work in street economies and their spatial parameters.

Second, a street economy is often conceived as a realm of "small-scale" work. Economists use the terms "microvending" or "microenterprises" when talking about street economies. These concepts assume that vendors have low levels of capital and labor, produce small volumes of goods and services, and serve small markets (Buss 1999). Given this set of assumptions, street vending is conceived as occurring in the context of a neighborhood, or more specifically, in a poor neighborhood. We do not find this to be the case for all forms of street vending in Dakar. On one occasion in 2009, I (Suzanne) shadowed a street vendor for a day. During this experience, it became evident that some street vendors' markets are constructed through social networks and not geographic locations. I observed the vendor interact with friends in the vendor's neighborhood of residence. I followed him into the offices of acquaintances whom he met on a bus ride. I also observed him deal with individuals whom we randomly met in the streets around Sandaga, the city's primary public market hall. The notion that a street economy may be defined in terms of vending in a small and poor neighborhood is contradicted by these observations.

Third, a street economy conjures up images of vending on roads and street corners and in plazas. But street vending entails a mixture of street and other urban space. I (Suzanne) observed transactions in an out-of-the-way place in one of the ministries, because ambulant vending is not permitted in government offices. I also observed sales completed through a series of visits to clients' residences, and others were advanced by chance encounters with friends in the streets. In other words, the space of the street economy is not necessarily a road or even a physical space. Rather, it is the product of the trails of social relations formed in the processes of buying and selling.

In short, several assumptions about location, scale, and qualities of space help to illuminate street economies, but these do not provide a clear view of their boundaries. As we suggest in the description above and in the rest of this chapter, attending to various qualities of social relations and their spatial reach sharpens a view of street vending and the boundaries of the street economy.

Scholarship on transnationalism has explored the properties and powers of the social relations that are created by transnational flows of people, money, things, and ideas and help to produce and reproduce translocal and transnational "fields of social relations" (Glick Schiller, Basch, and Blanc 1992). Translocal and transnational fields of social relations are not free floating, but rooted in particular spaces and shaped by particular political, economic, historical, and spatial processes. Luis Eduardo Guarnizo and Michael Peter Smith (1998:11) note, "Transnational practices, while connecting collectivities located in more than one national territory, are embodied in specific social relations established between specific people, situated in unequivocal localities, at historically determined times. The 'locality' thus needs to be further conceptualized." This chapter builds on the observation that locality needs to be further conceptualized in studies of street economies. It explores the meaning of locality and its boundaries by tracing the spatial and social relations in Centenaire's street economy.

DETECTING RACISM

An experience during fieldwork drew our attention to the racial dimensions of social relations among street vendors and shopkeepers in Centenaire. On some visits to the field, Lydia interviewed the Chinese shopkeepers in Mandarin, and Suzanne interviewed Senegalese street vendors and others in Wolof and French. These conversations often occurred simultaneously, and when participants needed to attend to customers, we would use those moments to update each other on the information we were gathering in the interviews.

On one occasion, we were interviewing individuals standing just inches apart from each other. The Chinese shopkeeper spoke negatively about the work ethic of Senegalese street vendors. Meanwhile, and unbeknownst to him, his Senegalese employee was harshly criticizing him for being racist toward Senegalese. The negative comments from both parties were delivered between laughter, smiles, and interactions with people who wandered by the shop. Although the Senegalese young woman is not a street vendor and therefore her relationship to the Chinese shopkeeper is particular, the experience of observing the two, inches apart from each other, simultaneously putting down the other without the other knowing, fueled our interest in expressions of social relations in Centenaire, particularly those involving street vendors.

The expression "veiled racism" describes this situation and resonates with Eduardo Bonilla-Silva's (2003:9) discussion of color-blind racism and its role in reinforcing the social relations and practices of white privilege in American society. He suggests that although the government can put an end to institutionalized racism, privileged groups evoke other structures in society to reinforce their power. References such as a "postracial society" and a "color-blind society" and other ideological expressions that on the surface appear to be liberal, in fact, reproduce traditional, uneven relations of power. Social relations in Centenaire are different from those in the United States; nonetheless, the practice of using veiled terms to express a negative view of others and a desire for a particular social order is the same.

In "Interrogating Racism," Leith Mullings (2005:677) notes that concealment is perhaps the most noteworthy aspect of contemporary racism and is a common characteristic of racism in former, colonial metropoles. In the case of Centenaire, smiles and superficial acts of kindness hide negative views that street vendors and Chinese shopkeepers have of each other. Language differences help to conceal negative thoughts, although some Chinese merchants communicate effectively in Wolof and French and understand many street vendors' expressions. A desire to maintain power and privilege is easily read in Chinese shopkeepers' expressions because stark forms of racism are sometimes expressed. In contrast, Senegalese street vendors express some xenophobic views of Chinese shopkeepers. But more often, they talk about teranga—welcoming and embracing the "stranger." On the one hand, teranga may be read as a neutral expression of hospitality that resonates with the notion that street vendors benefit from Chinese shopkeepers and therefore have social relations of cooperation and solidarity. On the other hand, in the context of a host of historical processes that shape the current conditions of Dakar's economy and street vendors' access to space and power in Centenaire, teranga reads as an expression of cooperation that masks the anticipation of and preparation for competition.

The semiconcealed nature of shopkeepers' and street vendors' views is about to change. A documentary highlighting the racialized expressions of Chinese merchants (Huffman and Zhou 2005) is on the Internet for international populations to view. Similarly, a Senegalese consumer protection association (ASCOSEN), which is explicitly against Senegalese xenophobia toward Chinese traders, communicates the positive and negative aspects of social relations in Centenaire to Senegalese in diaspora and other international supporters of the organization. In short, an international community is increasingly made aware of social relations in Centenaire even though shopkeepers and vendors conceal their views by speaking languages that are not understood by everyone in the market.

Reflecting on these observations, we began to examine expressions of social relations in Centenaire more broadly. The research for this chapter was conducted in Dakar during 2005, 2006, and 2009. During this time, we carried out fifty-three interviews with Chinese shopkeepers. We conducted approximately three-fourths of the interviews with men. More than half of these interviews were with middle-aged men, many of whom had worked in other parts of Africa and Europe. Most of the women we interviewed were middle-aged individuals who had come to Dakar to work alongside their husbands. We interviewed several young couples raising small children in Senegal and spoke with several who had arranged for their children to be raised in China. We conducted thirty briefer interviews with Senegalese street vendors, entrepreneurs with small kiosks, and employees in Chinese shops. Although there are Senegalese women selling in the street and working for Chinese shopkeepers, during the times of our fieldwork, there were never more than two or three women doing this work. The majority of Senegalese working in Centenaire are men. All of our interviews, therefore, were with men. Most of the interviews were with youths in their twenties and thirties.

In addition to interviews with individuals working in Centenaire, we conducted six one-hour, open-ended interviews with key leaders in trade in Dakar's informal economy and with two leaders in the Chinese business community in Dakar. With our participants, we discussed the informalization of Dakar, social relations in the market, and interactions with the Senegalese government, among other topics.

All of the interviews with Senegalese were conducted in Wolof (the lingua franca of Senegal) and/or French. Interviews with Chinese shopkeepers were conducted mostly in Mandarin, which was not always the first language of the traders; however, most of the people we met could communicate effectively in this language. A few Chinese participants were interviewed in combinations of English and Mandarin or of French and Wolof because they were fluent in these languages and wanted to accommodate the researchers. In sum, fieldwork in Centenaire involved multiple languages and cultural expertise. This further highlights the globalized nature of Dakar's street economy.

CENTENAIRE FROM ABOVE AND BELOW

There are many perspectives from which to consider Centenaire. One view is to see it as a commercial street produced by urbanization. When viewed from this perspective, Centenaire is located outside downtown Dakar but within the boundaries of the "center city." The center city includes areas near Point de Dakar, where the colonial city was first developed, and the residential neighborhoods called the Libertés (e.g., Liberté I–VI). This belt of housing formed the outer limits of Dakar until approximately 1970, when the pace of urbanization accelerated. Since the 1970s, the areas between the traditional center city and the suburbs have been filled in with houses and businesses, although the development of essential infrastructure such as schools, hospitals, and markets has been limited. From this perspective, Centenaire is viewed as an unplanned, organic response to the need for new infrastructure.

Linda Seligmann (2004:28) suggests that in order to fully grasp the structures and practices of markets, it is constructive to look at them from "above, below, and within." We interpret this as a call to examine commercial spaces in terms of the transnational (or "global") and translocal processes and grassroots movements that shape them. In the following section, we discuss processes from above and below that shaped the emergence of Centenaire. We then discuss how space and social relations in Centenaire are structured by processes occurring "within."

From Above

Dakar's colonial urban planning shaped the development of Centenaire as a site open to foreign commerce. Under French colonial rule, Senegal's cities were largely developed to support groundnut agriculture, which was controlled by the French and structured to benefit France. The French government encouraged Lebanese entrepreneurs to work in the groundnut economy in Senegal. Their strong presence in the economy helped to create a hierarchy of entrepreneurs marked by ethnicity and race: French entrepreneurs controlled the majority of wealth and power; Lebanese traders had some control in the economy by working in the packaging and transportation sectors; and Senegalese farmers had limited wealth and power because their work was low paying and low status (Boumedouha 1990). Colonialism established the uneven relations of power upon which Senegal was built, defining it as a place that accommodates foreign entrepreneurs. The recent arrival of Chinese businesspeople to Centenaire is an extension of this historic dynamic of accommodation.

Current trends in the global political economy illuminate why Senegal is open to Chinese trading in Centenaire. China, to reposition itself in the global economy, seeks to reestablish a strong presence in many African economies. As one aspect of this process, Chinese companies offer to boost African economies by building new infrastructure. In Senegal, for example, Chinese entrepreneurs propose building a new international airport and developing large-scale horticultural projects. Chinese projects are expected to help jumpstart economic growth, which would help to lessen Senegal's deep debt.

Small-scale Chinese trading is not a piece of this process that is explicitly agreed upon by the governments of China and Senegal, especially because it creates competition for local Senegalese traders. From the Chinese point of view, however, small-scale trading aids economic development in China. In fact, although many Chinese immigrants in Centenaire come from areas with long histories of trading migrations (e.g., Fujian, Zheijian, Hong Kong, and Shanghai), many more come from newly developing provinces in China such as Henan, Hebei, and Jilin.

These immigrants talk about sending remittances to China and prolonging their stay abroad for the sake of their families in China. In other words, the global political economy has given rise to the development of a Chinese "transnational community" (Guarnizo and Smith 1998) in Centenaire that is tied to and contributes to the reproduction of political, economic, and social structures in China. This informal development strategy for

China is vast and complex, yet the Senegalese government overlooks it in order to reap the benefits of higher-level investments from China. In this light, Centenaire is again viewed as an unplanned, organic outcome of a host of processes from "above."

In the 1980s and 1990s, global processes influenced the creation of Centenaire from another direction. In exchange for loans and aid from the World Bank and International Monetary Fund, Senegal was required to implement structural adjustment programs, which adversely affected the economy. They diminished the power of local manufacturing, increased dependency on foreign imports, and drove up the price of basic goods, which forced many into the margins of the economy. Though accurate statistics are lacking, approximately 35.5 percent of the population lives under the national poverty line, and 60.3 percent lives on two dollars a day (UNDP 2010:178). Economic decline compels many in Senegal to rely on the informal economy for their livelihood. The transformation of Centenaire responds to the need for new vending spaces for the growing number of people who work in the informal economy in Dakar.

Senegalese with limited resources in Dakar also rely on Centenaire for consumption. With the prices of bread, gas, and electricity increasing, the opportunity to buy new inexpensive clothing in Centenaire is no small contribution to the survival of people with limited income. This need for inexpensive goods also fits China's need for new outlets for low-capital commodities. The recent growth in manufacturing in China challenges Chinese merchants to find new groups of consumers. For this reason, Chinese merchants are establishing trading communities in many areas that are new to the Chinese diaspora (Dobler 2005; Haugen and Carling 2005). The emergence of Centenaire is a part of these broader economic developments in China and various parts of Africa.

In addition to affecting people with few economic resources, neoliberal economic policies affect the middle class in Dakar. When structural adjustment policies required the government to downsize and withdraw from traditional welfare programs, retired civil servants were left without pensions and other public servants without jobs. As a result, some members of a shrinking middle class turn their homes into alternative sources of income. Throughout Dakar, homeowners convert single-family houses into apartment buildings and home/workshop or home/vending spaces. Property owners along the Boulevard Général Charles de Gaulle participate in this by filling in the spacious courtyards of their homes with basic cement block shops that they then rent to Chinese businesspeople who are willing to pay rents above the market price. Although Centenaire was originally zoned for residential purposes, changes in the economy spurred by global political and economic processes, repurposed the neighborhood for commerce.

From Below

If processes from above help explain the creation of Centenaire, then processes from below show how social relations developed in the neighborhood. In response to the rapid urbanization and the lack of employment in Dakar, the Senegalese government planned to invigorate the economy by strengthening tourism. The plan to make Dakar a more attractive global city involves developing new consumption sites in the city, alleviating traffic congestion in the downtown area, and controlling street vending near Sandaga. In the early 2000s, Dakar's municipality proposed closing down the Sandaga market hall for repairs. It was suggested that traders relocate to some of the newly developed commercial centers in the city. Senegalese traders refused to follow the plan because they did not have the capital to pay the slightly higher rents in the new buildings. In the meantime, Chinese vendors moved into some of the new commercial centers and residential rental properties along Centenaire.

The spatial distribution of Chinese entrepreneurs has prompted Senegalese traders to attack the government for permitting Chinese traders to work in Dakar. UNACOIS (L'Union nationale des commerçants et industriels du Sénégal), an association exclusively for traders who work in Senegal's informal economy, argues that Chinese entrepreneurs engage in illegal business practices such as bribery and tax evasion. Since they break the law, UNACOIS argues, they should be deported.

Leaders of ASCOSEN (Association des consommateurs du Sénégal), Senegal's leading consumer protection association, disagree with UNACOIS's views. In the view of Momar Ndao, the leader of ASCOSEN, Chinese trading democratizes consumption in Dakar: "Air conditioners used to be for the rich. Now more people can afford them.... It is also part of our culture to dress up and to look *sanse*. The Chinese give everyone a chance to practice these traditions since more people can afford their new clothing.... Chinese trading gives consumers a choice. Before, our own traders controlled what we could buy. They set the prices. They controlled the market like a mafia."[1] Ndao adds that UNACOIS's emphasis on bribery and evasion of taxes is "hypocritical" because it is well known that many Senegalese traders employ these same practices.[2]

In March of 2005, ASCOSEN sponsored a march against "racism" against Chinese businesspeople in Dakar. Regarding the purpose of this protest, Ndao comments, "We have to set an example at home. If we do not treat visitors in Senegal with respect, how can we expect others to treat Senegalese who live abroad?" It is well known in Dakar that Senegalese in the diaspora experience much racism. Academics document how Senegalese street vendors in particular are viewed by host countries as a threatening "other" (Riccio 1999). In Ndao's eyes, negative views of Chinese in Dakar are connected to and fuel disparaging views of Senegalese immigrants—many of whom are street vendors—in Europe and the United States. Thus, he believes, Senegalese in general, but traders in particular, must become more tolerant of Chinese merchants in Dakar.

In 2009, Chinese traders in Dakar responded to this debate by forming the Chinese Business Association of Senegal (CBAS). There are, in fact, many Chinese business associations in Dakar, but this particular association represents Chinese merchants along Centenaire and in Gare Petersen. Unlike other associations, it has a social justice agenda. For example, in 2007 a Chinese shopkeeper was murdered in Dakar. This was actually the fourth Chinese shopkeeper to have been murdered since 2000. The CBAS decided to protest these crimes by organizing a three-day walk-out in Centenaire.[3] Some Senegalese shopkeepers also closed their doors to the public as an act of solidarity with the Chinese vendors.

This brief sketch of movements from below explains the context in which concealing and revealing expressions of social relations emerge along Centenaire. Conflicts between Senegalese traders, consumers, and the government, as well as conflicts between Senegalese and Chinese businesspeople, mobilize people to organize and to cast their conflicts in racialized and xenophobic terms, as well as in terms of masked hospitality. The view from above and below shows the transnational, translocal, and grassroots processes that created Centenaire and its particular cultural vibe. These views also locate street vendors in Centenaire's grid of power relations.

FROM WITHIN: CENTENAIRE

Street economies are cultural *places* that shape and are shaped by social processes. Although streets are frequently celebrated, if not romanticized, as forms of urban space in studies of urbanism, very few analyses of actual streets tell us about the relationships between cities and societies (Fyfe 1998:1). Our detailed description of Centenaire brings the street into view for the case of at least one street economy.

Centenaire, also called the Boulevard Général Charles de Gaulle, runs from the avenue Malik Sy to Colobane and is a neighborhood known as the center of secondhand clothing distribution (figure 9.1).[4] The boulevard is

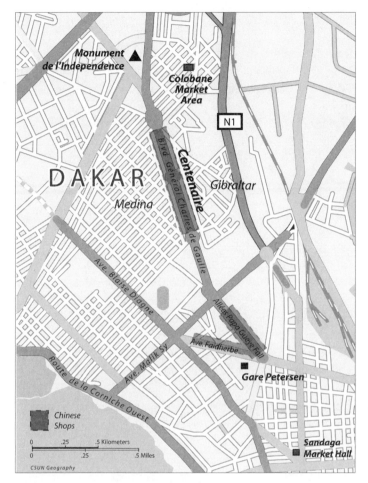

FIGURE 9.1
Map of Dakar. Map: Steve Graves.

approximately a mile long. Shady trees line the road, suggesting that there were once intentions to develop a more manicured landscape. Instead of grass, the spaces between the main boulevard and peripheral roads are covered with sand. Some parts of the boulevard have nicely laid cement sidewalks. In some parts, the sidewalk is broken. In other parts, there is no sidewalk at all, just bare ground.

To the west of the boulevard lies Medina. In 1914, an outbreak of bubonic plague in downtown Dakar was used to justify moving African families in the center of the city to Medina, a remote area with minimal infrastructure (Betts 1971; Curtin 1985). Later, Medina developed the reputation of being an overcrowded "*quartier populaire.*" It is now the location of many immigrants from Mali and Guinea. The neighborhood is well known for its animated street life, with women pounding millet and washing clothing in village-styled collectivities in open lots and groups of youths with *djembe* drums and soccer balls competing for street space with herds of goats and sheep.

To the east of the boulevard is Gibraltar, a middle-class neighborhood. Large single-family houses support spacious courtyards and car garages. The homes are enclosed by walls adorned with decorative, imported ceramic tiles, potted plants, and bougainvillea. The streets feature an upscale bakery that offers fresh croissant, brioche, and refrigerated drinks and a butcher shop that displays neatly cut meats. The neighborhood is noticeably quiet. During the day, the children are in school. Animals do not wander freely in Gibraltar.

The spatial layout of the Boulevard Général Charles de Gaulle invokes Baron Haussmann's designs of the boulevards of Second Empire Paris. Haussmann created open and wide boulevards in order to increase the state's control over rebels, who tended to hide in the corners of narrow, winding streets. The wide-open boulevard gave the army access to the city and a means to control through surveillance (Fyfe 1998:2). Although Centenaire's boulevard may not have been built for the same purposes, it has military associations. For example, the neighborhood is named after a general, and it is the site of Senegal's Independence Day parade. On April 4, military troops march down the boulevard while military aircraft fly overhead. The parade culminates at the end of the road near the obelisk, the Monument of Independence. The military symbols along Centenaire remind inhabitants of the power of the nation-state. The reference to General Charles de Gaulle honors Senegal's connection with France, and at the same time, the Monument of Independence reminds viewers that Senegal is a free nation. Yet, the symbols of state power are falling apart. The cement on the obelisk needs reinforcement. Sidewalks are cracked, and landscaping on the boulevard is neglected. Military aircraft appear old and excessively noisy, and troops' uniforms look worn and frayed. This scenery reminds Senegalese citizens that state power is declining. In relation to Chinese shopkeepers in Centenaire, the scenery suggests that the state has little control over Chinese claims to space. At the same time, the military symbols, too, provide a context for shopkeepers. Although the symbols may be read as signifying state power in decline, these also remind Chinese vendors that they are not at home. Indeed, many Chinese shopkeepers hesitate to complain about the proximity of street vendors to their shops because they feel that, as immigrants, they have limited claims to space in the city.

Baron Haussmann also designed boulevards in Paris as barricades to protect bourgeois private property and social order. In Dakar, this principle was at work before Chinese merchants entered the neighborhood. The Allées du Centenaire separated middle-class residents of Gibraltar from "others" in Medina. Today, this principle of divide and protect is still in effect. However, the populations have changed. Chinese merchants rent apartments in Gibraltar and enjoy the short walk to work. In contrast, many Senegalese street vendors live in the suburbs of Dakar and travel more than an hour on crowded and exhaust-filled converted lorries in order to get to Centenaire. Although the demographics have changed, the spatial design of Centenaire reinforces a particular social order in the area that privileges Chinese shopkeepers and disadvantages Senegalese street vendors.

Spatial Organization

Social practices give meanings to spaces and transform them into places. In the section that follows, we describe how street vendors and shopkeepers in Centenaire use space in different ways and what this means for their identities and social relations.

Chinese shopkeepers use space in ways that appear to mute their presence in Centenaire. For example, there are no decorative archways marking the entrance to "Chinatown." There are few store fronts with the red and gold decorations that are typically displayed in Chinatown shops in other parts of the world. In Centenaire, most shopkeepers do not have any signs above their store or on the door to advertise their merchandise. One vendor explained that every time he puts up signs or posters, they are torn down by youths in the neighborhood. At least one shop did have a sign, but it is now painted over. This sign captures the idea that Chinese shopkeepers have an ambiguous presence in the neighborhood.

Ambiguous Chinese identities are reflected in the way that businesspeople relate to the space of their shop. Vendors sit inside spaces that appear to be for storage rather than for shopping. In some shops, there is nothing more than a large window through which Chinese shopkeepers communicate with customers. Merchandise is placed on the window ledge for shoppers to inspect. Shops that are more like open garage spaces are closed off by a row of high display cases. The display cases act as spaces to feature merchandise, but they also serve as barricades that separate Chinese shopkeepers from Senegalese customers and keep Chinese shopkeepers partially hidden from view.

The Boulevard Général Charles de Gaulle is a long road across which Chinese businesspeople transport goods from one shop to another all day long. Their means for transporting goods adds to their ambiguous identity in the neighborhood. Several years ago, bicycles manufactured in China were popularly used to transport merchandise in Centenaire. The bicycles are distinctly Chinese, with a large cart on the back featuring Chinese lettering. But now, a fuel-powered scooter from China is replacing the old-fashioned bicycle. When the scooters zip by on the street, everyone stops to observe them. On the one hand, the scooters draw attention to Chinese businesspeople because these vehicles are new to Dakar. On the other hand, they contribute to the ambiguous identity of Chinese merchants, for they flash by and then quickly disappear. The new mode of transportation makes Chinese business more efficient but also makes it challenging to locate Chinese merchants in the neighborhood.

The ambiguous presence of Chinese shopkeepers in Centenaire contrasts to the broadcast presence of Senegalese vendors in the market. Being exposed is intrinsic to working in the streets. Even so, there are many ways that Senegalese vendors increase their visibility in the streets. They do this by challenging the expected use of public space. In Centenaire, Senegalese vendors make use of spaces that shoppers ordinarily walk through. They set up their displays of goods on the sidewalks and very close to the Chinese shops, leaving very little room for people to move through. This is striking because the peripheral roads of the boulevard provide ample space for street vendors and parts of the boulevard are underutilized (figure 9.2). Yet, the vendors close up space, thereby directing attention to themselves and their displays of goods.

When vendors take advantage of the boulevard's spacious peripheral road, they create elaborate displays of merchandise that further call attention to their presence in the market. For example, in one vendor's display, I counted approximately seventy-five pairs of shoes spread out on a cardboard platform that was carefully balanced on a series of cardboard boxes. The vendor had taken the time to separate the pairs so that he could place, for example, a left pink shoe in one corner of the display and the right pink shoe in a different corner. This strategy of separating pairs of shoes enables vendors to create compelling displays by maximizing the color and design of what is otherwise limited merchandise. At the same time, it minimizes the possibility of theft. Such elaborate displays of goods also suggest that street vendors see themselves as "installed" in the neighborhood. In the absence of structures such as kiosks or market stalls, a creative arrangement of goods reinforces claims to space.

FIGURE 9.2
Street vendors in Centenaire. Photo by Suzanne Scheld.

Another way in which they call attention to themselves is by gravitat-ing toward vendors selling similar products. In effect, this principle shapes Centenaire's reputation as a commercial area for clothing and footwear. *Biahou* (mixed goods) used to be sold in Centenaire and Gare Petersen, but now there is an emphasis on clothing and footwear in Centenaire. In the context of the boulevard, Senegalese street vendors make an additional distinction. Vendors selling secondhand clothing tend to gather at the northern end of the west side of the boulevard, an area that is closest to

Colobane, a neighborhood that is the center of secondhand clothing distribution in Dakar.

On the one hand, selling in proximity to other vendors who offer similar products invites competition. On the other hand, Senegalese vendors believe that working together draws consumers into vending areas. Once they are there, it is a matter of luck whom customers decide to buy from. Once an exchange has been made, a new social tie is created. Consumers will often go out of their way to honor that relationship rather than buy merchandise from someone else. In this light, there is an advantage to situating oneself nearby others selling similar goods. Although this principle is not followed throughout Centenaire, it contributes to secondhand clothing vendors concentrating in one area and developing their own system of assistance within their group. For example, these vendors claim particular spaces along the sidewalk. In case someone is late to work, for example, another vendor will reserve the space until he arrives. Overall, product distinctions mapped on to space make vendors more visible in a space that is otherwise busy and complex.

Whereas Chinese vendors have an ambiguous presence in Centenaire because of their motorized transportation, Senegalese street vendors make their presence known by their use of wheelbarrows. When they are not working, for example, Senegalese vendors transform flat wheelbarrows, typically used to cart merchandise, into cots for midday siestas. When it is especially hot in the afternoon, many bodies are draped over carts parked under trees. As this demonstrates, many aspects of life are conducted during work in the streets, including napping, eating, praying, and urinating.

The visibility and ambiguity of vendors in Centenaire are partly due to the difference between vending outside on the street and inside a shop. Yet, expanding visibility and diminishing presence are also strategies that shopkeepers and street vendors use to make the most of the spaces they are able to get in Centenaire. There are significant power differences between the groups. For example, Chinese shopkeepers have sufficient capital to rent permanent structures and deal in larger volumes of merchandise than street vendors. Street vendors control public space, whereas Chinese shopkeepers' control over space is limited to private space. Despite these differences, shopkeepers and street vendors depend on each other to a certain extent and have developed a way to work together.

VENDORS' PERCEPTIONS

Developing a way of working together does not necessarily mean that there are strong bonds of solidarity between vendors. However, some

Chinese and Senegalese do have strong bonds mediated through genuine acts of sharing and cooperation. For example, we saw Chinese shopkeepers providing street vendors with umbrellas and chairs and at the end of the day providing free storage space in their shops for street vendors' merchandise. We met Chinese youths, men in their mid-twenties, who had developed a remarkable affinity for Senegalese culture. One of these youths, Alassane, as he was called by his Senegalese friends, speaks fluent Wolof, adores *ceebu-jën* (Senegalese fish and rice), and walks with a swagger that is associated with Senegalese youthful "cool." We also interviewed Chinese with Senegalese spouses and close professional and personal relationships with urban residents. In addition to this, we interviewed Senegalese who were impressed with the Chinese entrepreneurial spirit and wished to know more about Chinese culture. In short, it is incorrect to suggest that Chinese and Senegalese entrepreneurs cannot understand or appreciate each other and that there is no sense of solidarity in Centenaire. Nonetheless, when talking to entrepreneurs in the context of their specific social world, we see a pattern of mutually disparaging views held by shopkeepers and street vendors.

In conversations with Chinese shopkeepers, for example, we heard direct and indirect expressions of racism toward Senegalese street vendors. A middle-aged woman from Henan describes Senegalese in Centenaire: "Those black people…they are not civilized. The kids do not go to school, and they are dirty and messy." Another middle-aged woman commented, "The locals are primitive. Not like people in China. The whole day, you don't know what they are thinking…they don't use their brains much. All of the women are fat…all they do is sit at home and get fat…they don't exercise." These comments were especially disturbing since both these women hire Wolof-speaking Senegalese assistants to help make sales and to keep their shops in order.

Not all of the discriminatory comments from Chinese traders refer to skin color and body types. Modern racism often involves systems of rank based on cultural categories of differences. The shift to cultural categories is an outcome of "intra" and "inter" nation-state–building processes (Mullings 2005:672). Indeed, Chinese traders point to cultural differences between Chinese and Senegalese as a means of comparison. For example, Chinese traders describe themselves as superior to Senegalese in business. One Chinese trader in Centenaire commented, "Chinese are outstanding when it comes to doing business…. We are helping the economy here and in China." This comment overlooks the complex and particular underlying political and economic circumstances that allow some traders to have success while others struggle. In fact, many Chinese traders would return to China if it were not for their debt. Nonetheless, the comment suggests that Chinese traders are "naturally" superior traders and Senegalese are not. We frequently heard comments to the effect that Senegalese are easily duped, because street vendors willingly source inexpensive, low-quality goods from Chinese traders. One Chinese trader bragged about his power to push low-quality goods to Senegalese street vendors: "The goods that won't sell in China are the ones we want to sell in Africa!"

Another way that Chinese traders put down Senegalese revolves around the logics of Senegalese street vending. Some vendors labeled the Senegalese approach to street vending with paternalistic terms such as "innocent" and "primitive" behavior. One trader sarcastically called Senegalese street vending "special." Yet another expressed the notion that the Senegalese approach to street vending is undisciplined behavior that needs control. This Henan trader commented, "There's no way that you can push them away.... We can't kick them away, and the police won't help."

In addition to putting down Senegalese approaches to selling, Chinese vendors criticized Senegalese approaches to consumption. Some Chinese vendors view Senegalese consumers as the noble savage whose innate goodness is corrupted by the influences of civilization. A trader from Shanghai and long-time resident in Dakar asserted, "In the past, they [Senegalese] were friendlier. Now there are more fights. In the past, people didn't have money...now they have money, and they have become more materialistic.... When you have money, you have crime. And they are not like the Chinese. When they [Senegalese] have money, they spend...they overspend...they will buy until they don't even have a cent in their pocket." In his opinion, the nobility of Senegalese is undermined by desires for money and consumption. The Chinese view themselves as innately different from and better than Senegalese because their sense of morality and discipline is unaffected by the negative influences of civilization.

Another theme in Chinese expressions is the view of Senegalese as primitive and dependent upon the traders for a taste of civilization. A young man from Henan who worked in other parts of Africa and had lived in Dakar for more than three years commented on the Chinese contribution to Senegal's economy: "The local people are eager to shop here, so we are helping by bringing new goods to them. Look, we are giving Senegalese an opportunity to see new beautiful shoes!" The emphasis on shoes as a marker of difference may be an innocent association made by a vendor working in a market that has a focus on footwear. From another perspective, there is a long history in West Africa of shoes' symbolizing the difference between the "civilized" and "primitive," especially in Senegal, where in the mid 1800s, French doctors and administrators perceived the Senegalese Tirailleurs (sharpshooters in the French army) as too primitive to know how to make the best use of their boots (Fogarty and Osborne 2003:221–223). Given this history, it is easy for Senegalese street vendors to interpret the Chinese shopkeepers' comments as derogatory and insulting.

Senegalese street vendors similarly utter disparaging comments about Chinese shopkeepers. Chinese merchants are often called bandits because they are perceived to be smuggling noodles, Chinese medicines, and other goods that are important to a Chinese lifestyle and are not available in Senegal. The word "Chinatown," for example, uttered in English in the midst of a phrase spoken in Wolof, communicates a negative view of Chinese merchants in Centenaire.

An understanding of the Senegalese notion of teranga is helpful to explain this negative perception of Chinese shopkeepers. Teranga is an explicit cultural practice that Senegalese observe, to greater or lesser degree. It entails helping a visitor discover Senegal, feel at home in Senegal, or accomplish the goals that are set for his or her particular visit. Teranga is performed by rearranging personal plans in order to accompany a visitor on a tour of Dakar or a visit to the markets or to ensure safe arrival at a meeting or conference. It involves invitations to share food, meet family, and experience "the Senegalese reality." It may also be characterized as a form of social networking since a main feature of teranga is sharing social contacts with visitors to help them advance their goals. In the eyes of Senegalese street vendors, who frame themselves as open to sharing, neighbors who distance themselves and go to great lengths to sustain themselves with illegally imported cultural foods are viewed as suspicious "others" who may cause harm.

As an explicit cultural practice, teranga is spoken about in everyday conversations. It is mentioned in the discourse of foreign relations and in popular culture. Senegalese street vendors also mention teranga as one of the reasons it is acceptable for Chinese merchants to operate businesses in Centenaire. For example, one young man selling shoes commented, "Senegal is the land of teranga. Anyone can do business here if they want. Teranga is our culture. True…at first, we were not happy about the Chinese, but it's not a problem anymore."

Over time, foreigners have contributed to creating and exacerbating social and economic inequalities in Senegal. The production of social and economic inequalities is evidenced in aspects of the history of French colonialism and Lebanese migration to Senegal, as French and Lebanese entrepreneurs often benefited from the Senegalese groundnut economy more than Senegalese farmers. It is also evidenced in the recent history of international development efforts in Senegal. For example, the implementation of structural adjustment programs and other World Bank and International Monetary Fund policies between the 1980s and today has permitted foreign investors to acquire former state-owned enterprises in Senegal. The privatization of public utilities has exacerbated poverty by driving up the cost of electricity and other basic services but produced profits for foreign entrepreneurs. Despite some of the inequalities produced by foreign interventions in Senegal, teranga persists as a strong cultural practice in Senegal. Teranga may be interpreted as an expression that masks the anticipation that inequalities may develop as a result of "contact." When street vendors speak of teranga as a justification for Chinese trading in Centenaire, such expressions also imply agency. The position of welcoming newcomers is a proactive stance in a situation of change. In the context where political and economic power in the city is limited, teranga prompts a person to look for possibilities and the means to make the most of limited resources. This practice of exploitation in the context of accommodation appears to be at work as Senegalese street vendors sell goods in close proximity to their suppliers and tolerate disparaging views of their approach to business.

THE TRANSLOCAL/TRANSNATIONAL STREET ECONOMY

This chapter approaches Centenaire from above, below, and within in order to demonstrate the embedded nature of the street economy. We argue a specific set of transnational, translocal, grassroots processes are intertwined with the everyday spatial practices and expressions of social relations that characterize Centenaire. If this conjuncture of processes and practices transforms the Boulevard Général Charles de Gaulle into a vibrant cultural place, what kind of place is it? It is a market with no market hall, a commercial area with no commercial zoning, a contested space with both cooperation and disharmony. Market values, human values, the shape of physical space, and human relationships to space are the strongest forces structuring Centenaire, which otherwise appears to be amorphous, eclectic, and elusive. In short, it is a hard-to-define place.

The residents of Dakar simplify the issue of identification by calling Centenaire "Chinatown." But this name has contradictory and problematic meanings and does not capture the essence of the market. In fact, this international name overlooks the contributions of half the local population working there. Referring to Centenaire as Chinatown is a way of constructing Chinese as the "other" and also constructs street vendors as invisible. Indeed, street vendors contribute to creating this new commercial space, its particular dynamics, and its power in shaping broader cultural and economic activity in the city.

Chinese and Senegalese entrepreneurs have other ways of talking about Centenaire. Although voice is important, little attention is devoted to it in the work on street economies. Street vendors tend to be cast by the public as voiceless actors in the city. They are "seen but not heard" (Brown and Lyons 2010), or they are beginning to be heard as they develop means of representation through political organizing (Lindell 2010a). This chapter considers another quality of voice in street economies—everyday self-expressions. We hear Chinese traders putting down street vendors as a means to assert their right to Dakar's informal economy and their position in the global social order as international businesspeople. But Senegalese street vendors have other concerns. Their opportunities for work in Dakar are limited, and vending in semiregulated public space is risky. Vending in Centenaire is further complicated by the need to negotiate with foreign traders whose status in the city is unclear. In this light, ordinary voices, as well as political voices, provide a means for understanding street vendors' agency, especially in an insecure and ambiguous economic milieu.

Street vendors' voices are assumed to be muted, but this study suggests that voices in a street economy carry over far distances through transnational social relations. Although this study focuses on interactions rooted in Dakar, thick description of Centenaire and discourses of global and local social orders casts light on the global reach of social formations in a street economy. This account makes the case that street economies, though difficult to define, must be conceived in broader terms than physical location. Increasingly, the street economy in Dakar is a translocal/transnational space.

Notes

1. *Sanse* is a Wolof word derived from the French word *changer* (to change). It refers to the act of dressing to impress. Ndao's use of the word "mafia" is a figure of speech. In Ndao's view, Mouride traders have too much control over prices in the market.

2. Interview with Momar Ndao conducted in Dakar on March 11, 2006.

3. Interview with George Qian conducted in Dakar on March 25, 2009.

4. I wish to thank Steve Graves for making the map of Dakar, Khadim Diaw for his help in the field, and the College of Social and Behavioral Science at CSUN for supporting this project.

10

The World Cup 2010, "World Class Cities," and Street Vendors in South Africa

Ilda Lindell, Maria Hedman,
and Kyle-Nathan Verboomen

Street vending, a source of livelihood for growing numbers of urban dwellers in the Global South, is being redefined in many places as not belonging in the modern city. Vendors commonly have been exposed to raids and confiscations, but government hostility is intensifying in many cities across the South, where sporadic crackdowns have given way to more systematic interventions. Bromley and Mackie (2009:1485) speak of a "determined policy of displacement" resulting in unprecedented mass removal of street traders from central areas in many Latin American cities. Sometimes these interventions have the character of urban campaigns directed from government offices specially created to ensure their implementation. Recent campaigns, like "City Decongestion" in Accra, "City Sunshine" in Calcutta, and "Operation Restore Order" in Zimbabwe, have street vendors among their major targets (Kamete and Lindell 2010; Potts 2008; Roy 2004).

Although motives and triggers for such actions vary, recent intensifications are related to the spread of neoliberal entrepreneurial forms of urban governance. Such forms of urban governance are influenced by a rationale that views cities as key economic locations that places them in competition with one another for corporate investment (Brenner and Theodore 2002). In the South, local governments are faced with the challenge "to perform as global centers of production that must compete internationally for corporate location and, at the same time, generate local economic development opportunities for their citizens" (McCarney 2003:39). Albeit, this balance is difficult to strike, but there also has been a marked shift in urban governance from concerns with redistribution and welfare toward concerns with city competitiveness (Crossa 2009; Purcell 2002).

Local governments apply a range of "entrepreneurial strategies" to increase the capacity of their cities to attract international visitors and investments. These strategies include investing in cultural and recreational structures like sport stadiums and shopping malls to turn cities into attractive "places in which to…visit, invest, play and consume" (Crossa 2009:45). They include physical reshaping to transform key city areas from sites of work and production to sites of leisure and consumption. Beautification and revitalization of key areas in cities of the Global South have often been accompanied by the relocation or eviction of street vendors (Bromley and Mackie 2009; Crossa 2009). Such interventions are perceived as critical to changing a city image of chaos and decay into an image of order and prosperity. They constitute a reimagining of the city and of key areas within it that steers away from popular uses and the needs of the majority of urban residents. In short, the city has become "a product;… something to be sold, promoted and marketed" (Crossa 2009:45).

In this context, place marketing has become a common entrepreneurial strategy for governments to promote their cities in the international arena. Hosting major international events is one way for governments to market their cities. Most studies of this topic have examined the importance of place marketing in the competition for "world class" status in cities in the North. However, the assumption of a global hierarchy of cities in which Southern centers occupy too marginalized a postion to afford such aspirations has deterred investigations of such strategies in the urban South. Yet, in recent years, nations and cities in the South have sought to host international events (Black 2007) as a means to boost their image, change international (negative) perceptions, and project an image of being places for tourists and investors.

Decisions to host mega-events are influenced by internationally circulating frames of reference (Kamete and Lindell 2010). Black (2007) has shown that bidding discourses for mega–sport events in three different countries shared references to aspirations to "world class city" status and international competitiveness. Because hosting international events increases exposure to global media and the flow of international visitors, city governments strive to project an image of their city as modern and attractive. They embark on urban intervention projects ranging from evictions to urban renewal that adversely affect the livelihoods of the urban poor, particularly people earning a living on the city streets (Bromley 2000; Hansen 2004; Kamete and Lindell 2010). Such projects treat street vending as a nuisance to be eradicated and an unhealthy deviation from internationally accepted standards of urbanism.

Focusing on place marketing, this chapter analyzes how an international sport event, the World Cup, and its interventions affected the livelihoods of street vendors. Drawing on the 2010 World Cup competition in South Africa and specifically on experiences in two host cities, Port Elizabeth and Durban, the chapter examines the social, political, and economic dynamics set into motion by place marketing strategies. In these cities, key vending areas were targeted for beautification and renewal. These interventions aimed to transform the areas into sites of leisure and consumption, and the initiatives were highly varied, including both demolition and upgrading of vending structures. We demonstrate the processes through which the majority of traders were kept out of the most profitable areas and prevented from benefiting economically from such a high-profile event. We argue that the economic and political exclusion of street vendors during the event took place through transformations in urban governance and discursive practices that legitimated the event on the one hand and criminalized vendors on the other. We also discuss the role of collective organizing in challenging unfavorable interventions and discourses and highlight how the varying ability of the traders to organize effectively in these two cities affected the outcome.

The chapter draws on interviews with traders, association leaders, and activists in both cities. Immediately before the World Cup, Hedman interviewed ten street vendors in Port Elizabeth about their expectations and perceptions of the event. The interviewees were women of varying ages who conducted street sales in different parts of Port Elizabeth. Hedman carried out these interviews during an internship with StreetNet International (April to June 2010). The texts of the interviews were published by the same organization (Hedman 2010). We cite Hedman's 2010 publication when we refer to these interviews. This chapter also draws on insights Hedman gained during her internship with the "World Class Cities for All" campaign (WCCA), which involved her in meetings with urban authorities, traders' workshops, and other activities of the campaign.

Our research continued in February and March 2011, including interviews by Verboomen with about twenty traders on Durban's beachfront, local government officials, and association leaders; we also interviewed campaign activists in both cities. During the years prior to the World Cup

2010, Lindell interviewed the coordinator of StreetNet International, the organization that initiated the campaign (WCCA), and organization representatives, focusing on their plans and preparations for the event. From 2009, Lindell followed developments relating to the 2010 event through contacts with the organizations and Internet searches. We also collected documentation from government archives in Durban and Port Elizabeth.

THE WORLD CUP AND THE MANUFACTURING OF "WORLD CLASS CITIES"

The hosting of the World Cup 2010 was influenced by rationales and discourses to legitimate the event and mobilize support among international and domestic audiences. One important discourse referred to the image-making potential of the event (Black 2007; Cornelissen 2007; van der Westhuizen 2007). Proponents of this argument maintained that hosting the event would improve the position and image of South Africa and its cities throughout the world. The event would raise the host cities to the status of "world class cities" and "place South African cities in a global hierarchy of competitive metropolitan economies"; the organizers claimed that hosting the World Cup would change tourists' and investors' perceptions of the country and project an image of South Africa as a modern nation (van der Westhuizen 2007:333). This justified heavy investment in mega-projects, such as football stadiums, that were considered key vehicles for marketing the nation and its cities, serving as symbols of prosperity and technological capacity and as icons for the cities. Alegi (2008:397) describes the World Cup as "a national project" driven by South African elites and "aimed at enhancing the prestige and credibility of the South African nation-state and its leadership." Such a national project required and warranted the active involvement of the national state and the deployment of its resources.

In public discourse, the World Cup was presented as bringing political and economic benefits to the country. The event was described as a moment of inclusion with the potential to "transcend historical divisions" and social cleavages in South African society, strengthening national identity, unity, and cohesion (Black 2007:267; Kersting 2007). In addition to contributing to nation-building, the Cup would also "strengthen and consolidate [South African] democracy" (Black 2007:267, quoting Danny Jordan, chief executive officer of the Local Organizing Committee). Economic growth would result from an increased inflow of investments. These economic benefits were assumed to trickle down, and the dominant message was that the World Cup would create jobs and economic benefit for everyone.

Generally, hosting the event was expected to propel urban development and provide "a unique opportunity to fasttrack development in...cities and large towns" and develop low-income urban areas (Black 2007:271; Maenning and du Plessis 2009). Yet, the "urban development" initiatives and interventions were mainly in tune with and subordinated to "world class city" ideals and associated views of cityness.

When the World Cup selection committee accepted South Africa's bid in 2004, the country's nine host cities (Durban, Cape Town, Johannesburg, Nelson Mandela Bay, Mangaung, Tshwane, Nelspruit, Rustenburg, and Polokwane) initiated significant transformations to prepare for the mega-event. Firstly, they mobilized national resources for massive investments in infrastructure, mainly in transport and high-standard sport facilities in line with the requirements of the Fédération Internationale de Football Association (FIFA). Secondly, urban authorities implemented beautification and rejuvenation projects to raise their cities to the status of "world class cities." Thirdly, host cities had to form a new institution, the Local Organising Committee, that in collaboration with local and central government agencies ensured that preparations complied with FIFA regulations. Fourthly, as part of host cities' agreement to observe FIFA guidelines, local governments had to approve FIFA by-laws, that is, regulations specifically guiding the World Cup 2010. These by-laws established demarcation zones, regulated access to event zones, and contained strict regulations for street vending. They granted exclusive rights to FIFA's partners and sponsors as specified in FIFA's Rights Protection Programme (FIFA 2010). This program supported corporate rights holders, including FIFA partners (Coca Cola; Emirates), FIFA World Cup sponsors (McDonald's; Castrol), and national sponsors (Telkom; Prasa). As a result of contributing, each rights holder had exclusive access to profit opportunities. Partners and sponsors enjoyed immunity from competition within the demarcated zones of the host cities; these included areas surrounding stadiums, fan parks (areas managed by FIFA where the public could watch the football games live on large television screens), public viewing areas, and fan boulevard walkways. The Rights Protection Programme explicitly sought to prevent organized "ambush marketing" (unlawful and intrusive behavior), counterfeiters, and unauthorized traders.

GRASSROOTS CONTESTATIONS: "WORLD CLASS CITIES FOR ALL"

During the preparations for the event, "World Class Cities for All" was launched by StreetNet International, an international federation of organizations of street vendors from across the Global South. The aim of the campaign was to promote participation by street vendors and other marginalized groups in the preparations for the World Cup (StreetNet International n.d.). Challenging the "world class cities" narrative, the campaign stressed that it was detrimental to the urban poor and claimed their right to be included in the event. The campaign sought to mobilize a range of organizations, including street vendors' associations, trade unions, and social movements. It facilitated the creation of traders' organizations, as occurred in Port Elizabeth. In other cases, the campaign resulted in stronger associations with a stronger leadership and long-term goals (StreetNet International n.d.).

Campaign activities, including workshops, demonstrations, and protest marches, were carried out in all the host cities. Through such activities, street vendors and their organizations presented their demands to local authorities and pressed for inclusive policies. Bargaining forums were formed between street vendor associations and local and national government departments to encourage negotiation and social dialogue. The campaign also sought to unite traders in a common front, a challenging task, given the diverse trader population in terms of nationality, race, ethnicity, sex, age, income, and employment background. Although important achievements were made, the ability to organize collectively against unfavorable policies and interventions varied considerably between the two cities, Durban and Port Elizabeth.

STREET VENDORS IN PORT ELIZABETH: "THIS WORLD CUP IS NOT FOR US"

Port Elizabeth is part of the Nelson Mandela Bay Metropolitan Municipality, comprising the cities Uitenhage, Dispatch, and Port Elizabeth. The population in the metropolitan area is estimated to be more than one and a half million, with more than one million in Port Elizabeth alone (Nelson Mandela Metropolitan University n.d.). Port Elizabeth is the commercial capital of the Eastern Cape Province, an important center for the automobile industry, and a major transport hub in the province, with a port linking the city to other national and international destinations. The economy of Port Elizabeth is based primarily on manufacturing, with automotive manufacturing being the most important industry, and tourism also plays an important economic role. However, the Eastern Cape is the poorest province in South Africa in terms of average household monthly earnings (Hirschowitz 2000).

For decades, street vendors have worked the streets of Port Elizabeth. As elsewhere in urban South Africa during the apartheid years, street vending was stricly controlled by local and national regulations. The traders we interviewed in Port Elizabeth told us that the number of vendors had increased over the preceding ten to twenty years. Most of them explained that the municipality has always had a negative attitude toward street sellers, and they complained about how local authorities repeatedly subjected them to harassment and forced displacement.

In preparation for the World Cup, the municipal government undertook several infrastructure and beautification projects, including the renovation of dilapidated housing in key areas of the city and the renewal of major tourist attraction facilities. The city also invested in the construction of an upscale football stadium, its first facility for hosting large sport events (Project 2010 2009a, 2009b).

As part of host city obligations, the Nelson Mandela Bay Metropolitan Municipality had to observe the FIFA by-laws issued in January 2009 in a Local Authority Notice (Province of the Eastern Cape 2009). The by-laws that were to be in effect during the event sought "to enable an *orderly* and *efficient* staging and hosting" of the event (2009:5; emphasis added). Among other things, the by-laws introduced detailed regulations for street trading in "Public Open Spaces and City Beautification" and "Controlled Access Sites." For example, street traders were not allowed to occupy, display their goods in, or erect structures in a public road or an amenity area or to leave their goods overnight; vendors could not operate "in contravention of a sign...displayed by the Municipality for the purpose of these By-laws" (2009:32).

The by-laws issued prohibitions on street vendors, identifying several categories of "Restricted and Prohibited Trading Areas." Unless vendors had written authorization from the municipality, they were not allowed to operate in, among others, Exclusion Zones, that is, areas in the proximity of the football stadium; Controlled Access Sites, including the stadium, the FIFA Fan Park, and the sites of other official events; Restricted Areas; Prohibited Areas; and gardens and parks "to which the public has a right of access" (Province of the Eastern Cape 2009:34). The by-laws gave the municipality the authority to demarcate such Restricted and Prohibited Areas with FIFA's approval (2009:35, 42) and gave "authorized officials" considerable authority, for example, to evict street vendors and confiscate their goods if they were perceived to be in contravention of the by-laws (2009:38–39). Recovering confiscated goods was difficult, entailing costs and proof of ownership; if goods were handed over to someone else "in good faith," the vendor had no "right of redress against the Municipality" (2009:39). Disrespecting the by-laws resulted in heavy penalties, such as fines of 10,000 Rand ($US1,430) (maximum) and/or imprisonment for six months (maximum) or, in the case of reincidence, twelve months and 15,000 Rand ($US2,150) for every day of infraction (2009:40).

The by-laws clearly made street traders the main target of these directives. In effect, street vending activities in areas close to the World Cup events were criminalized and heavily penalized. The by-laws protected business owners from competition from street vendors (Province of the Eastern Cape 2009:33) and granted FIFA and its corporate associates exclusive rights to operate in event areas: FIFA is "the lawful owner of the world-wide Marketing Rights, Media Rights and all other commercial rights in respect of the Competition" (2009:4).

In preparation for the mega-event and in accordance with the by-laws, the municipality established several Restricted and Prohibited Trading Areas in the city, including a Fan Park at St. Georges Park and a Commercial Exclusion Zone (figure 10.1) surrounding the new stadium, "to create a zone around the outside of the Stadiums which is protected on Match Days from *ambush marketing* and *unauthorized* commercial activity (which is *unfairly* attempting to ride on the back of the success of the event by targeting the large number of spectators coming to the stadium)" (Nelson Mandela Bay Municipality 2009; emphasis added). Street vendors, who formerly had access to these areas, were prohibited from trading there during the games; many were evicted or prevented from continuing their operations if they defied the ban. Reclassified as "unauthorized," "unfair," and "ambush marketing," street vending became associated with illegal if not criminal behavior. Street vendors were well aware of their criminalization, according to one of the interviewees: "People have the impression that street vendors are criminals, but that is completely wrong" (Hedman 2010:25).

The street vendors we interviewed felt disappointed and betrayed. Several mentioned promises by the municipality. Thelma, a mother of four and a vendor since the 1980s who had completed nursing and computer courses, declared, "The World Cup will come and the municipality has promised that we will get a lot of money from that. The government said that everybody is going to get richer by that time. I want it to come so we can see if it is true" (Hedman 2010:8).

With the support of the WCCA campaign, street vendors in Port Elizabeth formed an association, the Nelson Mandela Bay Street Vendors Association (NMBSVA). In March 2010, they organized a demonstration to protest the evictions and poor working conditions, submitting a petition to the municipality to demand consultation and inclusion (StreetNet

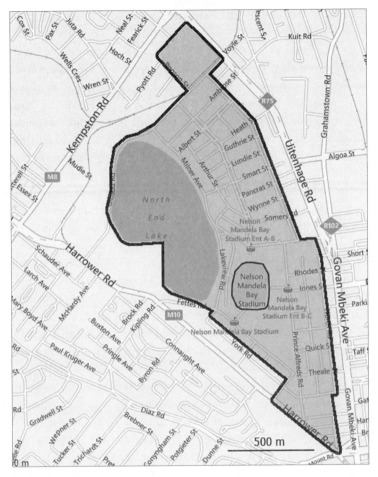

FIGURE 10.1

The Commercial Exclusion Zone, 2010, Port Elizabeth. Map drawn by the authors (on background by Bing Maps).

International n.d.; interview with WCCA campaign coordinator April 2011). Some weeks later, the city government declared that informal traders selling food, drinks, crafts, and merchandise could apply for permits to operate in the Fan Zone and at the FIFA Fan Fest at St. Georges Park during the duration of the World Cup (StreetNet International n.d.). This gave the street vendors some hope, and several of the interviewed traders had completed such forms. But vendors complained that the municipality did not follow up on this decreee. Thirty-year-old Bianca, who sold drinks, potato chips, and fruit at the central bus terminal in Port Elizabeth, explained "I filled in that form to sell in the Fan Park, but what is happening with that? I have not heard anything; we are still waiting for the results and it is only eleven days to go now" (Hedman 2010:21). Other vendors expressed similar doubts. A few days before kick-off, at a meeting with the municipality (which Hedman attended), informal traders were informed that during the event, street vending would not be allowed at the FIFA Fan Park, at the stadium, or in the Exclusion Zone surrounding it. Traders operating in those areas would be removed and not provided alternative vending places or compensation for loss of income. Although the prohibition was supposed to be in effect only during the event, street vendors were removed from these areas well in advance of the games (StreetNet International n.d.).

Most of the vendors we interviewed wanted to sell at the Fan Park and in and around the football stadium because large crowds would assemble there. Ilundas, a vendor in her forties who operated at the bus terminal and sole provider for two dependents, made this clear: "We street vendors want to have something for us in the stadiums" (Hedman 2010:11). The vendors resented their exclusion from these income-generating opportunities. Said Bianca, "The municipality and the government said the World Cup will benefit even us the poor, but I do not see that now because they said we cannot sell our goods close to or in the stadium. We will not have access to those areas" (Hedman 2010:21).

Julia, an elderly woman selling meat from her stand in the township of Veerplus, articulated her feelings of exclusion and powerlessness: "World Cup or no World Cup, it is still the same poor situation for me. We are not allowed next to the stadium and I do not have any access to sell to the tourists.... So, I really do not feel that the World Cup is for me.... I will just stay here because I heard that I cannot go anywhere near the stadium" (Hedman 2010:18–9). Majola, a woman of influence among traders as the chairperson of the vendors' association, lamented, "I'm not feeling all right about the World Cup; this event is taking the business away from the streets and the rules of the FIFA World Cup are very strict to us street vendors. We cannot be close to the stadium and we are not allowed to sell in the stadium.... The tourists will be around the stadium, not here. There are boundaries and I do not think I can get any closer to the stadium. It is very unfortunate for me" (Hedman 2010:5–6). She continued, "I feel that we street vendors do not have a part in the World Cup; it is not for us. It is okay if the World Cup never comes here again because we do not benefit from it" (Hedman 2010:5). Majola echoed the views of many vendors, stating, "The World Cup makes poor people even poorer. It is only rich people who will benefit from this World Cup" (Hedman 2010:6).

Indeed, several vendors felt that street sellers were being discriminated against and that large business interests were being protected. Thelma pointed out, "The government, the FIFA committee, they did not consider us street vendors. Because there in the stadium they do not care about the street vendors; they only consider those people who already have got lots of money. Like Coke has got space there, and Nando's has got space there, but the street vendors do not have space there.... They want us far away from the stadium. They did not consider us" (Hedman 2010:8). Veronica, a vendor for twenty-five years selling fruits and vegetables in central Port Elizabeth, expressed similar sentiments: "Hey, you know, you do not feel nice about the World Cup when you do not have money.... They are using the already established companies instead of us street vendors to benefit from this World Cup" (Hedman 2010:17).

Feelings of exclusion were not simply about being denied access to income opportunties. Rather, most vendors resented that their needs were not considered in the World Cup planning and that they were not informed, listened to, or consulted about decisions that affect their lives and opportunities. Majola said, "Not involving us is the main reason why I feel that the World Cup is not for us poor people" (Hedman 2010:6). Ilundas said, "We fight the municipality to let us benefit from the World Cup, but I never hear anything from them. I do not know what they are saying about us" (Hedman 2010:11). There was widespread disillusionment with the local government. Nokuthula, who at the bus terminal sold vegetables, fruits, and hats that she knits herself, exclaimed, "That local government, they do nothing for us!... I want a government that supports us street vendors" (Hedman 2010:12, 13).

The interviewed traders, several of whom were members of the NMBSVA, expressed hope that their new association might enable them to make demands on the local government more effectively and to collectively express their grievances. At the time of the interviews, the association had members operating in different parts of Port Elizabeth. Its chairperson explained, "If you have an association you have a better chance to be part of the decision-making and the processes that lead to the World Cup. Unfortunately we started our association very late and now it seems like we can not be part of the process" (Hedman 2010:6).

Indeed, the creation of the association, with the support of the WCCA, seems to have marked an important moment. A WCCA officer who had been active in Port Elizabeth was interviewed in April 2011. He commented that, previously, the vendors "were very much disconnected, operating in small groups or as individuals." With the creation of the association, they

FIGURE 10.2

A traders' workshop in Port Elizabeth to discuss World Cup 2010 interventions. Photo: Maria Hedman, Port Elizabeth, South Africa, 2010.

were able to have meetings (figure 10.2) and bargain. For the first time, the mayor of this city went to a meeting with street vendors and talked to them. A WCCA officer explained, "Politicians now know about the circumstances of street vendors.... They know that there is a public perception among the street vendors that they did not benefit [from the World Cup]."

Although the association managed to capture the attention of authorities, questions remain about its strength and viability beyond the WCCA campaign. Comparing the situation with other areas of South Africa where social movements are strong, a campaign officer noted, "Here in Port Elizabeth, we do not actually receive that much [support]." The officer explained that advocacy is hampered by the membership, which consists primarly of elderly women who have limited experience with organizations and by-laws. The association was also dealing with a metropolitan government described by activists as particularly harsh toward traders, again, in comparison with the attitudes of other local governments in South Africa. This WCCA officer added that the Port Elizabeth authorities do not recognize street vendors and their organization, stating, "This association is under attack...from the municipality."

In sum, the enactment of new by-laws that criminalized street vendors made it difficult for those in Port Elizabeth to benefit economically from the sporting event. The traders maintained that the World Cup was designed to benefit large businesses; street vendors felt betrayed by the urban authorities and excluded from the planning of the event. And their recently formed association was unable to signficantly improve their opportunities.

DURBAN: FROM COLLABORATIVE PLANNING TO STRICT CONTROL AND DEMOLITION

The city of Durban and neighboring towns are part of the eThekwini Metropolitan Municipality. The population of more than three million is highly diverse culturally and includes a large Asian community, reflecting the particular history of the city. One of the largest cities in South Africa, Durban is the main economic and administrative center in the province of KwaZulu-Natal. Operating the country's largest port, the city is an important node of international trade. It also attracts a major share of South Africa's international and national tourism, thanks to its climate and local attractions (including its beachfront area). Durban's diversified economy comprises a substantial commercial and financial sector and a large manufacturing sector (CEROI 2000). However, the official rates of unemployment are high. Although the municipal government has been committed to providing equal opportunities to all citizens (Robinson 2008), inequality in the city continues to be evident, not least in terms of access to basic services.

Many people are compelled to make a living in the informal economy through activities such as domestic work, trading, and catering (CEROI 2000). Street vending is an important source of income for many households in Durban (Skinner 2008, 2009). In most cases, this work is a low-income activity pursued by Africans, particularly women. Restricted during the apartheid era, street vendors began to experience greater freedom of operation in the late 1980s (Skinner 2009). In the 1990s, the local government adopted a development-oriented approach toward vending. But as Caroline Skinner (2008) has noted, this approach was followed by a restrictive and less tolerant attitude in which preparations for the World Cup played a role.

Unlike Port Elizabeth, Durban was already well acquainted with the hosting of international sport events. With the hosting of the World Cup 2010, the city sought to market itself as "a global sport city" (Alegi 2008:408). To match this high ambition, Durban invested large sums of money in infrastructure, constructing or upgrading multifunctional sport arenas and stadiums, and several urban renewal projects, including the revitalization of eThekwini's beachfront and theme park and the redevelopment of the Warwick Junction area (Maenning and du Plessis 2009). These developments set into motion transformations that reversed earlier progressive practices.

From the mid-1990s and during the next decade, the postapartheid Durban authorities adopted a progressive stance toward urban vendors and engaged in collaborative and inclusive planning involving detailed and regular consultations with increasingly strong and articulate traders' organizations (Skinner 2008, 2009). The Durban government's informal-economy policy document of 2001 declared an "overall policy move away from sanction and control, toward support and the creation of new opportunities" and expressed an intent to revise street trader by-laws to reflect this move (quoted in Skinner 2008:237). One well-known outcome of this progressive stance was the Warwick Junction Urban Renewal Project, which promoted trading in public space and the needs of the poor (Skinner 2009:104). Improving conditions for traders in that area, the project became internationally acclaimed for its "best practice" in managing and supporting street vending (StreetNet International and WIEGO n.d.).

In Skinner's 2008 review of relations between the Durban authorities and street traders, she demonstrates, and others confirm (e.g., StreetNet International 2007), that the local government adopted a less tolerant attitude toward traders from 2004, the year that South Africa was declared the host for the World Cup 2010. This change of attitude partly reflected "a modernist vision of the city" that was growing in strength within the Durban authorities as they prepared to host the World Cup (Skinner 2009:107–108). From that year onward, more vendors' goods were confiscated, and more street vendors were removed from Durban's Central Business Districts (CBDs) and from the beachfront (Horn 2009; Skinner 2008). Because only a limited number of trading permits had been issued, the majority of traders in the city were considered to be illegal and were exposed to raids (StreetNet International 2007). Deteriorating opportunities for dialogue between the Durban authorities and street vendors organizations made it increasingly difficult for the organizations to ensure the constitutional rights of street vendors (Horn 2009; StreetNet International 2007).

In preparation for the World Cup 2010, two vending areas in Durban targeted for intervention were the beachfront and the Warwick Junction area. Contrasting interventions took place in these two areas: demolition in one and upgrading in the other. Even then, both interventions were shaped by the same intent and rationale, which considered traders' needs to be peripheral.

In anticipation of the standards the city wished to project for the World Cup 2010, Durban's beachfront was the site of an important top-down intervention. For more than twenty years, numerous vendors had operated in this beach market area (StreetNet International 2007). Most were middle-aged African women selling beadwork, curios, and clothes to tourists. Because of its strategic location on the beachfront and proximity to two major World Cup–related events or sites—the Fan Park and the beach festival—the Durban authorities and the Local Organizing Committee decided that the beachfront market had a function to fill but that it needed to be "upgraded." They intended to revamp the location to accommodate a large influx of World Cup visitors. New vending stands were to be built, and vendors were to operate in a strictly controlled setting in line with FIFA recommendations. Product vendors were to be placed strategically throughout the market (Shine 2010). Vendors were required to hold a permit to operate at the beachfront market. The plans were to be implemented and supervised by the Business Support Unit (BSU), a unit within Durban municipal government established to support local and informal businesses.

The traders we interviewed complained that they were neither consulted about the reconstruction plans nor informed by the BSU. Most of them did not hold permits but operated on the premises of absent permit holders, and only the latter were invited by the BSU to information meetings. A leader of the Durban branch of the South African Self-Employed Women Association (SASEWA), an association that was active in the WCCA campaign and with many members at the beachfront, explained, "They do not invite us to get our views.... They invite us to tell us the rules, not to get our views."

The reconstruction of the beachfront market took three months. During that period, January to April 2010, the vendors were relocated to a temporary market at Pavilion Square. Almost all the vendors with whom we talked complained that they were unable to earn enough income because the temporary location was a "secluded area." Many of the relocated vendors remained at home, waiting until the reconstruction of the beach market was completed. Because of the poor income opportunities at the temporary site, the vendors organized themselves, according to one of the interviewees, and managed to get the BSU to provide them with vending spaces at the beachfront before the reconstruction was actually finalized.

Anticipating returning to the beachfront in time for the World Cup, the vendors had high expectations of making considerable profit, given the

FIGURE 10.3

Trading at the upgraded beachfront, 2011, Durban. Photo: Kyle-Nathan Verboomen, 2011.

advantageous location of their renovated market location. The SASEWA leader explained how local and government officials and the media had built up and supported vendors' expectations: "On the radio, they said that thousands of people will come here to South Africa and we will gain a lot from them." But most of the vendors at the beachfront reported decreasing earnings during the games. They identified several causes, including restrictive fencing around the Fan Park and constraining regulations regarding the hours of operation. Expecting an influx of customers, many traders had taken loans to increase their stock and were left with large debts because of unsold goods. The vendors were also dissatisfied with the poor design of the new shelters (figure 10.3), which exposed them and their goods to weather hazards, even though the rent had doubled.

The Early Morning Market, a fresh produce market at Warwick Junction, a major transportation node in Durban, was targeted for a different kind of intervention. The site of an internationally praised project (the Warwick Junction Urban Renewal Project), it was now targeted for demolition to create space for a shopping mall. Breaking with "the consultative practices that...characterized council-trader relations" in earlier years, the municipality informed the traders, without previous consultation, that they would be evicted on April 6, 2009 (StreetNet International and WIEGO n.d.).

The municipality attributed the lack of consultation to the World Cup 2010 deadlines and was accused of bypassing several "legislative and procedural requirements" in the process (Skinner 2009:106; StreetNet International and WIEGO n.d.). Durban police used tear gas and rubber bullets on protesting and resisting traders and denied them the right to march (Skinner 2009:107).

As the sport event drew closer, controls and restrictions intensified and Durban adopted the stringent FIFA by-laws. Much as in Port Elizabeth, according to a media article, "Durban street traders [were] warned not to engage in *ambush marketing* during the FIFA World Cup 2010 or else they could face possible fines" (Malukela 2010; emphasis added). Street traders were informed about prohibited trading areas and the illegality of advertising their enterprises at controlled access sites and in areas within one hundred meters of the FIFA Fan Park. During sport match days, street traders were expected to continue operating at their permanent trading sites. This was reported in the local media: "If the street traders had to trade away from their official premises or if they had to sell other objects for which they are not authorized to trade, they would be going against the by-laws" (Malukela 2010). In this way, the regulations curtailed both the mobility and the product diversification that are crucial for the viability of street vendors' livelihoods. Compared with the earlier progressive informal-economy policy of the Durban authorities, with its explicit intention of moving "away from sanction and control" (Skinner 2008:237), these by-laws represented a dramatic shift in the opposite direction.

Durban's informal traders persistently expressed their discontent with the way they were treated (Lindell, Hedman, and Verboomen 2010). As a result of World Cup 2010–related interventions, large numbers of vendors were removed from their usual sites of operation, disrupting their livelihoods and client networks. They resented mistreatment by the police, income loss, lack of information, and poor consultation. Dissaftisfaction grew and culminated in violent confrontations between street vendors and municipal police (StreetNet International 2007). During the years preceding the event, traders associations organized several large demonstrations (Horn 2009; interview with association leader). According to some sources, gatherings assembled as many as five thousand informal workers. Leaders of vendor associations like SASEWA and Masibambisane Traders Organisation (MATO) explained that they used the organizations in Durban to repeatedly approach the authorities to discuss conditions surrounding the World Cup 2010. Yet, relations with the Durban authorities deteriorated. A leader in SASEWA explained, "[When authorities announced their beautification plans, they proceeded] cleaning this town so that those people who are visiting us see that our town is beautiful. So they shove our members away because they say they are not clean."

Another petition, sponsored by StreetNet International and WIEGO (Women in Informal Employment: Globalizing and Organizing), to save the Early Morning Market requested the municipality to reconsider plans for the area, resume the consultative relations of the past, and "recognize the contribution of public-space trading and markets to the City" (StreetNet International and WIEGO n.d.). The petition argued that trading in and around the market supports the livelihoods of "households in poorer parts of the city [and] provide[s] goods [at] affordable prices to poorer commuters." Advocates argued, "Fresh produce has been traded on this site since 1880 making it a critical part of city heritage" and "an iconic site on the landscape of Durban [that] should be recognized as a national monument" (StreetNet International and WIEGO n.d.). Traders at Warwick Junction and their associations were supported by a broad constellation of actors reaching far beyond the market—middle-class individuals, concerned researchers and professionals, the Legal Resources Centre, the trade union movement, politicians, and the international advocacy networks WIEGO and StreetNet International, including the "World Class Cities for All" campaign launched by the latter (Skinner 2009; personal comunication with Francie Lund 2010). As a result of these major and concerted contestations, the market was not demolished before the World Cup (Dardagan 2010).

The centenary celebration of the market offered a symbolically important moment in the struggle. When the eThekwini Municipality indicated that it did not want the sport event to be held, the Early Morning Market Traders Association (EMMTA) took the matter to court and won the case, enabling it to stage a large-scale celebration that gathered hundreds of traders and garnered media coverage (even if city officials declined to attend) (Dardagan 2010; Kubheka and Sikakane 2010; Saib 2010). One trader expressed optimism: "After today's celebration, I know we will stay in the market for a long time." The traders used the media attention to threaten to "boycott the 2011 local government elections unless their demands [were] met" (Saib 2010).

WHOSE "WORLD CLASS CITIES"? GOVERNING AND CONTESTING EXCLUSION

The hosting of the World Cup 2010 was an excellent opportunity for place marketing and for improving the international competitiveness of South African cities. In preparation for the event and the global exposure it entailed, the authorities embarked on a range of "entrepreneurial strategies." These included large investments in sport stadiums and other event-related infrastructure and the physical transformation and "revitalization" of key city areas, all to project an image of modern and prosperous cities. In the pursuit of "world class city" status, the hosting cities were reimagined without regard to the needs and aspirations of vulnerable urban groups. Trading areas in key city locations were reconceived in tune with those ideals, targeted for diverse interventions. Given Durban's strategic location and appeal to tourists, its beachfront market was incorporated and retained as a vending area. Its traders were considered part of the performing population for the event. The area was "upgraded," redesigned, and refashioned to serve the interests of tourists and event organizers rather than the needs of the traders. During the event, traders operating in these locations did so under strict control, subordinated to FIFA's ordinances. In the end, their incomes suffered from the temporary relocation during the reconstruction and declined during the event itself.

In other areas and more commonly, street traders were regarded as irrelevant to the event and unsuitable for a modern city image. Practices of displacement, demolition, fencing, and prohibition helped make street vending activities invisible because they were categorized as not belonging in a "world class" city." In both cities, street vendors were prevented from operating in profitable areas like fan parks and close to stadiums, and many vendors were removed from their work sites (StreetNet International 2007). In Durban, the Early Morning Market at Warwick Junction was targeted for demolition, and the area was redefined from being a place for public trading of critical importance to the poor to a place for middle-class consumption.

In both Durban and Port Elizabeth, interventions were designed largely without consulting the affected traders and without taking their needs into consideration. The case of Durban even suggests a drastic reversal of the progressive urban policies of earlier years. Some traders and their association leaders found this governance style reminiscent of the apartheid era (Shine 2010; Sunday Tribune 2009).

The exclusion of street vendors was not an unintended consequence, but the result of significant changes in city governance. The FIFA by-laws, which targeted mainly vendors, became the legal instrument to exclude them from income-generating opportunities related to the event. Indeed, FIFA's Local Organizing Committee was created to ensure that these regulations and FIFA's requirements were implemented. The marginalization of vendors was also enabled by a criminalizing discourse that was used by both FIFA and government officials to construct vendor activities as "ambush marketing," "unfair," "unauthorised," intrusive, and unlawful. Vendors were faced with an unprecedented constellation of powerful actors and interests: an unsupportive local government backed by a nation-state with great stakes in the event and with both parties subjected to FIFA's conditionalities. The influence of external actors on urban governance was particularly notorious in this case (Alegi 2008; Cornelissen 2007). FIFA exerted great control over the planning of the event, redirecting initial objectives and strongly influencing local decision making. The considerable power of FIFA and of sponsor firms needs to be understood in the context of a rapidly expanding "global sport economy, which is dominated by a few large transnational corporations," providing "a distinct corporate underpinning to the hosting of major sport events" (Cornelissen 2007:246).

In spite of the powerful forces working against street vendors, they were not passive. The "World Class Cities for All" campaign directly challenged the exclusionist premises of dominant world-class city visions. Vendors' organizations, often backed by larger organizations like StreetNet International, handed in petitions, demonstrated, and protested. This chapter demonstrates that vendors can achieve some of their goals by organizing collectively and using strategies across a broad front. Compared with Port Elizabeth, traders in Durban were more successful in their collective actions. They were backed by a coalition of actors in a city with a substantive and vibrant civil society. Their long experience in collective organizing and their past achievements assisted them in upholding the Warwick Junction market as a city icon and challenging the dominance of stadiums and shopping malls in the "world class city" imaginaries of the urban elites.

In Port Elizabeth, the traders lacked organizational experience. Their ability to mobilize broad support from civil society was more limited. These differences suggest that the extent of traders' past success in organizing collectively with a strong and experienced leadership and in mobilizing broad support from other social actors affects their abilities to withstand unfavorable policies and interventions during such mega-events. This conclusion is supported by another case study by Hedman (2011), in Cape Town, in which she shows how World Cup interventions on traders differed between two areas, partly as a result of different levels of collective organizing. In short, traders' capacity to mobilize collective resistance cannot be generalized.

Acknowledgments

The authors thank Francie Lund, Caroline Skinner, and Pat Horn for valuable support and all respondents, including traders, association leaders, and municipal officials for sharing their views. The Swedish International Development Cooperation Agency sponsored fieldwork through a Minor Field Studies grant and through a program on poverty, inequality and social exclusion, administered by The Nordic Africa Institute, Sweden. Stefan Ene kindly assisted with the images.

11

Street Economies in the Urban Global South

Where Are They *Heading and Where Are* We *Heading?*

Florence E. Babb

The young Tunisian fruit vendor who responded to the indignities he experienced at the hands of local authorities by publicly setting himself on fire in December 2010 sparked a wave of rebellion that, many claim, helped launch the Arab Revolution (Fahim 2011). As a result of an online video that "went viral," no street vendor has received so much international media attention or been credited with such a feat of heroism. As Hansen, Little, and Milgram note in their introduction to this volume (chapter 1), the vendor's defiant and desperate act brings to light the hardships that those depending on street economies for their livelihood endure on a daily basis—as research on the subject also makes abundantly clear. While this man's story helped inspire political uprisings throughout the Middle East, it also set in dramatic relief what our seminar at the School for Advanced Research a few months later aimed to discuss: the urban poverty and social inequality in which street vendors are entrenched, the enduring perception that they constitute a social problem, and their continued efforts to stand up to power as individuals and as part of movements for change.

Our seminar, "Street Economies, Politics, and Social Movements in the Urban Global South," drew together participants with a wealth of experience, both pioneering and recent, on the subject. Anthropologists and cultural geographers alike, we have carried out research and contributed to conceptualizations and reconceptualizations of the relationship of street vendors to the larger publics of which they are a part, to the informal and formal economies vendors serve to support, and to social and political movements in which street vendors engage. Although some evidence suggests that today's vendors continue to struggle for a livelihood in much the same way they did decades ago when research on the subject gained hold, more recent work compels us to ask what it is that appears to be changing in the contemporary context. Notwithstanding the abundant contradictions in the relations of vendors to the wider societies they are part of, there is unmistakably a quickening pace of urbanization and globalization, drawing ever more vendors to city streets in an effort to get by or even improve their life chances. Moreover, transnational flows of media and new technologies of communication have meant changing practices and expectations for street vendors. Governing authorities have likewise adopted new means of controlling or removing vendors in neoliberal contexts where city space is at a premium.

My own early experience may be illustrative of our changing analytical orientations and viewpoints. When I set out in 1977 to conduct doctoral research on marketers and street vendors in Peru, there were few conceptual frameworks to guide me. I took from feminist theory and Marxist political economy an interest in examining women in Peruvian markets at the nexus of reproduction and production, which I found to be a powerful starting point. It was only after I returned home, however, that I came across several salient theoretical works that further informed what I had seen in field research: the articulated and often ambivalent connection between informal and formal economies, and the value of interrogating the binaries that inevitably fall short in on-the-ground analysis. A special issue of the journal *World Development* (1978b) edited by SAR seminar discussant Ray Bromley and Bromley and Gerry's *Casual Work and Poverty in Third World Cities* (1979) provided critical tools for analyzing small-scale vendors and service providers who filled the streets of cities in the Global South, identifying them as often exploited workers in urban political economies who were nonetheless vilified for rising prices, urban congestion, and other social ills.

These emergent theoretical frameworks offered a way to think more productively about, for example, those shopkeepers I discovered in Andean Peru who ventured out (or hired others to set out) on the streets to draw buyers and increase sales. In the language of the day, they were a mix of petty entrepreneurs and proletarians—the latter, indeed, were hired laborers rather than self-employed, as they might appear to casual observers. Using a petty commodity production and commerce model and learning more about the diverse actors in these street economies, I found that a decidedly more complex social reality was revealed. My work (Babb 1984, 1986, 1987a, 1987b) and that of others, for example, Clark (1988c, 1994), as well as Hannah Lessinger and Josephine and Alan Smart (in Clark 1988c), was inspired by such a rethinking of earlier models of informal and formal sectors, and traditional and modern markets across diverse societies.

More recently, some of us who are seasoned scholars have joined with younger scholars in an effort to shed light on still greater social complexity than was generally recognized a quarter century ago. Although class, and sometimes gender and race, figured in our earlier analyses of marketers and vendors, we rarely went on to explore the conditions of postcoloniality underlying cultural identity formation and social movements among the urban poor. Two landmark anthologies edited by seminar participants had a significant impact: Gracia Clark's *Traders Versus the State* (1988c) addressed the widespread tensions between marketers and the states that sought to regulate their activity, and Linda Seligmann's *Women Traders in Cross-Cultural Perspective* (2001) examined the central part played by women in market and street trade. As a contributor to those anthologies, I joined with others in calling for greater attention to nuanced cultural questions that economic anthropologists and fellow travelers had often overlooked (Babb 1988, 2001). These works may have begun by considering class, gender, and race as disparate categories, but our ethnographic material led us to examine these social vectors more deeply as multiple and overlapping sites of cultural and political subjectivity formation.

Ethnography has been a key methodology for those gathering original data on the under-examined population of street vendors in the urban Global South. The approach has enabled us to generate thickly descriptive material and powerful narratives of the lives of vendors in diverse social locations—as well as to put our ethnographic studies into broader conversation so that comparative analysis and interpretation are possible. Participants at the SAR seminar have contributed significantly to the body of place-specific ethnographic work, historically informed and contemporary in focus, which guides us in our present inquiry (Babb 1998[1989]; Clark 1994; Hansen 2000; Little 2004a; Seligmann 2004). Without excessive privileging of ethnography but acknowledging the critical interventions of historians, economists, and others, it is fair to say that anthropologists' and cultural geographers' emphasis on everyday forms of economic participation has been instrumental in challenging preconceived notions regarding street vending. Ethnographic research into the nuances of social interaction elucidates some of the most vexing problems of urban poverty and social exclusion in the era of globalization.

I begin with these points of reference because they can serve as benchmarks, indexing questions that have been advanced in recent years and that our current work builds upon or challenges. Notably, many key findings of the research presented in this book's eight ethnographic and analytical chapters bear some resemblance to those in earlier studies. Yet, without a doubt, global contexts and conditions have changed, and our ways of perceiving the work and lives of street vendors have had to change as well. In what follows, I chart several main themes addressed at the SAR seminar and attempt to give a sense of the fruitful conversations we had as we considered specific cases and then went on to propose comparative analyses. I conclude with discussion of some of the most promising directions taken and where we may be headed from here.

WHAT IS NEW IN THIS APPROACH TO STREET ECONOMIES?

In several important respects, this collection charts a new direction in studies of urban street lives and livelihoods in the context of contemporary neoliberal globalization. I would like to begin, however, by noting some significant connections with past contributions to the research on street vendors and marketers. Some anthropologists and others who pioneered in the field, for example, contributors to Bohannan and Dalton's *Markets in Africa* (1962), had a tendency to exoticize cultures and social practices. This was owing less to a taste for the folkloric than to their participation in the formalist-substantivist debate in economic anthropology; many were eager to show that the tools of classical economics were insufficient to account for qualitatively different market systems. Over the decades, scholars, anthropologists and geographers among them, with a more critical or Marxist orientation carried out work on street vending and marketing that went further in examining the relationships of petty trade to wider economies. The work of Sidney Mintz (1955, 1971), spanning decades, inspired others working on street trading to consider broad structural differences of gender, class, and race in society. And Caroline Moser (1977) was a prominent forerunner in critically examining notions of dual economy and marginality, in her research on petty traders. Along with Bromley and Gerry, Moser (1978) was a key contributor to the groundbreaking issue of *World Development* offering a theoretical assessment of the debate over whether the informal sector or petty commodity production was a more valuable framework for examining small-scale producers and sellers of goods.

My own work and that of many others are greatly indebted to the productive discussion that culminated in the volume co-edited by Bromley and

Gerry (1979). Thus, I find it important to link the work that appears in this volume to an intellectual genealogy that goes back half a century and became stronger in recent decades. Although the focus of earlier research was often petty manufacturing and marketing rather than street trade per se, I would argue that notwithstanding the different locales where work has been carried out, we are heirs to this knowledge production in the past.

A notable aspect of the approach taken in this volume and found in some earlier strands of research is that it recognizes the embeddedness of street vending in the broader contours of economy and society, from the everyday and local to the transnational. Contributors to the SAR discussion of street economies in the Global South began by delineating the research subject and, in doing so, agreed that the focus would be on street economies and lives rather than on marketplace traders, who generally work in more stable and officially sanctioned areas. Although the street as location may draw sellers seeking a higher concentration of commercial traffic, more mobility, and fewer fixed costs, street vendors occupy particularly vulnerable places in the public sector. They are exposed to the elements and to harsh treatment by officials who would often prefer to get them out of the way. They may be subjected to public scorn because they are viewed as visible evidence of social problems that more privileged sectors would rather not see, even if those sectors are dependent on the retail sales in the hands of street vendors. This is so in socialist and postsocialist societies where street vending is often viewed as evidence of the state's failure to develop the economy (Turner, chapter 8, and Hansen and Nchito, chapter 4, this volume), just as it is in capitalist-oriented societies (Clark, chapter 3, and Milgram, chapter 5, this volume). Widespread ambivalence and contradiction about suitable uses of the street surround vendors, who might well be led to ask (in the manner of Saskia Sassen 1996b), "Whose streets are they?"

In this volume, contributors focus on vendors of goods ranging from agricultural products to mass-produced merchandise, who participate in the often competitive, if small-scale, world of neoliberal capitalism and socialism. Most petty retailers are self-employed, and some are hired to sell for others or are in other ways beholden to larger wholesale interests. What engaged our interest from the beginning was the question of what exactly should count as street economies and just how are these economies and informal street trade changing in recent times. Although it is difficult to generalize, we agreed that street economies are fundamentally place specific, even if we might quibble over whether, for example, those selling in the doorways of homes, at the threshold to the street, are properly part of street economies. The evidence brought to bear in contributors' case studies shows the diversity of the individuals participating in street economies, yet we also discover the widespread and familiar intensification of economic activity *and* of government hostility to this activity on city streets in the urban Global South. Contestations over space are central to the dramas on view among street vendors, authorities, and wider publics in many of the places discussed—see Clark (chapter 3) on long-term conflicts in and around the Kumasi Central Market, Milgram (chapter 5) on the struggles of Baguio City traders and the city government over rights to public space, and Turner (chapter 8) on the modernization drive to control vendors in Hanoi. As such, contestations are central to our assessment of street economies today. Given the already broad scope of our SAR seminar, other prominent aspects of street lives, including illicit drug sales and sex work, were not taken up in the discussion.

CULTURE, DIFFERENCE, AND POWER

Economists studying marketers and traders are frequently criticized for their analytical disregard for individual and cultural differences, but anthropologists and cultural geographers have long taken into account the interplay of the economic with the social and cultural. Even so, earlier research often spent more effort in establishing typologies of vending and vendors than in documenting the often ambiguous sites where culture and power are negotiated among participants in street economies. By now, theorizations of culture and power have advanced in our disciplines to the point that it is difficult to ignore sites where even those occupying very unequal places in the social landscape jockey for economic and political advantage.

We see such interplay addressed in all the cases presented here in this volume, among traders and their publics in Kumasi, Ghana (Clark, chapter 3), Lusaka, Zambia (Hansen and Nchito, chapter 4), Dakar, Senegal (Scheld and Siu, chapter 9), Antigua, Guatemala (Little, chapter 6), Baguio City, Philippines (Milgram, chapter 5), Cusco, Peru (Seligmann, chapter 7), Hanoi, Vietnam (Turner, chapter 8), and in cities in South Africa (Lindell, Hedmen, and Verboomen, chapter 10). Class differences in relationships between vendors and urban consumers are perhaps the most visible form of difference (in plain view) in daily interfaces of street economies yet are commonly taken for granted as part of the social landscape. Gender, since the emergence of feminist scholarship in the 1970s, has received more specific attention particularly because street economies are frequently populated by a disproportionate number of women traders (Clark, Seligman, Little, Milgram, Turner). Race may still be the most under-theorized social vector in work on street vendors, though it figures importantly in the work of Scheld and Siu, who discuss the alternately tense *and* collaborative relations of Senegalese and Chinese traders in Dakar. Likewise, the work of Lindell, Hedman, and Verboomen shows that in South Africa's Durban and Port Elizabeth, race continues to be highly salient. Notably, in these cases, transnational relations may either aggravate or ameliorate histories of racial tension. In Dakar, both jealousy and admiration of Chinese traders' success provoke Senegalese to confront their xenophobia, and Chinese must overcome racialized attitudes toward African sellers. In contrast, in South Africa during the exhilarating time of the 2010 World Cup competition, local street vendors encountered both further repression of their activity and opportunities to market the postapartheid brand to eager visitors to the country.

It may not be coincidental that postcolonial and poststructuralist scholarship appears to have a greater influence in the contributions of Africanists and Asianists to the seminar discussion and to this volume. The histories of the regions where they work in the Global South have influenced scholars of Africa and Asia to consider the subaltern in particularly nuanced ways. For example, like those just mentioned, Turner found in her research in Hanoi everyday forms of resistance that referenced social status and heritage. Even so, we may see in the Latin Americanist contributions of Little and Seligmann attention to changing conditions of indigeneity and how they impact street vending and tourism in the heritage cities of Antigua and Cusco. More is said of their research in the next section, but here we may note these works' attention to shifting political identities and alliances as indigenous Mayas and Andeans launch counter-offensives on social exclusion by means of the recent marketability of their "traditional" heritage. I would emphasize the growing attention in these accounts to how actors in urban street economies put social and cultural differences to strategic use, whether to gain a competitive edge or to form alliances in globalized contexts. Of course, those inclined toward poststructuralism must be mindful of romanticizing street economies as a sort of analytical "paradise"—fluid and in a state of permanent becoming or transition—as Karen Hansen aptly pointed out in our SAR seminar.

CULTURAL IDENTITY AND COMMODIFICATION

With the turn from the more distinctly political-economic approaches of several decades ago to a closer engagement with the cultural, identity has featured much more prominently in studies of street vendors' lives and work. We have seen that vendors have much at stake when they strategize to sell on the streets: not only goods but also branding themselves as those worthy of selling certain items, to the point of commodifying themselves as artisans and sellers in regional economies. This is particularly notable when tourism creates desires to consume the "other" and indigenous sellers gain cultural capital by adorning themselves in "traditional" dress (Little, Seligmann). The recognition of vendors striving to brand and commodify both goods and selves has led analysts back to political economy, but in new ways. The contributions to this volume are excellent examples of such hybrid approaches, which are concerned with meaning and materiality, culture and economy.

Where traders capitalize on their iconic relationship to specific locations, as in the cases of Antigua and Cusco noted above, the politics of place may have special resonance. Cultural heritage and identity are grounds for asserting rights to space and to carving out a livelihood, though middle-class and elite publics and officials may lack sympathy for the impoverished indigenous bodies congesting city streets, even if they are calling cards for international tourism. Little and Seligmann reveal the tensions that often accompany the increasingly saturated street economies in the cities where they have carried out research. Likewise, Lindell, Hedman, and Verboomen shed light on South Africa's efforts to promote its cities as products, indeed, as world-class cities, in an effort at place making. Their work, like that of other contributors (Clark, Hansen and Nchito, Milgram, Turner), comments on periodic street clearances of vendors in the name of beautification and public order. Thus, although vendors may be celebrated as part of national patrimony (indigenous emblems of a treasured past in Guatemala and Peru or as recently enfranchised racial groups in South Africa), they are frequently treated as unwanted and in need of regulation by neoliberal governments. The increasing criminalization of street vendors is often the end result of such campaigns and clearances.

Turner's work on the everyday negotiations among street vendors in Hanoi, Vietnam, introduces the concept of "identity management" to discuss both the officials' hostile efforts to contain vendor activity and the vendors' strategies for asserting their economic rights and cultural-political identities. Similar struggles over defining boundaries and identities—as either unruly and marginal individuals or as hard-working and worthy citizens—can be observed in other cases taken up in this volume (Hansen and Nchito; Lindell, Hedman, and Verboomen; Milgram). In this collection and elsewhere, Little has reminded us not to underestimate the self-representation of vendors, whose status as "traditional" can be as carefully constructed as their more "modern" demeanor when they are out of the public (and tourist) eye.

STREET VENDORS AND NEW SOCIAL MOVEMENTS

The engagement of street vendors in social protest is not a new phenomenon, and we have many historical examples of vendors participating in food riots and opposition to taxation, as well as in trade unions. For example, Clark offers evidence of the deep roots of social protest from her historical research on responses to clearance campaigns during Ghana's colonial period and, later, to postcolonial modernization efforts at regulating street vending. Nonetheless, with the recent emergence of social movements, social actors including women, youth, indigenous and racial minorities, and others who have been economically marginalized are coming to be more visible in vendors' associations and broader-based social movements. Among the issues they address are workers' rights and human rights, specifically, their right as vendors to the use of public space, and the relationship of public culture and civil society in a time of rapid urbanization and globalization. In this regard, Ray Bromley has called our attention to the salience of generational differences, along with other vectors of social difference, in accounting for rising or diminishing expectations and levels of activism.

Our focus on contestations over space followed from the evidence of heightened tensions in ever more crowded streets in the urban Global South and the growing difficulties of vendors seeking to make a living when they are confronted with competition from other vendors and hostility from authorities. Despite these obstacles to organizing, beleaguered actors in street economies come together around common interests. South African vendors' participation in StreetNet International's campaign "World Class Cities for All," initiated in 2006 and calling for the inclusion of low-income constituencies in policy planning, captured with unusual eloquence the spirit of urban social movements in which street vendors have played a part (Lindell, Hedman, and Verboomen). Even when participants in street economies do not embrace social movement activity, their resistance to dominant cultural norms may be expressed through dress, language use, or simply their stalwart presence on the street.

In some cases, street vendors' local and regional associations have transnational dimensions, as we have seen among vendors in Dakar and Durban (Scheld and Siu; Lindell, Hedman, and Verboomen); there, city vendors are enmeshed in global relationships, which can either inhibit or enhance participation in forms of resistance and social movements. A notable example of activist street vendors and their advocates mobilizing across international borders is an association initiated in 1997, Women in Informal Employment: Globalizing and Organizing, known as WIEGO.

The organization is committed to research and social action addressing informal labor and urban poverty; indeed, following our SAR seminar in March 2011, participants Bromley and Lindell went on from Santa Fe to an international gathering in South Africa called by WIEGO, where scholars and organizers engaged in a discussion of ways to build transnational networks for political mobilization. If there is one striking difference between the cases reported more than two decades ago in Clark's *Traders Versus the State* (1988c) and those discussed in this volume, it may be that the earlier volume focused on local, regional, and national levels whereas the current volume includes cases of the political engagement across national borders of vendors who reveal a growing transnational consciousness.

NEW DIRECTIONS AND CONCEPTUAL FRAMEWORKS

A number of perspectives advanced in the SAR seminar and in this volume have roots in findings from past scholarship, for example, in research on the political economy of informality and in feminist analysis of interlocking systems of production and reproduction. Several of us pointed to the continuing relevance of our earlier work on clashes between traders and states and on the frequent scapegoating of street vendors for rising prices, as well as urban congestion and unhygienic conditions. Referring to one such insight from past research, Bromley cautioned that the informal sector, despite predictions of its expansion during times of high underemployment, may have a saturation point at which expansion no longer occurs. And Seligmann brought our attention back to the household as a key unit of analysis in which economic diversification by age and gender continues to condition participation in street economies. Furthermore, as I suggested in the seminar, these points lead us to question once again who has the right to make a living on the streets when informal economies reach the saturation point. Will women, youth, and racial and national minorities be the ones squeezed out of street economies when neoliberal globalization and hostile governments constrain certain demographic groups as economically active populations?

The new terms of engagement that characterize street economies in the twenty-first century have required new insights and modes of analysis. Where we find intensified economic activity, cultural commodification, and new urban social movements gaining force in the Global South, we have assessed which responses of vendors and their allies are most fruitful in building networks of solidarity; which practices, from the local to the transnational, are enabling urban planners and governments to establish reasonable limits on street activities without imposing harsh and exclusionary measures. As scholars, we have needed to ask how well we are contending with the new conditions surrounding street economies and what part our research findings and analyses will play in ameliorating the crises that cities in the Global South are now experiencing.

Contributors to this volume have gone far in addressing these questions and in pointing the way toward further research and conceptual development. Calling on theorists ranging from Clifford Geertz and James Scott, to Michel de Certeau, Henri Lefebvre, and David Harvey, they give critical emphasis to public space as the ground on which street economies turn and they insist, on placing the so-called informal sector of activity at the center of analysis. To these two key aspects of the works presented, I would add that the ethnographic method has enabled this diverse group of anthropologists and geographers to delve more deeply into the relationships of street vendors and their wider publics. The approach has helped bring forward the voices of participants in street economies, often illuminating contemporary discourses of livelihood and human rights in the face of neoliberal market and state relations. Documenting local-level activities has led us to diverse locations including on-the-street negotiations, NGOs working with and on behalf of street vendors, and Internet sites used by vendors to stimulate broader awareness and discussion of the problems they confront in their everyday lives.

Finally, and vital to our project, contributors have shifted from the narrower attention to street vendors and their work lives toward examination of urban street economies as a still growing phenomenon, the implications of which extend from the individual vendor to transnational axes of culture and power. With the fast pace of urbanization, vibrant and innovative efforts at making a livelihood at the local level are still constrained by a host of impediments to vendors' success, or even survival. The broader conceptual framework offered here has enabled us to recognize the subtle ways in which contestations in the streets of the urban Global South are taking new forms with different outcomes. New technologies of communication include cellphones, used by vendors to alert others about crackdowns, and the Internet, for mobilizing on a broader scale. The growth in numbers of vendors can be a liability or an asset in organizing, just as assertions of cultural rights can be strategically risky or empowering. Similarly, going global through collaboration with NGOs and transnational social movements may be a drain on the energies of weary participants in street economies, but it can also provide valuable networks of support, including the consuming public and policy makers.

This volume should inspire further efforts to generate the sort of rich and provocative research and analysis that are offered here. Moreover, it should reset the terms of discussion to address urban street economies in the Global South as they are found today—often unruly in appearance but revealing a cultural logic that gives shape to meaning and materiality in the lives of many, both on and off city streets.

References

Abraham, Itty, and Willem van Schendel

2005   Introduction: The Making of Illicitness. *In* Illicit Flows and Criminal Things: States, Borders, and the Other Side of Globalization. Willem van Schendel and Itty Abraham, eds. Pp. 1–37. Bloomington: University of Indiana Press.

Agathangelou, Anna M., and Nevzat Soguk

2011   Rocking the Kasbah: Insurrectional Politics, the "Arab Streets," and Global Revolution in the 21st Century. Globalizations 8(5):551–558.

Agoot, Liza

2008a   Mayor Asked to Locate Vending Places in the City. Baguio Midland Courier, February 10: 20, 39.

2008b   "Do Not Kill Us," Market Peddlers Ask City Officials; City Officials Discuss Options for Vending. Baguio Midland Courier, October 19: 24, 45.

2010   Mayor Wants an End to Collection of Kwartais [Rent]. Baguio Midland Courier, July 11: 16, 36.

Alegi, Peter

2008   A Nation to Be Reckoned With: The Politics of the World Cup Stadium Construction in Cape Town and Durban, South Africa. African Studies 67(3):397–422.

Anchishkin, A., ed.

1980   National Economic Planning. Moscow: Progress Publishers.

Anderson, Christopher

2008   The Effects of Tourism on the Cusco Region of Peru. University of Wisconsin-La Crosse Journal of Undergraduate Research. http://www.uwlax.edu/urc/JUR-online/PDF/2008/anderson.pdf, accessed December 12, 2012.

Anderson, Jay

1984   Time Machines: The World of Living History. Nashville: The American Association for State and Local History.

REFERENCES

Babb, Florence E.

1984   Women in the Marketplace: Petty Commerce in Peru. Special issue on
         the political economy of women, Review of Radical Political Economics.
         16(1):45–59.

1986   Producers and Reproducers: Andean Marketwomen in the Economy. *In*
         Women and Change in Latin America. June Nash and Helen I. Safa, eds.
         Pp. 53–64. South Hadley: Bergin and Garvey.

1987a   From the Field to the Cooking Pot: Economic Crisis and the Threat to
         Marketers in Peru. Ethnology 26(2):137–149.

1987b   Marketers as Producers: The Labor Process and Proletarianization of
         Peruvian Marketwomen. *In* Perspectives in U.S. Marxist Anthropology. David
         Hakken and Johanna Lessinger, eds. Pp. 166–185. Boulder: Westview.

1988   From the Field to the Cooking Pot: Economic Crisis and the Threat to
         Marketers in Peru. *In* Traders Versus the State: Anthropological Approaches
         to Unofficial Economies. Gracia Clark, ed. Pp. 17–40. Boulder: Westview.

1998[1989] Between Field and Cooking Pot: The Political Economy of Marketwomen
         in Peru. Rev. edition. Austin: University of Texas Press.

2001   Market/places as Gendered Spaces: Market/women's Studies Over Two
         Decades. *In* Women Traders in Cross-Cultural Perspective: Mediating
         Identities, Marketing Wares. Linda J. Seligmann, ed. Pp. 228–239. Stanford:
         Stanford University Press.

2011   The Tourism Encounter: Fashioning Latin American Nations and Histories.
         Stanford: Stanford University Press.

Baguio Midland Courier staff

2010   Study to Decongest Market Ongoing. Baguio Midland Courier, May 8: 3.

Balisacan, Arsenio M.

1995   Anatomy of Poverty during Adjustment: The Case of the Philippines.
         Economic Development and Cultural Change 44(1):33–62.

Barker, Joshua

2009   Introduction: Street Life. City & Society 21(2):155–162.

Bayat, Asef

2004   Globalization and the Politics of the Informals in the Global South. *In*
         Urban Informality: Transnational Perspectives from the Middle East, Latin
         America, and South Asia. Ananya Roy and Nezar Alsayyad, eds. Pp. 79–102.
         Lanham: Lexington Books.

BBC

2012   Nông dân về Hà Nội khiếu kiện [Farmers' claim to Hanoi]. BBC News
         Vietnam. http://www.bbc.co.uk/vietnamese/vietnam/2012/02/120221
         _ecopark_protest.shtml, accessed July 10, 2012.

Bebbington, Anthony

2009   Poverty Reduction and Social Movements: A Framework with Cases.
         Manchester: University of Manchester, Institute for Development Policy and

Management / Brooks World Poverty Institute. http://www.sed.manchester
.ac.uk/research/socialmovements, accessed September 23, 2010.

Becker, Marc
2011   Pachakutik: Indigenous Movements and Electoral Politics in Ecuador.
        Lanham: Rowman and Littlefield.

Bell, Rick, Lance Jay Brown, Lynne Elizabeth, and Ron Schiffman, eds.
2012   Beyond Zuccotti Park: Freedom of Assembly and the Occupation of Public
        Space. Oakland: New Village Press.

Berger, Dina, and Andrew Grant Wood, eds.
2010   Holiday in Mexico: Critical Reflections on Tourism and Tourist Encounters.
        Durham: Duke University Press.

Bernstein, Henry, and Terence J. Byres
2001   From Peasant Studies to Agrarian Change. Journal of Agrarian Change
        1:1–56.

Betts, Raymond
1971   Establishment of the Medina in Dakar, Senegal, 1914. Africa 61:143–152.

Beveridge, Andrew A., and Anthony R. Oberschall
1979   African Businessmen and Development in Zambia. Princeton: Princeton
        University Press.

Bhowmik, Sharit K.
2005   Street Vendors in Asia: A Review. Economic and Political Weekly, May 28–
        June 4: 2256–2264.

Bhowmik, Sharit, ed.
2010   Street Vendors in the Global Urban Economy. London and New York:
        Routledge.

Black, David
2007   The Symbolic Politics of Sport Mega-events: 2010 in Comparative
        Perspective. Politikon 34(3):261–276.

Blomley, Nicholas
2011   Rights of Passage: Sidewalks and the Regulation of Public Flow. London and
        New York: Routledge.

Bohannan, Paul J., and George Dalton, eds.
1962   Markets in Africa: Eight Subsistence Economies in Transition. Evanston:
        Northwestern University Press.

Bonham, Carl, Christopher Edmonds, and James Mak
2006   The Impact of 9/11 and Other Terrible Global Events on Tourism in the
        U.S. and Hawaii. East-West Center Working Papers, Economics Series, 87.
        Honolulu: East-West Center.

Bonilla-Silva, Eduardo
2003   Racism Without Racists: Color-Blind Racism and the Persistence of Racial
        Inequality in the United States. Lanham, Boulder, New York, Oxford:
        Rowman & Littlefield.

REFERENCES

Boumedouha, Said
1990   Adjustment to West African Realities: The Lebanese in Senegal. Africa: Journal of the International African Institute 60:538–549.

Brenner, Neil, and Nick Theodore
2002   Cities and the Geographies of "Actually Existing Neoliberalism." Antipode 34(3):349–378.

Bromley, Ray
1978a   Organization, Regulation and Exploitation in the So-called "Urban Informal Sector": The Street Traders of Cali, Colombia. World Development 6(9/10):1161–1172.

2000   Street Vending and Public Policy: A Global Review. International Journal of Sociology and Social Policy 20(1/2):1–29.

2007   Foreword. *In* Street Entrepreneurs: People, Place and Politics in Local and Global Perspectives. John C. Cross and Alfonso Morales, eds. Pp. xv–xvii. London and New York: Routledge.

Bromley, Ray, ed.
1978b   World Development. Special issue on the urban informal sector, World Development 6(9/10).

1985   Planning for Small Enterprises in Third World Cities. Oxford: Pergamon.

Bromley, Ray, and Chris Gerry, eds.
1979   Casual Work and Poverty in Third World Cities. New York: John Wiley.

Bromley, Rosemary, and Peter Mackie
2009   Displacement and the New Spaces for Informal Trade in the Latin American City Centre. Urban Studies 46(7):1485–1506.

Brown, Alison
2006a   Challenging Street Livelihoods. *In* Contested Space: Street Trading, Public Space, and Livelihoods in Developing Cities. Alison Brown, ed. Pp. 3–16. Warwickshire: ITDG Publishing.

2006b   Urban Public Space in the Developing World—A Resource for the Poor. *In* Contested Space: Street Trading, Public Space, and Livelihoods in Developing Cities. Alison Brown, ed. Pp. 17–36. Warwickshire: ITDG Publishing.

Brown, Alison, ed.
2006c   Contested Space: Street Trading, Public Space, and Livelihoods in Developing Cities. Warwickshire: ITDG Publishing.

Brown, Alison, and Michal Lyons
2010   Seen But Not Heard: Urban Voice and Citizenship for Street Traders. *In* Africa's Informal Workers: Collective Agency, Alliances and Transnational Organizing in Urban Africa. Ilda Lindell, ed. Pp. 33–45. London: Zed Books.

Brown, Alison, Michal Lyons, and Ibrahima Dankoco
2010   Street Traders and the Emerging Spaces for Urban Voice and Citizenship in African Cities. Urban Studies 47(3):666–683.

Brown, Michael
2003   Who Owns Native Culture? Cambridge: Harvard University Press.

Bruner, Edward
2005   Culture on Tour: Ethnographies of Travel. Chicago: University of Chicago Press.

Buss, Terry
1999   Microenterprise in International Perspective: An Overview of the Issues. International Journal of Economic Development 1:1–28.

Butcher, Melissa, and Selvaraj Velayutham, eds.
2009   Dissent and Cultural Resistance in Asia's Cities. New York and London: Routledge.

Butler, Judith
1990   Gender Trouble: Feminism and the Subversion of Identity. New York: Routledge.

Calthorpe, Peter
2011   Urbanism in the Age of Climate Change. Washington, DC: Island Press.

Carmack, Robert M., ed.
1986   The Harvest of Violence: Maya Indians and the Guatemalan Crisis. Norman: University of Oklahoma Press.

Castells, Manuel, and Alejandro Portes
1989   World Underneath: The Origins, Dynamics and Effects of the Informal Economy. *In* The Informal Economy: Studies in Advanced and Less Developed Countries. Alejandro Portes, Manuel Castells, and L. A. Benton, eds. Pp. 11–40. Baltimore and London: Johns Hopkins University Press.

CEROI (Cities Environmental Reports on the Internet)
2000   Durban Metro State of the Environment and Development 1999. http://www.ceroi.net/reports/durban/drivers/economyl/state.htm, accessed July 9, 2011.

Chikulu, Bornwell
2009   Local Governance Reforms in Zambia: A Review. Commonwealth Journal of Local Governance 2:98–106.

City Government of Baguio
2000–2001 Tax Ordinance Number 2000–001: With Amendments as of March 2010. Baguio City: Office of the City Treasurer.
2008   Administrative Order No. 115, Series of 2008 (passed July 25). Implementing the Clearing of Passageways in the City Public Market. Baguio City: Public Order and Safety Division / Office of the City Treasurer / Baguio City Police Office.

REFERENCES

2009 Baguio City Public Market Summit. Baguio Convention Center, April 25–26. Baguio City: Office of the City Mayor.

Clark, Gracia

1988a Introduction. *In* Traders Versus the State: Anthropological Approaches to Unofficial Economies. Gracia Clark, ed. Pp. 1–22. Boulder: Westview.

1988b Kumasi Market Traders' Response to 1979 Price Control of Local Foodstuffs in Ghana. *In* Traders Versus the State: Anthropological Approaches to Unofficial Economies. Gracia Clark, ed. Pp. 57–79. Boulder: Westview.

1989 Money, Sex and Cooking: Manipulation of the Paid/Unpaid Boundary by Asante Market Women. *In* The Social Economy of Consumption. Benjamin Orlove and H. Rutz, eds. Pp. 323–348. Monographs in Economic Anthropology, 6. Lanham: University Press of America.

1994 Onions Are My Husband: Survival and Accumulation by West African Market Women. Chicago: University of Chicago Press.

1999 Mothering, Work and Gender in Urban Asante Ideology and Practice. American Anthropologist 101(4):717–729.

2010 African Market Women: Seven Life Stories from Ghana. Bloomington: Indiana University Press.

Clark, Gracia, ed.

1988c Traders Versus the State: Anthropological Approaches to Unofficial Economies. Boulder: Westview.

Cohen, Margot

2003 Neat Streets. Far Eastern Economic Review 166(21):38.

Collins, John

2007 The Sounds of Tradition: Arbitrariness and Agency in a Brazilian Cultural Heritage Center. Ethnos 72(3):383–407.

2008 "But What If I Should Need to Defecate in Your Neighborhood, Madame?" Empire, Redemption, and the "Tradition of the Oppressed" in a Brazilian World Heritage Site. Cultural Anthropology 23(2):279–328.

Comaroff, John, and Jean Comaroff

2009 Ethnicity, Inc. Chicago: University of Chicago Press.

Connerton, Paul

2009 How Modernity Forgets. Cambridge: Cambridge University Press.

Cornejo, Andrea

2010 Intangible Fruits of Peruvian Economic Development. Washington, DC: Council on Hemispheric Affairs. http://www.coha.org/intangible-fruits-of -peruvian-economic-development/, accessed October 27, 2010.

Cornelissen, Scarlett

2007 Crafting Legacies: The Changing Political Economy of Global Sport and the 2010 FIFA World Cup. Politikon 34(3):241–259.

Cross, John C.

1998   Informal Politics: Street Vendors and the State in Mexico City. Stanford: Stanford University Press.

2000   Street Vendors, Modernity and Postmodernity: Conflict and Compromise in the Global Economy. International Journal of Sociology and Social Policy 1(2):30–52.

Cross, John C., and Marina Karides

2007   Capitalism, Modernity, and the "Appropriate" Use of Space. In Street Entrepreneurs: People, Place and Politics in Local and Global Perspectives. John C. Cross and Alfonso Morales, eds. Pp. 19–35. London and New York: Routledge.

Cross, John C., and Alfonso Morales, eds.

2007   Street Entrepreneurs: People, Place and Politics in Local and Global Perspectives. London and New York: Routledge.

Crossa, Veronica

2009   Resisting the Entrepreneurial City: Street Vendors' Struggle in Mexico City's Historic Center. International Journal of Urban and Regional Research 33(1):43–63.

CSO (Central Statistical Office)

2003   Migration and Urbanization: 2000 Census Report. Lusaka: Central Statistical Office.

2006   Living Conditions Monitoring Surveys. Poverty in Zambia 1991–2006. http://www.zamstats.gov.zm/lcm.php, accessed October 29, 2010.

Curtin, Philip D.

1985   Medical Knowledge and Urban Planning in Tropical Africa. The American Historical Review 90:594–613.

Daniere, Amrita, and Mike Douglass

2009   Urbanization and Civic Space in Asia. In The Politics of Civic Space in Asia: Building Urban Communities. Amrita Daniere and Mike Douglass, eds. Pp. 1–19. London and New York: Routledge.

Dardagan, Colleen

2010   Sweet Victory for Durban's 100-Year-Old Market. The Mercury, May 20. http://www.streetnet.org.za/wp-content/uploads/2010/06/Mercury20052010.jpg, accessed January 21, 2011.

Dasgupta, Nandini

1992   Petty Trading in the Third World: The Case of Calcutta. Aldershot: Avebury.

De Boeck, Filip

2011   Inhabiting Ocular Ground: Kinshasa's Future in the Light of Congo's Spectral Urban Politics. Cultural Anthropology 26(7):263–286.

de Certeau, Michel

1984   The Practice of Everyday Life. S. Rendall, trans. Berkeley: University of California Press.

References

de la Cadena, Marisol
1991   Las mujeres son más indias: Etnicidad y género en una comunidad del Cusco. Revista Andina 9(1):7–29.

de Langen, Marius
2005   Urban Road Infrastructure Policies in Africa: The Importance of Mainstreaming Pedestrian Infrastructure and Traffic Calming Facilities. Urban Transport Policy and Practice 11(2):17–32.

de Soto, Hernando
1989   The Other Path: The Invisible Revolution in the Third World. New York: Harper and Row.

Dear, Michael
1997   Post-modern Bloodlines. *In* Space and Social Theory: Interpreting Modernity and Postmodernity. G. Benko and U. Strohmayer, eds. Pp. 49–71. Oxford: Blackwell.

Debord, Guy
2005[1970] The Society of the Spectacle. New translation by Ken Knabb. London: Rebel Press.

Dewey, Alice G.
1962   Peasant Marketing in Java. New York: Free Press of Glencoe.

DiGregorio, Michael R.
1994   Urban Harvest: Recycling as a Peasant Industry in Northern Vietnam. East-West Center Occasional Papers, 17. Honolulu: East-West Center.

DIRCETUR (Dirección Regional de Comercio Exterior y Turismo-Cusco)
2011   Boletín estadístico de turismo, 2010.

Dobler, Gregor
2005   South-South Business Relations in Practice: Chinese Merchants in Oshikango, Namibia. http://www.eldis.org/vfile/upload/1/document /0708/DOC22353.pdf, accessed January 5, 2011.

Dobson, Richard, and Caroline Skinner with Jilian Nicholson
2009   Working in Warwick: Including Street Traders in Urban Plans. Durban: University of KwaZulu-Natal, School of Development Studies.

Donovan, Michael G.
2008   Informal Cities and the Contestation of Public Space: The Case of Bogota's Street Vendors, 1988–2003. Urban Studies 45(1):29–51.

Drummond, Lisa
1993   Women, the Household Economy, and the Informal Sector in Hanoi. Unpublished MA thesis, University of British Columbia.

Drummond, Lisa, and Nguyen Thi Lien
2008   Uses and Understandings of Public Space among Young People in Hanoi, Vietnam. *In* The Politics of Civic Space in Asia: Building Urban

Communities. Amrita Daniere and Mike Douglass, eds. Pp. 175–196. London and New York: Routledge.

Duany, Andres, and Elizabeth Plater-Zyberk
1991   Towns and Town-Making Principles. New York: Rizzoli.

Edelman, Marc
2001   Social Movements: Changing Paradigms and Forms of Politics. Annual Review of Anthropology 30:285–317.

Edensor, Tim
1998   The Culture of the Indian Street. *In* Images of the Street: Planning, Identity, and Control in Public Space. Nicholas R. Fyfe, ed. Pp. 205–253. London and New York: Routledge.
2001   Performing Tourism, Staging Tourism: (Re)producing Tourist Space and Practice. Tourist Studies 1(1):59–81.

Elden, Stuart
2001   Politics, Philosophy, Geography: Henri Lefebvre in Recent Anglo-American Scholarship. Antipode 33:809–825.

Elyachar, Julia
2005   Markets of Dispossession: NGOs, Economic Development, and the State in Cairo. Durham: Duke University Press.

EIR (Economist Intelligence Report)
2010   Country Report. Zambia. October 2010. London: Economist Intelligence Unit.

Evangelista, Geronimo
2010   Market Development, a Challenge to New City Government. Baguio Midland Courier, July 25: 5, 40.

Fahim, Kareem
2011   Slap to a Man's Pride Set Off Tumult in Tunisia. New York Times, January 22. http://www.nytimes.com/2011/01/22/world/africa/22sidi .html?pagewanted+all, accessed December 5, 2011.

Fainstein, Susan S., and Dennis Judd
1999   Global Forces, Local Strategies, and Urban Tourism. *In* The Tourist City. Dennis Judd and Susan Fainstein, eds. Pp. 1–20. New Haven and London: Yale University Press.

Fernandez, Manny
2010   Vendor vs. Vendor: Who Deserves Credit? New York Times, May 4. http:// cityroom.blogs.nytimes.com/2010/05/04/vendor-vs-vendor-who-deserves -credit/, accessed August 19, 2012.

FIFA (Fédération International de Football Association)
2010   The FIFA Rights Protection Programme at the 2010 FIFA World Cup South Africa. http://www.fifa.com/mm/document/affederation/marketing /01/18/98/99/ march2010rightsprotection_a5_20100308.pdf, accessed July 4, 2010.

REFERENCES

Fogarty, Richard, and Michael A. Osborne
2003   Construction and Function of Race in French Military Medicine, 1830–1920. *In* The Color of Liberty: Histories of Race in France. Sue Peabody and Tyler Stovall, eds. Pp. 206–236. Durham: Duke University Press.

Foucault, Michel
1991   Governmentality. *In* The Foucault Effect: Studies in Governmentality. Graham Burchell, Colin Gordon, and Peter Miller, eds. Pp. 87–104. Chicago: University of Chicago Press.

Freeman, Carla
2007   The "Reputation" of Neoliberalism. American Ethnologist 34(2):252–267.

Fussell, Paul
1980   Abroad. Oxford: Oxford University Press.

Fyfe, Nicholas R.
1998   Introduction: Reading the Street. *In* Images of the Street: Planning, Identity and Control in Public Space. Nicholas R. Fyfe, ed. Pp. 1–12. London and New York: Routledge.

Garnier, Tony
1917   Une Cité Industrielle [An Industrial City]. Paris: Vincent.

Geertz, Clifford
1963   Peddlers and Princes: Social Change and Economic Modernization in Two Indonesian Towns. Chicago: University of Chicago Press.

Gilbert, Alan
2004   Love in the Time of Enhanced Capital Flows: Reflections on the Links between Liberalization and Informality. *In* Urban Informality: Transnational Perspectives from the Middle East, Latin America, and South Asia. Ananya Roy and Nezar AlSayyad, eds. Pp. 33–66. Lanham: Lexington Books.

Glick Schiller, Nina, Linda Basch, and Cristina Szanton Blanc
1992   Transnationalism: A New Analytical Framework for Understanding Migration. *In* Toward a Transnational Perspective on Migration: Race, Class, Ethnicity and Nationalism Reconsidered. Nina Glick Schiller, Linda Basch, and Cristina Szanton Blanc, eds. Pp. 1–24. New York: New York Academy of Science.

Gomez, Lailany
2009   First-Quarter Debt Rises as Govt Jacks Up Borrowings. The Manila Times, June 17: B1–B2.

Gonzalez, Carmen G.
2009   Squatters, Pirates, and Entrepreneurs: Is Informality the Solution to the Urban Housing Crisis? Inter-American Law Review 40(2):239–260.

Gotham, Kevin Fox
2002   Marketing Mardi Gras: Commodification, Spectacle and the Political Economy of Tourism in New Orleans. Urban Studies 39(10):1735–1756.

2005   Theorizing Urban Spectacles: Festivals, Tourism and the Transformation of
            Urban Space. City 9(2):225–246.

Gotham, Kevin Fox, and Daniel A. Krier
2008   From the Culture Industry to the Society of the Spectacle: Critical Theory
            and the Situationalist International. Current Perspectives in Social Theory
            25:155–192.

Gramsci, Antonio
1971   Selections from the Prison Notebooks of Antonio Gramsci. Quintin Hoare
            and Geoffrey Nowell Smith, trans. and eds. New York: International
            Publishers.

Griffith, Abigail
2010   The Struggle between Indigenous Folkways and National Law: Resolving
            the Past and the Present. Washington, DC: Council on Hemispheric Affairs.
            June 21. http://www.coha.org/, accessed July 16, 2010.

Guarnizo, Luis Eduardo, and Michael Peter Smith
1998   The Locations of Transnationalism. *In* Transnationalism from Below. Luis
            Eduardo Guarnizo and Michael Peter Smith, eds. Pp. 3–34. New Brunswick:
            Transaction.

Gupta, Akhil, and James Ferguson, eds.
1997   Culture, Power, Place: Explorations in Critical Anthropology. Durham and
            London: Duke University Press.

Hale, Charles
2006   Más Que un Indio: Racial Ambivalence and Neoliberal Multiculturalism in
            Guatemala. Santa Fe: SAR Press.

Hall, Peter
1988   Cities of Tomorrow. London: Blackwell.

Handler, Richard, and Eric Gable
1997   The New History in an Old Museum: Creating the Past at Colonial
            Williamsburg. Durham: Duke University Press.

Hansen, Karen Tranberg
2000   Salaula: The World of Secondhand Clothing in Zambia. Chicago: University
            of Chicago Press.

2004   Who Rules the Streets? The Politics of Vending Space in Lusaka. *In*
            Reconsidering Informality: Perspectives from Urban Africa. Karen Tranberg
            Hansen and Mariken Vaa, eds. Pp. 62–80. Uppsala: Nordic Africa Institute.

2008a   The Informalization of Lusaka's Economy: Regime Change, Ultra Modern
            Markets, and Street Vending, 1972–2004. *In* One Zambia, Many Histories:
            Towards a History of Post-Colonial Zambia. Jan-Bart Gewald, Marja Hinfelaar,
            and Giacomo Macola, eds. Pp. 213–239. Leiden: Brill.

2010   Changing Youth Dynamics in Lusaka's Informal Economy in the Context of
            Economic Liberalization. African Studies Quarterly 11(2&3):13–27.

REFERENCES

Hansen, Karen Tranberg, ed.
2008b   Youth and the City in the Global South. Bloomington: Indiana University Press.

Harper, Malcolm
1998   Profit for the Poor: Cases in Micro-finance. London: ITDG Publishing.

Hart, Keith
1973   Informal Income Opportunities and Urban Employment in Ghana. Journal of Modern African Studies 11(1):61–89.
2010   Informal Economy. *In* The Human Economy: A Citizen's Guide. Keith Hart, Jean-Louis Laville, and Antonio David Cattani, eds. Pp. 142–153. Cambridge and Malden: Polity.

Harvey, David
2005   A Brief History of Neoliberalism. Oxford: Oxford University Press.
2006   Space as a Keyword. *In* David Harvey: A Critical Reader. Noel Castree and Derek Gregory, eds. Pp. 270–293. Malden and Oxford: Blackwell.

Haugen, Heidi Ø, and Jorgen Carling
2005   On the Edge of the Chinese Diaspora: The Surge of Baihou Business in an African City. Ethnic and Racial Studies 28:639–662.

Hedman, Maria
2010   This World Cup Is Not for Us Poor People: Interviews with Street Traders in Port Elizabeth and Pretoria, South Africa. Durban: ProPrint.
2011   "The World Cup Only Benefited the Already Rich and McDonald's": Impacts of the 2010 FIFA World Cup on Cape Town's Informal Traders. Masters thesis, Stockholm University.

Heyman, Josiah McC., and Alan Smart
1999   States and Illegal Practices: An Overview. *In* States and Illegal Practices. Josiah McC. Heyman, ed. Pp. 1–24. Oxford and New York: Berg.

Higgs, Peter
2003   Footpath Traders in a Hanoi Neighbourhood. *In* Consuming Urban Culture in Contemporary Vietnam. Lisa Drummond and Mandy Thomas, eds. Pp. 75–88. London: RoutledgeCurzon.

Hill, Matthew J.
2007   Re-imagining Old Havana: World Heritage and the Production of Scale in Late Socialist Cuba. *In* Deciphering the Global: Its Scale, Spaces and Subjects. Saskia Sassen, ed. Pp. 86–109. New York: Routledge.

Hill, Michael D.
2007   Contesting Patrimony: Cusco's Mystical Tourist Industry and the Politics of Incanismo. Ethnos 72(4):433–460.

Hill, Polly
1969   Hidden Trade in Hausaland. Man, n.s., 4(3):392–409.

Hirschowitz, Ros
2000   Measuring Poverty in South Africa. Pretoria: Statistics of South Africa.

Holston, James

1989   The Modernist City: An Anthropological Critique of Brasília. Chicago: University of Chicago Press.

2002   The Modernist City and the Death of the Street. *In* Theorizing the City: The New Urban Anthropology Reader. Setha Low, ed. Pp. 245–276. New Brunswick: Rutgers University Press.

Horn, Pat

2009   Street Vendors' Support for Schack Dwellers. Abahlali baseMjondolo, October 21. http://www.abahlali.org/node/5931, accessed July 7, 2010.

Huffman, Brent, and Xiaoli Zhou

2005   The Colony. http://www.youtube.com/watch?v=bz0bhb5m3pQ, accessed December 20, 2010.

Hunt, Stacey

2009   Citizenship's Place: The State's Creation of Public Space and Street Vendors' Culture of Informality in Bogota, Columbia. Environment and Planning D: Society and Space 27:331–351.

Hutchcroft, Paul D., and Joel Rocamora

2012   Patronage-Based Parties and the Democratic Deficit in the Philippines: Origins, Evolution, and the Imperatives of Reform. *In* Routledge Handbook of Southeast Asian Politics. Richard Robison, ed. Pp. 97–119. London and New York: Routledge.

INEI (Instituto Nacional de Estadística e Informática Perú)

2008   Censos Nacionales 2007, XI de Población y VI de Vivienda. Sistema de Consulta de Principales Indicadores Demográficos, Sociales y Económicos. http://www.inei.gob.pe/, accessed October 21, 2010.

International Labour Office (ILO)

1972   Employment, Incomes and Equality: A Strategy for Increasing Productive Employment in Kenya. Geneva: ILO.

Jackson, Jean, and Kay Warren

2005   Indigenous Movements in Latin America, 1992–2004: Controversies, Ironies, New Directions. Annual Review of Anthropology 34:549–573.

Jacobs, Jane

1961   The Death and Life of Great American Cities. New York: Random House.

Janicke, Kiraz

2009   Peru: Discontent Rages On. Peru en Movimiento, June 23. http://peru-enmovimiento.blogspot.com/2009/06/peru-discontent-rages-on.html, accessed August 20, 2010.

Jensen, Rolf, and Donald M. Peppard, Jr.

2003   Hanoi's Informal Sector and the Vietnamese Economy: A Case Study of Roving Street Vendors. Journal of Asian and African Studies 38(1):71–84.

REFERENCES

Kamete, Amin Y.

2008   Planning Versus Youth: Stamping Out Spatial Unruliness in Harare. Geoforum 39:1721–1733.

Kamete, Amin, and Ilda Lindell

2010   The Politics of "Non-planning" Strategies in African Cities: International and Local Dimensions in Harare and Maputo. Journal of Southern African Studies 36(4):889–912.

Katzin, Margaret F.

1959   The Jamaican Country Higgler. Social and Economic Studies 8:421–440.

Kerkvliet, Benjamin J. T.

2005   The Power of Everyday Politics: How Vietnamese Peasants Transformed National Policy. Ithaca: Cornell University Press.

2009   Everyday Politics in Peasant Societies (and Ours). Journal of Peasant Studies 36(1):227–243.

Kersting, Norbert

2007   Sport and National Identity: A Comparison of the 2006 and 2010 FIFA World Cups. Politikon 34(3):277–293.

Khayesi, Meleckidzedeck, Heiner Monheil, and Johannes Michael Nebe

2010   Negotiating "Streets for All" in Urban Transport Planning: The Case for Pedestrians, Cyclists and Street Vendors in Nairobi, Kenya. Antipode 42(1):103–126.

Koh, David

2004a   Urban Government: Ward-Level Administration in Hanoi. *In* Beyond Hanoi: Local Government in Vietnam. Benjamin J. Tria Kerkvliet and David G. Marr, eds. Pp. 197–228. Singapore: Institute of Southeast Asian Studies.

2004b   Illegal Construction in Hanoi and Hanoi Wards. European Journal of East Asian Studies 3(2):337–369.

2006   Wards of Hanoi. Singapore: Institute of Southeast Asian Studies.

2008   The Pavement as Civic Space: History and Dynamics in the City of Hanoi. *In* Globalization, the City and Civil Society in Pacific Asia: The Social Production of Civic Spaces. Mike Douglass, Ho Kong Chong, and Giok Ling Ooi, eds. Pp. 145–174. London and New York: Routledge.

KPHB (Kumasi Public Health Board minutes, accessed in the National Archives, Kumasi, Ghana)

1926a   No. 2513, July 13.

1926b   No. 2513, August 12.

1926c   No. 2513, August 28.

1926d   No. 2513, November 16.

1930a   No. 2513, March 12.

1930b   No. 2513, September 24.

1930c   No. 2513, October 29.

1931   No. 2513, Petition, five female bakers to Chief Commissioner Ashanti, April 27.

1932a   No. 2866, May 26.

1932b   No. 2866, October 26.

1934   No. 2866, January 29.

Krier, Leon
1992   Architecture and Urban Design, 1967–1992. London: Academy Editions.

Kubheka, Anelisa, and Nomvula Sikakane
2010   Court Win Sweetens Celebration: Market Traders Fete 100 Years. Daily News, May 20. http://www.streetnet.org.za/wp-content/uploads/2010/06/DN20052010.jpg, accessed January 21, 2011.

Kusakabe, Kyoko
2006   Policy Issues in Street Vending: An Overview of Studies in Thailand, Cambodia and Mongolia. Informal Economy, Poverty and Employment. Bangkok: International Labor Office.

Laking, Jimmy
2008   City's "Zero Vending" Policy Reinforced amid Opposition. Baguio Midland Courier, February 3: 1, 35.

Lazar, Sian
2008   El Alto, Rebel City: Self and Citizenship in Andean Bolivia. Durham: Duke University Press.

Le Corbusier
1933   La Ville Radieuse [The Radiant City]. Paris: Vincent Fréal & Cie.

Lefebvre, Henri
1991   The Production of Space. Donald Nicholson-Smith, trans. Cambridge: Blackwell.

Leshkowich, Ann Marie
2005   Feminine Disorder: State Campaigns Against Street Traders in Socialist and Late Socialist Việt Nam. In Việt Nam: Women's Realities. G. Bousquet and N. Taylor, eds. Pp. 187–207. Paris: Les Indes Savantes.

2011   Making Class and Gender: (Market) Socialist Enframing of Traders in Ho Chi Minh City. American Anthropologist 113(2):277–290.

Lewis, Harold MacLean
1949   Planning the Modern City. 2 vols. New York: John Wiley.

Lewis, W. Arthur
1954   Economic Development with Unlimited Supplies of Labour. Manchester School of Economics and Social Studies 22:139–191.

Li Tana
1996   Peasants on the Move: Rural-Urban Migration in the Hanoi Region. Occasional Paper 91. Singapore: Institute of Southeast Asian Studies.

REFERENCES

Lindell, Ilda

2010a   Introduction: The Changing Politics of Informality—Collective Organizing, Alliances and Scales of Engagement. *In* Africa's Informal Workers: Collective Agency and Transnational Organizing in Urban Africa. Ilda Lindell, ed. Pp. 1–30. London: Zed Books.

2010b   Between Exit and Voice: Informality and the Spaces of Popular Agency. African Studies Quarterly 11(2/3):1–11.

Lindell, Ilda, ed.

2010c   Africa's Informal Workers: Collective Agency, Alliances and Transnational Organizing in Urban Africa. London: Zed Books.

Lindell, Ilda, Maria Hedman, and Kyle-Nathan Verboomen

2010   The World Cup 2010 and the Urban Poor: "World Class Cities" for All? Uppsala: The Nordic Africa Institute.

Liporada, Isagani

2008a   Marikina Market Becomes Model in Anti-vending. Sun Star Baguio, March 3: 2.

2008b   Execs Backtrack; Allow Vendors Back in Market. Baguio Midland Courier, November 9: 1, 48.

Lipsky, Michael

1980   Street-Level Bureaucracy: Dilemmas of the Individual in Public Services. New York: Russell.

Lipton, Michael

1977   Why Poor People Stay Poor: A Study of Urban Bias in World Development. London: Temple Smith.

Little, Walter E.

2004a   Mayas in the Marketplace: Tourism, Globalization, and Cultural Identity. Austin: University of Texas Press.

2004b   Outside of Social Movements: Dilemmas of Indigenous Handicraft Vendors in Guatemala. American Ethnologist 31(1):43–59.

2008a   Crime, Maya Handicraft Vendors, and the Social Re/Construction of Market Spaces in a Tourism Town. *In* Economies and the Transformation of Landscape. Society for Economic Anthropology Monograph Series, 25. Lisa Cliggett and Christopher A. Pool, eds. Pp. 267–290. Walnut Creek: AltaMira.

2008b   A Visual Political Economy of Maya Representations in Guatemala, 1931–1944. Ethnohistory 55(4):633–663.

2008c   Living within the Mundo Maya Development Project: Strategies of Maya Handicraft Vendors. Latin American Perspectives 35(3):87–102.

2009   Contesting Heritage in Antigua, Guatemala. *In* Cultural Tourism in Latin America: The Politics of Space and Imagery. Michael Baud and Annelou Ypeij, eds. Pp. 217–244. Leiden: Brill Publishers.

Little, Walter E., and Timothy J. Smith, eds.
2009   Mayas in Postwar Guatemala: Harvest of Violence Revisited. Tuscaloosa: University of Alabama Press.

Lloyd-Evans, Sally
2008   Geographies of the Contemporary Informal Sector in the Global South: Gender, Employment Relationships and Social Protection. Geography Compass 2(6):1885–1906.

Low, Setha
1996   The Anthropology of Cities: Imagining and Theorizing the City. Annual Review of Anthropology 25:383–409.

Lucas, Daxim
2009   Corruption Is Top Issue for Next President, Says Survey. Philippine Daily Inquirer, July 10: A7.

MacCannell, Dean
1976   The Tourist: A New Theory of the Leisure Class. New York: Shocken.

Maenning, Wolfgang, and Stan du Plessis
2009   Sports Stadia, Sporting Events and Urban Development: International Experience and the Ambitions of Durban. Urban Forum 20(1):61–76.

Malukela, Slindile
2010   FIFA by-laws for street traders. IOL News, February 5. http://www.iol.co.az /news/south-africa/fifa-by-laws-for-street-traders-1.472638, accessed January 21, 2011.

Marx, Karl, and Friedrich Engels
1998[1848] The Communist Manifesto. New York: Monthly Review Press.

Maxwell, Keely, and Annelou Ypeij
2009   Caught between Nature and Culture: Making a Living within the World Heritage Site of Machu Picchu, Peru. In The Politics of Space and Imagery. Michael Baud and Annelou Ypeij, eds. Pp. 177–196. Leiden and Boston: Brill.

Mayer, Enrique
2002   The Articulated Peasant: Household Economies in the Andes. Boulder: Westview.

McCann, Eugene J.
1999   Race, Protest, and Public Space: Contextualizing Lefebvre in the U.S. City. Antipode 31(2):163–184.

McCarney, Patricia
2003   Confronting Critical Disjunctures in the Governance of Cities. In Governance on the Ground: Innovations and Discontinuities in Cities of the Developing World. Patricia McCarney and Richard Stren, eds. Pp. 31–55. Baltimore and London: The Johns Hopkins University Press.

Meisch, Lynn
2002   Andean Entrepreneurs: Otavalo Merchants and Musicians in the Global Arena. Austin: University of Texas Press.

REFERENCES

Merrifield, Andrew

1993   Place and Space: A Lefebvrian Reconciliation. Transactions of the Institute of British Geographers 18:516–531.

1997   Between Process and Individuation: Translating Metaphors and Narratives of Urban Space. Antipode 29(4):417–436.

2006   Henri Lefebvre: A Critical Introduction. London: Routledge.

Middleton, Alan

2003   Informal Traders and Planners in the Regeneration of Historic City Centres: The Case of Quito, Ecuador. Progress in Planning 59:71–123.

Mihalyi, Louis J.

1975   The Pedlars of Lusaka. Zambian Geographical Journal 29/30:111–125.

Milgram, B. Lynne

2004   Refashioning Commodities: Women and the Sourcing and Circulation of Secondhand Clothing in the Philippines. Anthropologica 46(2):123–136.

2008   Activating Frontier Livelihoods: Women and the Transnational Secondhand Clothing Trade between Hong Kong and the Philippines. Urban Anthropology and Studies of Cultural Systems and World Economic Development 37(1):5–47.

2009   Negotiating Urban Activism: Women, Vending and the Transformation of Streetscapes in the Urban Philippines. In Dissent and Cultural Resistance in Asia's Cities. Melissa Butcher and Selvaraj Velayutham, eds. Pp. 110–127. London and New York: Routledge.

Mills, Mary Beth

2008   Claiming Space: Navigating Landscapes of Power and Citizenship in Thai Labor Activism. Urban Anthropology and Studies of Cultural Systems and World Economic Development 37(1):89–128.

Mintz, Sidney

1955   The Jamaican Internal Marketing Pattern: Some Notes and Hypotheses. Social and Economic Studies 4:95–103.

1971   Men, Women, and Trade. Comparative Studies in Society and History 13:247–269.

Mitchell, Carrie

2008   Altered Landscapes, Altered Livelihoods: The Shifting Experience of Informal Waste Collecting During Hanoi's Urban Transition. Geoforum 39:2019–2029.

Mitchell, Don

1995   The End of Public Space? People's Park, Definitions of Public, and Democracy. Annals of the Association of American Geographers 85:108–133.

Mitullah, Winnie

2004   A Review of Street Trade in Africa. Report: Women in Informal Employment

Globalising and Organising. Boston: WIEGO / Kennedy School of Government, Harvard University.

Montoya Rojas, Rodrigo

2009 Con los rostros pintados: Tercera rebellion Amazónica en el Perú (Agosto 2008–Junio 2009). Lima: Ediciones Lucha Indígena.

Morales, Alfonso

2007 Law, Deviance, and Defining Vendors and Vending. *In* Street Entrepreneurs: People, Place and Politics in Local and Global Perspectives. John C. Cross and Alfonso Morales, eds. Pp. 262–267. London and New York: Routledge.

Moser, Caroline

1977 The Dual Economy and Marginality Debate and the Contribution of Micro Analysis: Market Sellers in Bogotá. Development and Change 8:465–489.

1978 Informal Sector or Petty Commodity Production: Dualism or Dependence in Urban Development? World Development 6(9/10):1041–1064.

M4P (Making Markets Work Better for the Poor)

2007 Street Vending in Hanoi—Reconciling Contradictory Concerns. Markets and Development Bulletin 13. http://www.markets4poor.org/?name=public ation&op=viewDetailNews&id=574, accessed April 22, 2010.

Mullings, Leith

2005 Interrogating Racism: Toward an Antiracist Anthropology. Annual Review of Anthropology 34:667–693.

Mutale, Emmanuel

2004 The Management of Urban Development in Zambia. Farnam: Ashgate.

N.d. Host Cities Watch. http://www.streetnet.org.za/?p=532, accessed January 21, 2011.

NAA6 (National Archives, Accra)

1947 No. 0028 SF8. Irregularities in Import Control, motion by Hon. Dr. J. B. Danquah, Legislative Council, March 26.

NAK14 (National Archives, Kumasi)

1930 No. 2504, item 34. Chief Commissioner, Ashanti, to Commissioner, Western Province, Ashanti, September 25.

NAK6 (National Archives, Kumasi)

1914 No. 1315. Kumasi Town Council. Changes proposed by Superintending Sanitary Engineer on visit to Kumasi, July.

NAK8 (National Archives, Kumasi)

1951 No. 2866. Hawkers' Controllers to President, Kumasi Town Council, June 4.

Nash, June

2007 Social Movements in Global Circuits. *In* Practicing Ethnography in a Globalizing World. June Nash, ed. Pp. 137–164. Lanham: AltaMira.

REFERENCES

Nchito, Wilma S.

2002   New Markets, New Practices: A Study of Management Practices in the New Markets of Lusaka, Zambia. Unpublished paper presented at workshop on urban governance, gender, and markets, organized by the Nordic Africa Institute and held in Bamako, Mali, September 8–12.

2011   Formalizing Informal Trading Places in the Urban Sector: An Analysis of Trading Spaces and Places in Lusaka, Zambia. *In* The Legal Empowerment Agenda: Poverty, Labour and the Informal Economy in Africa. Dan Banik, ed. Pp. 87–106. Farnham: Ashgate.

Nchito, Wilma S., and Karen Tranberg Hansen

2010   Passport Please: The Cross-Border Traders Association in Zambia. *In* Africa's Informal Workers: Collective Agency, Alliances and Transnational Organizing in Urban Africa. Ilda Lindell, ed. Pp. 169–183. London: Zed Books.

Nelson Mandela Bay Municipality

2009   Commercial Exclusion Zone. http://www.nelsonmandelabay.gov.za /fifaworldcup/Content.aspx?objID=290, accessed January 21, 2011.

Nelson Mandela Metropolitan University

N.d.   Port Elizabeth. http://www.nmmu.ac.za/default.asp?id=4167&bhcp=1, accessed July 9, 2011.

New Seven Wonders of the World

2007   http://www.new7wonders.com, accessed October 23, 2010.

Niñal, Lorenzo

2008   "Illegal" Vending Allowed by City's Tax Ordinance. Sun Star Baguio, January 23: 1, 9.

Olivera, Oscar (in collaboration with Tom Lewis)

2004   Cochabamba! Water War in Bolivia. Cambridge: South End Press.

Olson, Ernie

2008   POSD Assistant Heard Cries Foul after Writer Claims POSD Men Receive Payola from Vendors. Baguio Sun Star, November 9: 1, 11.

ONPE (Oficina Nacional de Procesos Electorales)

2011   Información Electoral y Elecciones: Segunda Elección Presidencial 2011. http://www.onpe.gob.pe/, accessed August 7, 2011.

Opiña, Rimaliza

2008   Vendors Denied Vending Rights at Market's Sari-sari Section. Sun Star Baguio, November 16: 2.

2009   Vendors Seek Bigger Markets. Sun Star Baguio, May 18: 6.

Palangchao, Harley

2008   Market Visit Shows Illegal Vendors Keep Coming Back. Baguio Midland Courier, October 19: 1, 46.

Pallares, Amalia

2002   From Peasant Struggles to Indian Resistance: The Ecuadorian Andes in the Late Twentieth Century. Norman: University of Oklahoma Press.

Peberdy, Sally

2000   Mobile Entrepreneurship: Informal Sector Cross-Border Trade and Street Trade in South Africa. Development Southern Africa 17(2):201–219.

People's Committee of Hanoi

2008   02/2008/QD-UBND Quyết định. Ban hành Quy định về quản lý hoạt động bán hàng rong trên địa bàn Thành phố Hà Nội [Decision. Promulgating regulation on management of street-selling activities in Hanoi].

Plattner, Stuart, ed.

1985   Markets and Marketing. Lanham: University Press of America.

Porter, Gina, Fergus Lyon, Fatima Adamu, and Lanre Obafemi

2010   Conflict and Cooperation in Market Spaces: Learning from the Operation of Local Networks of Civic Engagement in African Market Trade. Human Organization 69(1):31–42.

Postero, Nancy

2007   Now We Are Citizens: Indigenous Citizens in Postmulticultural Bolivia. Stanford: Stanford University Press.

Potts, Deborah

2008   The Urban Informal Sector in Sub-Saharan Africa: From Bad to Good (and Back Again?). Development Southern Africa 25(2):151–167.

Prime Minister of Vietnam

2008   Decision 490/QD-TTg, May 5, 2008. Quyết định 490/QĐ-TTg của Thủ tướng Chính phủ về việc phê duyệt Quy hoạch xây dựng vùng Thủ đô HN [Decision of the Prime Minister on the approval of construction planning for Hanoi Capital zone].

Prince Charles

1989   A Vision of Britain: A Personal View of Architecture. New York: Doubleday.

Project 2010

2009a   Port Elizabeth's Chance to Shine. September 30. http://www.project2010 .co.za/search.asp, accessed January 21, 2011.

2009b   Port Elisabeth: New R25m Deal for CBD Upgrade. September 8–9. http:// www.project2010.co.za/search.asp, accessed January 21, 2011.

Province of the Eastern Cape

2009   Local Authority Notice. Nelson Mandela Bay Metropolitan Municipality: 2010 FIFA World Cup South Africa By-Laws. Provincial Gazette No. 2050 (Extraordinary). King William's Town.

Purcell, Mark

2002   Excavating Lefebvre: The Right to the City and Its Urban Politics of the Inhabitant. Geojournal 58(2/3):99–108.

References

Ramón, Roxabel

2010   Paro contra Majes-Siguas II: Unos Siete Mil Turistas no Pudieron Desplazarse en Cusco. El Comercio, September 22.

Ramsamy, Edward

2006   The World Bank and Urban Development: From Projects to Policy. London and New York: Routledge.

Republic of the Philippines

1997–2001 Executive Order No. 452 (passed June 25, 2001). Providing for the Guidelines That Will Ensure the Security of Registered Vendors in the Workplace and Implementing Rules and Regulations. Manila: Republic of the Philippines, Office of the President.

Republic of Zambia

2006   Fifth National Development Plan 2006–2010: Broad Based Wealth and Job Creation through Citizenry Participation and Technological Advancement. Lusaka: Government Printer.

2007   Markets and Bus Stations Act (No. 7). Lusaka: Government Printer.

Resnick, Danielle

2011   In the Shadow of the City: Africa's Urban Poor in Opposition Strongholds. Journal of Modern African Studies 49(1):141–166.

Ribeiro, Gustavo Lins

2009   Non-hegemonic Globalizations: Alter-native Transnational Processes and Agents. Anthropological Theory 9(3):297–329.

Riccio, Bruno

1999   Senegalese Street Sellers, Racism, and the Discourse on "Irregular Trade" in Rimini. Modern Italy 4:225–239.

Rillorta, P.

2008   Illegal Vending, Who's to Blame? Baguio Midland Courier, May 18: 2, 42.

Robertson, Claire

1983   The Death of Makola and Other Tragedies: Male Strategies Against a Female-Dominated System. Canadian Journal of African Studies 17(3):469–495.

1984   Sharing the Same Bowl. Bloomington: Indiana University Press.

Robinson, Jennifer

2008   Developing Ordinary Cities: City Visioning Processes in Durban and Johannesburg. Environment and Planning A 40(1):74–87.

Rostow, Walt W.

1960   The Stages of Economic Growth: A Non-communist Manifesto. London: Cambridge University Press.

Roy, Ananya

2004   The Gentlemen's City: Urban Informality in the Calcutta of New Communism. In Urban Informality. Ananya Roy and N. Alsayyad, eds. Pp. 147–170. Lanham and Boulder: Lexington Books.

2005   Urban Informality: Toward an Epistemology of Planning. Journal of the American Planning Association 71(2):147–158.

Saib, Aarif
2010   Traders Threaten Elections Boycott: Fears for Future amid Market Centenary Celebration. Tribune Herald, May 28. http://www.streetnet .org.za/wp-content/uploads/2010/06/TribHerald23052010.jpg, accessed January 21, 2011.

Sassen, Saskia
1996a   Toward a Feminist Analytics of the Global Economy. Indiana Journal of Global Legal Studies 4(1):7–41.
1996b   Whose City Is It? Globalization and the Formation of New Claims. Public Culture 8(2):205–223.
2001   The Global City: New York, London and Tokyo: Princeton: Princeton University Press.

Schildkrout, Enid
1978   Roles of Children in Urban Kano. ASA Monograph 17. Series: Sex and Age as Principles of Social Differentiation. Jean LaFontaine, ed. London: Academic Press.

Scott, James C.
1976   The Moral Economy of the Peasant. New Haven: Yale University Press.
1985   Weapons of the Weak: Everyday Forms of Peasant Resistance. New Haven: Yale University Press.
1990   Domination and the Arts of Resistance: Hidden Transcripts. New Haven: Yale University Press.
1998   Seeing like a State: How Certain Schemes to Improve the Human Condition Have Failed. New Haven: Yale University Press.

Seligmann, Linda J.
1989   To Be In Between: The Cholas as Market Women in Peru. Comparative Studies in Society and History 31(4):694–721.
1995   Between Reform and Revolution: Political Struggles in the Peruvian Andes, 1969–1991. Stanford: Stanford University Press.
2000   Market Places, Social Spaces, in Cuzco, Peru. Urban Anthropology 29(1):1–68.
2004   Peruvian Street Lives: Culture, Power, and Economy among Market Women of Cuzco. Urbana and Chicago: University of Illinois Press.

Seligmann, Linda J., ed.
2001   Women Traders in Cross-Cultural Perspective: Mediating Identities, Marketing Wares. Stanford: Stanford University Press.

Shine
2010   World Cup Informal Trader By-laws Defined. February 18. http://www .shine2010.co.za/Community/blogs/goodnews/archive/2010/02/18/2010 -world-cup-informal-trader-by-laws defined.aspx, accessed March 9, 2010.

REFERENCES

Sicuani Noticias

2010   Artesanos Cusqueños Negocian con Empresarios Extranjeros. http://www
        .sicuaninoticias.com/, accessed September 25, 2010.

Silverman, Helaine

2002   Touring Ancient Times: The Present and Presented Past in Contemporary
        Peru. American Anthropologist 104(3):881–902.

Simon, Beatrice

2009   Sacamefotos and Tejedoras: Frontstage Performance and Backstage Meaning
        in a Peruvian Context. *In* The Politics of Space and Imagery. Michael Baud
        and Annelou Ypeij, eds. Pp. 117–140. Leiden and Boston: Brill.

Skinner, Caroline

2008   The Struggle for the Streets: Processes of Exclusion and Inclusion of
        Street Traders in Durban, South Africa. Development Southern Africa
        25(2):227–242.

2009   Challenging City Imaginaries: Street Traders' Struggles in Warwick Junction.
        Agenda 81(1):101–109.

Smart, Alan, and Josephine Smart

2005   Introduction. *In* Petty Capitalists and Globalization: Flexibility,
        Enterpreneurship, and Economic Development. Alan Smart and Josephine
        Smart, eds. Pp. 1–22. Albany: SUNY Press.

Smart, Josephine

1989   The Political Economy of Street Hawkers in Hong Kong. Hong Kong: Center
        for Asian Studies.

Soja, Edward

1996   Thirdspace: Journeys to Los Angeles and Other Real-and-Imagined Places.
        Malden: Blackwell.

Soubbotina, Tatyana P.

2004   Beyond Economic Growth: An Introduction to Sustainable Development.
        2nd edition. Washington, DC: World Bank.

Steel, Griet

2009   Dishing Up the City: Tourism and Street Vendors in Cuzco. *In* Cultural
        Tourism in Latin America: The Politics of Space and Imagery. Michael Baud
        and Annelou Ypeij, eds. Pp. 161–176. Leiden and Boston: Brill.

Stewart, Lynn

1995   Bodies, Visions, and Spatial Politics: A Review Essay on Henri Lefebvre's
        The Production of Space. Environment and Planning D: Society and Space
        13:609–618.

Stillerman, Joel

2006   The Politics of Space and Culture in Santiago, Chile's Street Markets.
        Qualitative Sociology 29:507–530.

Stoller, Paul

2002   Money Has No Smell: The Africanization of New York City. Chicago: University of Chicago Press.

Straits Times

2008   Supersized Ha Noi. Straits Times, July 6. http://www.mysinchew.com/node/13453, accessed June 24, 2010.

StreetNet International

2007   Durban's street wars—StreetNet International calls on eThekwini Metro to negotiate in good faith with street vendors Press statement. http://www.streetnet.org.za/wpcontent/pdf/Durban250707.htm, accessed June 25, 2007.

StreetNet International and WIEGO

N.d.   Save the Early Morning Market at Warwick Junction. http://www.ipetitions.com/petition/warwickjunction, accessed January 21, 2011.

Sunday Tribune

2009   Not Fair, Mr Mayor. Sunday Tribune, August 2, 2009. http://www.iol.co.za/index.php?from=rss_South%20Africa&set_id=1&click_id=13&art_id=vn20090802062338990C154440&page_number=1, accessed July 4, 2010.

Swanson, Kate

2007   Revanchist Urbanism Heads South: The Regulation of Indigenous Beggars and Street Vendors in Ecuador. Antipode 39(4):708–728.

Times of Zambia

2009   Cops Pursue, Conquer Lusaka Street Vendors. Times of Zambia, September 14.

2010   Modern Markets: A Source of Income for the Informal Sector. Times of Zambia, December 18:7.

Timothy, Dallen J.

1997   Selling to Tourists: Indonesian Street Vendors. Annals of Tourism Research 24(2):322–340.

Tostesen, Arne, Inge Tvedten, and Mariken Vaa, eds.

2001   Associational Life in African Cities: Popular Responses to the Urban Crisis. Uppsala: Nordic Africa Institute.

Trade Malpractices

1965   Report of the Commission of Enquiry into Trade Malpractices in Ghana. Accra: Government of Ghana.

Turner, Sarah

2009   Hanoi's Ancient Quarter Traders: Resilient Livelihoods in a Rapidly Transforming City. Urban Studies 46(5/6):1203–1221.

Turner, Sarah, and Laura Schoenberger

2011   Street Vendor Livelihoods and Everyday Politics in Hanoi, Vietnam: The Seeds of a Diverse Economy? Urban Studies 49(5):1027–1044.

REFERENCES

UNDP (United Nations Development Fund)
2010   Human Development Report 2009. http://hdr.undp.org/en/reports/global/hdr2010, accessed November 4, 2010.

UNESCO
2003   World Heritage. http://whc.unesco.org/en/list/273, accessed October 22, 2010.

UN-Habitat
2011   State of the World's Cities 2010/11: Bridging the Urban Divide. United Nations Human Settlement Programme. London: Earthscan.

Unwin, Tim
2000   A Waste of Space? Towards a Critique of the Social Production of Space. Transactions, Institute of British Geographers 25:11–29.

Van den Berghe, Pierre, and Jorge Flores Ochoa
2000   Tourism and Nativistic Ideology in Cuzco, Peru. Annals of Tourism Research 27(1):7–26.

van den Bogaert, Michael
1977   Barefoot Management: A Humanitarian Stand. Delhi: Action for Food Production (AFPRO).

van der Westhuizen, Janis
2007   Glitx, Glamour and the Gautrain: Mega-projects as Political Symbols. Politikon 34(3):333–351.

Van Horen, Basil
2005   City Profile. Hanoi. Cities 22(2):161–173.

Van Schendel, Willem, and Itty Abraham, eds.
2005   Illicit Flows and Criminal Things: States, Borders, and the Other Side of Globalization. Bloomington: Indiana University Press.

Vansina, Jan
1962   Trade and Markets among the Kuba. *In* Markets in Africa. Paul Bohannan and George Dalton, eds. Pp. 190–210. Evanston: Northwestern University Press.

Vickers, Adrian
1989   Bali: A Paradise Created. London: Periplus Editions.

VietnamNet
2009   Experts Surprised by Audacity of Proposed Hanoi Master Plan. July 17. http://english.vietnamnet.vn/tech/2007/10/751937/, accessed April 22, 2010.

Vietnam News
2008   Hanoi Bans Hawkers on Many Streets, Tourist Spots. Vietnam News, July 1. http://www.thanhniennews.com/society/?catid=3&newsid=39812, accessed April 22, 2010.

2009a 2008's Top Ten Events. Vietnam News, January 2. http://vietnamnews
.vnagency.com.vn/showarticle.php?num=08SOC020109, accessed April 22,
2010.

2009b Nation Gets New Year's Resolutions. Vietnam News, January 24. http://
vietnamnews.vnagency.com.vn/showarticle.php?num=07SOC240109,
accessed April 22, 2010.

Villar Campos, Alberto
2010 Abrir Hoy un Hotel en el Valle Sagrado Ya No Es Atractivo. El Comercio,
June 21: 20.

Warren, Kay B.
1998 Indigenous Movements and Their Critics: Pan-Maya Activism in Guatemala.
Princeton: Princeton University Press.

Weismantel, Mary
2001 Cholas and Pishtacos: Stories of Race and Sex in the Andes. Chicago:
University of Chicago Press.

Yessenova, Saulesh
2006 Hawkers and Containers in Azrya Vostoka: How "Bizarre" Is the Post-Soviet
Bazaar? Research in Economic Anthropology 24:37–59.

Zambia Daily Mail
2008 LCC Razes City Centre Market Stalls. Zambia Daily Mail, June 22.
2009a State Razes Illegal Stalls. Zambia Daily Mail, March 25.
2009b Will Street Vendors Disappear on June 10? Zambia Daily Mail, June 1.

Index

Accra, Ghana, 30, 32–34, 38, 43, 48, 179
activism, 8, 91, 134, 181, 190, 198, 209. *See also* public protests
Africa, 3, 9, 14, 21–22, 44, 48, 161, 163–64, 167–68, 174, 179, 204, 207. *See also* specific countries
age, 4, 210
agency, 90, 143, 176, 177
agricultural vendors, 116–18, 122, 129–31, 133, 135, 205
agriculture, 42–44, 51
Al-Jazeera, 18
Alegi, Peter, 182
ambulant vendors, 5; in Antigua, 99–100; in Cusco, Peru, 13; in Dakar, Senegal, 158–59; in Ghana, 32; in Hanoi, 144; in Philippines, 73–74, 76–77, 83, 86, 88–89, 91. *See also* itinerant vendors
Ambulatory Vendors Association of Antigua, Guatemala, 101
Andes, Peru, 132, 202, 207
"ant traders," 76
anthropology, 8–9, 96, 201, 203–04, 206, 211

Antigua, Guatemala, 12–13, 206, 208; and 1976 earthquake, 95; ethnic divisions of, 110, 113; historic center of, 96, 98–101, 106–07, 113; and ideologies of urban space, 98–100; as "Maya Antigua," 100, 102, 106, 114n2; as tourism spectacle, 93–95, 102, 105–07, 114; as World Heritage site, 94–95, 98, 103, 113. *See also* Ladinos; marketplaces; Maya vendors
Arab Spring, 17–18, 201
Arequipa, Peru, 119, 122, 127, 133–34
Argentina, 129
artisans, 21, 23–25, 100–102, 116, 122–25, 127–28, 129–31, 133–35, 136n2, 208. *See also* handicrafts
Asante people (Ghana), 11, 29–31, 33–35
Asantehene, 40
Ashanti Region, 31, 38
Asia, 9, 48, 73, 191, 207
Association des consommateurs du Sénégal (ASCOSEN), 161, 165–66
associations. *See* collective organizations
Atinga's Bar case study, 22
Australia, 50

School for Advanced Research Advanced Seminar Series

Published by SAR Press

CHACO & HOHOKAM: PREHISTORIC
REGIONAL SYSTEMS IN THE AMERICAN
SOUTHWEST
Patricia L. Crown & W. James Judge, eds.

RECAPTURING ANTHROPOLOGY: WORKING
IN THE PRESENT
Richard G. Fox, ed.

WAR IN THE TRIBAL ZONE: EXPANDING
STATES AND INDIGENOUS WARFARE
R. Brian Ferguson &
Neil L. Whitehead, eds.

IDEOLOGY AND PRE-COLUMBIAN
CIVILIZATIONS
Arthur A. Demarest &
Geoffrey W. Conrad, eds.

DREAMING: ANTHROPOLOGICAL AND
PSYCHOLOGICAL INTERPRETATIONS
Barbara Tedlock, ed.

HISTORICAL ECOLOGY: CULTURAL
KNOWLEDGE AND CHANGING LANDSCAPES
Carole L. Crumley, ed.

THEMES IN SOUTHWEST PREHISTORY
George J. Gumerman, ed.

MEMORY, HISTORY, AND OPPOSITION
UNDER STATE SOCIALISM
Rubie S. Watson, ed.

OTHER INTENTIONS: CULTURAL
CONTEXTS AND THE ATTRIBUTION OF
INNER STATES
Lawrence Rosen, ed.

LAST HUNTERS–FIRST FARMERS: NEW
PERSPECTIVES ON THE PREHISTORIC
TRANSITION TO AGRICULTURE
T. Douglas Price &
Anne Birgitte Gebauer, eds.

MAKING ALTERNATIVE HISTORIES:
THE PRACTICE OF ARCHAEOLOGY AND
HISTORY IN NON-WESTERN SETTINGS
Peter R. Schmidt & Thomas C. Patterson, eds.

CYBORGS & CITADELS: ANTHROPOLOGICAL
INTERVENTIONS IN EMERGING SCIENCES
AND TECHNOLOGIES
Gary Lee Downey & Joseph Dumit, eds.

SENSES OF PLACE
Steven Feld & Keith H. Basso, eds.

THE ORIGINS OF LANGUAGE: WHAT
NONHUMAN PRIMATES CAN TELL US
Barbara J. King, ed.

CRITICAL ANTHROPOLOGY NOW:
UNEXPECTED CONTEXTS, SHIFTING
CONSTITUENCIES, CHANGING AGENDAS
George E. Marcus, ed.

ARCHAIC STATES
Gary M. Feinman & Joyce Marcus, eds.

REGIMES OF LANGUAGE:
IDEOLOGIES, POLITIES, AND IDENTITIES
Paul V. Kroskrity, ed.

BIOLOGY, BRAINS, AND BEHAVIOR: THE
EVOLUTION OF HUMAN DEVELOPMENT
Sue Taylor Parker, Jonas Langer, &
Michael L. McKinney, eds.

WOMEN & MEN IN THE PREHISPANIC
SOUTHWEST: LABOR, POWER, & PRESTIGE
Patricia L. Crown, ed.

HISTORY IN PERSON: ENDURING
STRUGGLES, CONTENTIOUS PRACTICE,
INTIMATE IDENTITIES
Dorothy Holland & Jean Lave, eds.

THE EMPIRE OF THINGS: REGIMES OF
VALUE AND MATERIAL CULTURE
Fred R. Myers, ed.

CATASTROPHE & CULTURE: THE
ANTHROPOLOGY OF DISASTER
Susanna M. Hoffman &
Anthony Oliver-Smith, eds.

URUK MESOPOTAMIA & ITS NEIGHBORS:
CROSS-CULTURAL INTERACTIONS IN THE
ERA OF STATE FORMATION
Mitchell S. Rothman, ed.

REMAKING LIFE & DEATH: TOWARD AN
ANTHROPOLOGY OF THE BIOSCIENCES
Sarah Franklin & Margaret Lock, eds.

TIKAL: DYNASTIES, FOREIGNERS,
& AFFAIRS OF STATE: ADVANCING
MAYA ARCHAEOLOGY
Jeremy A. Sabloff, ed.

GRAY AREAS: ETHNOGRAPHIC
ENCOUNTERS WITH NURSING HOME
CULTURE
Philip B. Stafford, ed.

PLURALIZING ETHNOGRAPHY: COMPARISON
AND REPRESENTATION IN MAYA CULTURES,
HISTORIES, AND IDENTITIES
John M. Watanabe & Edward F. Fischer, eds.

AMERICAN ARRIVALS: ANTHROPOLOGY
ENGAGES THE NEW IMMIGRATION
Nancy Foner, ed.

VIOLENCE
Neil L. Whitehead, ed.

LAW & EMPIRE IN THE PACIFIC:
FIJI AND HAWAI'I
Sally Engle Merry & Donald Brenneis, eds.

ANTHROPOLOGY IN THE MARGINS
OF THE STATE
Veena Das & Deborah Poole, eds.

THE ARCHAEOLOGY OF COLONIAL
ENCOUNTERS: COMPARATIVE
PERSPECTIVES
Gil J. Stein, ed.

GLOBALIZATION, WATER, & HEALTH:
RESOURCE MANAGEMENT IN TIMES OF
SCARCITY
Linda Whiteford & Scott Whiteford, eds.

A CATALYST FOR IDEAS: ANTHROPOLOGICAL
ARCHAEOLOGY AND THE LEGACY OF
DOUGLAS W. SCHWARTZ
Vernon L. Scarborough, ed.

THE ARCHAEOLOGY OF CHACO CANYON:
AN ELEVENTH-CENTURY PUEBLO
REGIONAL CENTER
Stephen H. Lekson, ed.

COMMUNITY BUILDING IN THE TWENTY-
FIRST CENTURY
Stanley E. Hyland, ed.

AFRO-ATLANTIC DIALOGUES:
ANTHROPOLOGY IN THE DIASPORA
Kevin A. Yelvington, ed.

COPÁN: THE HISTORY OF AN ANCIENT
MAYA KINGDOM
E. Wyllys Andrews & William L. Fash, eds.

THE EVOLUTION OF HUMAN LIFE HISTORY
Kristen Hawkes & Richard R. Paine, eds.

THE SEDUCTIONS OF COMMUNITY:
EMANCIPATIONS, OPPRESSIONS,
QUANDARIES
Gerald W. Creed, ed.

THE GENDER OF GLOBALIZATION: WOMEN
NAVIGATING CULTURAL AND ECONOMIC
MARGINALITIES
*Nandini Gunewardena &
Ann Kingsolver, eds.*

NEW LANDSCAPES OF INEQUALITY:
NEOLIBERALISM AND THE EROSION OF
DEMOCRACY IN AMERICA
*Jane L. Collins, Micaela di Leonardo,
& Brett Williams, eds.*

IMPERIAL FORMATIONS
*Ann Laura Stoler, Carole McGranahan,
& Peter C. Perdue, eds.*

OPENING ARCHAEOLOGY: REPATRIATION'S
IMPACT ON CONTEMPORARY RESEARCH
AND PRACTICE
Thomas W. Killion, ed.

SMALL WORLDS: METHOD, MEANING,
& NARRATIVE IN MICROHISTORY
*James F. Brooks, Christopher R. N. DeCorse,
& John Walton, eds.*

MEMORY WORK: ARCHAEOLOGIES OF
MATERIAL PRACTICES
Barbara J. Mills & William H. Walker, eds.

FIGURING THE FUTURE: GLOBALIZATION
AND THE TEMPORALITIES OF CHILDREN
AND YOUTH
Jennifer Cole & Deborah Durham, eds.

TIMELY ASSETS: THE POLITICS OF
RESOURCES AND THEIR TEMPORALITIES
*Elizabeth Emma Ferry &
Mandana E. Limbert, eds.*

DEMOCRACY: ANTHROPOLOGICAL
APPROACHES
Julia Paley, ed.

CONFRONTING CANCER: METAPHORS,
INEQUALITY, AND ADVOCACY
Juliet McMullin & Diane Weiner, eds.

DEVELOPMENT & DISPOSSESSION: THE
CRISIS OF FORCED DISPLACEMENT AND
RESETTLEMENT
Anthony Oliver-Smith, ed.

GLOBAL HEALTH IN TIMES OF VIOLENCE
Barbara Rylko-Bauer, Linda Whiteford,
& Paul Farmer, eds.

THE EVOLUTION OF LEADERSHIP:
TRANSITIONS IN DECISION MAKING FROM
SMALL-SCALE TO MIDDLE-RANGE SOCIETIES
Kevin J. Vaughn, Jelmer W. Eerkins, &
John Kantner, eds.

ARCHAEOLOGY & CULTURAL RESOURCE
MANAGEMENT: VISIONS FOR THE FUTURE
Lynne Sebastian & William D. Lipe, eds.

ARCHAIC STATE INTERACTION: THE
EASTERN MEDITERRANEAN IN THE BRONZE
AGE
William A. Parkinson &
Michael L. Galaty, eds.

INDIANS & ENERGY: EXPLOITATION
AND OPPORTUNITY IN THE AMERICAN
SOUTHWEST
Sherry L. Smith & Brian Frehner, eds.

ROOTS OF CONFLICT: SOILS, AGRICULTURE,
AND SOCIOPOLITICAL COMPLEXITY IN
ANCIENT HAWAI'I
Patrick V. Kirch, ed.

PHARMACEUTICAL SELF: THE GLOBAL
SHAPING OF EXPERIENCE IN AN AGE OF
PSYCHOPHARMACOLOGY
Janis Jenkins, ed.

FORCES OF COMPASSION: HUMANITARI-
ANISM BETWEEN ETHICS AND POLITICS
Erica Bornstein & Peter Redfield, eds.

ENDURING CONQUESTS: RETHINKING THE
ARCHAEOLOGY OF RESISTANCE TO SPANISH
COLONIALISM IN THE AMERICAS
Matthew Liebmann &
Melissa S. Murphy, eds.

DANGEROUS LIAISONS: ANTHROPOLOGISTS
AND THE NATIONAL SECURITY STATE
Laura A. McNamara &
Robert A. Rubinstein, eds.

BREATHING NEW LIFE INTO THE EVIDENCE
OF DEATH: CONTEMPORARY APPROACHES
TO BIOARCHAEOLOGY
Aubrey Baadsgaard, Alexis T. Boutin, &
Jane E. Buikstra, eds.

THE SHAPE OF SCRIPT: HOW AND WHY
WRITING SYSTEMS CHANGE
Stephen D. Houston, ed.

NATURE, SCIENCE, AND RELIGION:
INTERSECTIONS SHAPING SOCIETY AND
THE ENVIRONMENT
Catherine M. Tucker, ed.

THE GLOBAL MIDDLE CLASSES:
THEORIZING THROUGH ETHNOGRAPHY
Rachel Heiman, Carla Freeman, &
Mark Liechty, eds.

KEYSTONE NATIONS: INDIGENOUS PEOPLES
AND SALMON ACROSS THE NORTH PACIFIC
Benedict J. Colombi & James F. Brooks, eds.

BIG HISTORIES, HUMAN LIVES: TACKLING
PROBLEMS OF SCALE IN ARCHAEOLOGY
John E. Robb & Timothy R. Pauketat, eds.

REASSEMBLING THE COLLECTION:
ETHNOGRAPHIC MUSEUMS AND
INDIGENOUS AGENCY
Rodney Harrison, Sarah Byrne, &
Anne Clarke, eds.

IMAGES THAT MOVE
Patricia Spyer & Mary Margaret Steedly, eds.

VITAL RELATIONS: MODERNITY AND THE
PERSISTENT LIFE OF KINSHIP
Susan McKinnon & Fenella Cannell, eds.

ANTHROPOLOGY OF RACE: GENES,
BIOLOGY, AND CULTURE
John Hartigan, ed.

Timeless Classics from SAR Press

Participants in the School for Advanced Research advanced seminar
"Street Economies, Politics, and Social Movements in the Urban Global
South" co-chaired by Karen Tranberg Hansen, Walter E. Little, and
B. Lynne Milgram, March 13–17, 2011. *Standing, from left*: Ray Bromley,
Suzanne Scheld, Sarah Turner, Florence E. Babb, Linda J. Seligmann,
Ilda Lindell, Gracia C. Clark; *seated, from left*: B. Lynne Milgram,
Karen Tranberg Hansen, Walter E. Little. Photograph by Jason S. Ordaz.